JAMES JOYCE'S WORLD

JAMES JOYCE'S WORLD

by

PATRICIA HUTCHINS

METHUEN AND CO. LTD
36 ESSEX STREET · STRAND · LONDON W.C.2

First published in 1957

CATALOGUE NO. 5880/U

PRINTED AND BOUND IN GREAT BRITAIN
BY BUTLER AND TANNER LTD, FROME AND LONDON

Loud,
  heap miseries upon us
  yet entwine our arts
  with laughters low!

James Joyce

CONTENTS

ILLUSTRATIONS

ILLUSTRATIONS

ACKNOWLEDGEMENTS

It would not have been possible to write this book without the co-operation of a great many people, and in acknowledging their help I must accept responsibility for any discrepancies which may remain in spite of our care. In particular I would thank Miss Harriet Shaw Weaver for unlimited patience and resourcefulness, Stuart Gilbert for advice and encouragement, and my husband, Robert Greacen, who believed it worth while from the beginning and assisted at every stage of the work.

The late Stanislaus Joyce provided a valuable commentary to the Dublin chapters which had formed the basis for my first short study, *James Joyce's Dublin*. Giorgio Joyce showed me Zürich and Madame Eugene Jolas gave considerable assistance where Joyce's life in France was concerned. L. A. G. Strong and Blanaid Salkeld also read drafts and the latter compiled useful notes on *Finnegans Wake*. I am also grateful to the staffs of the National Library of Ireland, the British Museum, the Lockwood Memorial Library, University of Buffalo and the Municipal Library of Vichy. In conjunction with Messrs Faber and Faber Ltd, the Trustees of the James Joyce Estate have given permission for the use of essential material and many individuals allowed other quotations. The photographers who accompanied various expeditions and others who provided portraits and snapshots are mentioned elsewhere.

I am also indebted to those who had known Joyce and his world or assisted in different ways. Among them were Samuel Beckett, Dr Richard Best, Frank Budgen, Mrs Casey, Sean O'Casey, Vincent Clarke, Mrs John Drinkwater, T. S. Eliot, W. G. Fallon, R. J. Gerrard, Bernard Gheerbrant, Madame Gillet, Mrs Kathleen Griffin, Dr Richard Hayes, Felix Hackett, Patrick Hinchy, M. J. C. Hodgart, J. M. Hone, Dr and Mrs Kerrigan, Valery Larbaud, Wyndham Lewis, William K. Magee, Richard de la Mare, Niall Montgomery, Mrs Monaghan, Alida Monro, David Marcus, Madame Monceau, Phyllis Moss, Kathleen Murray, Bernard Murray, J. Middleton Murry, J. J. O'Neill, Sir Harold Nicolson, George D. Painter, Ezra Pound, Madame Pontherier, Arthur Power,

ACKNOWLEDGEMENTS

Joseph Prescott, W. R. Rodgers, Mrs George Roberts, Monsieur and Madame Ronchon, and the Proprietors, Hôtel du Commerce, St Gérand-du-Puy, Mrs James Stephens, Madame Ludmila Savitzky, Walter Stucki, W. B. Stanford, Mr and Mrs Claud Sykes, Derek Stanford, William O'Sullivan, John J. Slocum, Owen Sheehy-Skeffington, Madame Vigneron, Carola Giedion Welcker, Mrs Marjorie Wells, Rebecca West, Dr C. G. Jung, and Mrs W. B. Yeats.

P. H.

INTRODUCTION

Most prefaces are written last, when the author has his general conclusions in mind. Unless a reader is familiar with the work and life of James Joyce, after these first few paragraphs he would do well to start in Cork. From there the book moves on to Dublin, out into Europe and back to Ireland again. It is an account of a journey which began perhaps in a house near the Vico Road in Dalkey, above the lovely little harbour of Coliemore, with its pale lion-coloured granite, and the wooded, Italian-like bays beyond. Here I met the hospitable Conan family and later became friendly with one of the daughters, Aileen, who lent me a book on Proust. This essay by Pierre Abraham, published by *Les Editions Rieder*, with its excellent illustrations, family portraits, photographs of Normandy, reproductions of manuscripts and notebooks, suggested that something similar should be made about Joyce's Dublin background—a few thousand words and numerous photographs. Once started, the text grew riverwise, from talk, books and a casual exploration of the city itself.

The friendly, domestic side of Dublin, with its peace and Victorian security, remained much as Joyce had known it. Not far from the beautiful Georgian squares and gardens were country lanes, fields and barns within the boundaries of the town. The canals and little rivers with their footpaths and trees, and at low tide the wide strands of the Bay, were remembered by Joyce in Pola or Trieste, beside the Zürichsee or as the light on some houses across the Seine brought back an early morning near the Pigeon House. There were many people whose eyes had once held the reality of the man himself. They could see a schoolboy running along the street to Belvedere or a student crossing St Stephen's Green towards University College, a young man who entered the National Library in white canvas tennis shoes and nautical cap. In some ways it was fortunate that Joyce did not return to Dublin in the nineteen-twenties for often these impressions have not been overlaid by those of an older, sadder Joyce with

I

his heavy glasses, his international reputation. Yet if much of Joyce's Dublin remains, its unity of period, the top-hats and wasp waists, an entire political structure, conventions, what one might call the metabolism of Irish life early in the century, has been completely changed. On looking at the newspapers, books and pictures of a time we have not shared, 'fadographs of a yestern scene' as Joyce said, one is struck by the inadequacy of the media which convey these images, making them seem as different from life as fashion drawings from clothes worn by people. We tend to wonder or laugh at the world they show, as if our present were the only one. Donald Davie,[1] for whom the book is 'the culminating masterpiece of naturalism', shows that 'in the world of *Ulysses*, facts that appear trivial are made important simply by being remembered with affection'. Part of Joyce's strength lay in the ability to use social phenomena and topographical landmarks as accurately as possible and yet to convey something of the re-issuing sameness of experience as it river-runs through one city, all cities, through his own and every generation.

With the publication of a short book, *James Joyce's Dublin*, and our removal to London, it seemed as if Joyce should now be left to the memoir writers and textual scholars. After a visit to the La Hune Gallery in Paris, where many of Joyce's manuscripts, part of his library and personal possessions were exhibited in 1949, the following year I assisted with a similar Exhibition at the Institute of Contemporary Arts in London. This put me in touch with a number of people who had known Joyce in England and abroad. Later I helped Miss Harriet Weaver and Stuart Gilbert to collect his correspondence for the edition to be published by Faber and Faber and the Viking Press. During further visits to Dublin, Belfast, and Galway, as a number of letters passed through my hands, I heard a good deal more talk. There were occasional disappointments, for instance the deliberate destruction of a collection which might have been of considerable interest to us. One of Joyce's Irish connections, either from religious scruples or more likely finding uncomplimentary references to himself, burnt all the writer's correspondence with a close relative, as well as autographed editions and perhaps photographs accumulated over a number of years. On protesting I was told that 'One genius is enough in a family'. When it was pointed out that a great deal of value had thus

---

[1] *The New Statesman and Nation*, April 10, 1954.

disappeared, he replied, 'I am perfectly satisfied in my own mind about what I have done.'

Although Joyce's autobiographical novel had caused them considerable embarrassment, for Dublin is a 'small place' in more ways than one, Joyce's relatives in Ireland are extremely loyal. Their explanations of his very alien development may not even satisfy themselves. It is hard to believe that someone known in a human, ordinary-seeming way, should either become an important name in literary history or now be passing through purgatory for it.

In some cases Joyce's letters were either too slight to preserve or had been lost. John Dulanty, then High Commissioner for Ireland, and friendly with Joyce and his family when they visited London, told me burglars had removed some, together with several cases of champagne, and doubtless had a lively evening. A cousin in North Wales had a letter written to Joyce's aunt, Mrs Josephine Murray, about religion, 'if only he could find it'. Yet the visit was not without compensations for he provided a clue to the origin of several autobiographical and other themes in *Finnegans Wake*. When I visited William Magee (John Eglinton, author of *Irish Literary Portraits* and other essays) at his home in Bournemouth, he had already contributed to the collection but told me how Joyce had remarked that each city had a characteristic ballad and asked for information about the lines,

> The Lord in his mercy be kind to Belfast,
>   Which sheltered the exile
> When through it he passed.[1]

On visits to Paris I would bring over some finds, or a note required by Stuart Gilbert, who was editing the letters. Walking from the Left Bank in winter time, with the Seine a yellowy-grey, the streets wet and windy, I thought 'That willow, those two small clocks like wristlet watches built into the east end of Notre Dame, the iron bridge with wooden planks like those to the Bull Wall, all this is "street furniture" as Joyce knew it. Odd that someone like myself, the product of so different an environment, should have become, as he might have put it, "one of my recording devils".' Then in the Gilberts' flat above the river, with a

---

[1] Perhaps a reference to Wolfe Tone who stayed there on his way to America.

3

view over the quays of white, crustacea-holding stone, as I sat in a chair Joyce had used, listening to the same pleasant, humorously interested voices, there came to mind Virginia Woolf's remark in one of her diaries, that writing is sometimes a kind of mediumship, a passageway between one form of consciousness and another.

The fact that I never met Mr or Mrs Joyce has given this work more variety in that they are presented through the reactions of other people. (If one can gather a good deal from the books a man owns, how much more revealing is his choice of friends!) On the other hand, there has been no chance to see in progress that combination of circumstances which we call an individual, to have formed an impression of what underlay the 'considerate Lord Chesterfield manners' as Mary Colum described them, nor to have guessed at the enigmatic quality which Stuart Gilbert and others had encountered there. It is clear that Joyce, like most Irishmen, had his share of pride, something which must hold the balance between personal dignity, honour, and a stubborn resistance to humility. Like St Columkille, Ireland's first spiritual exile, he gradually resolved the problems of his own nature, thus fulfilling that promise, whose measurements were hardly realized at the time, 'to forge in the smithy of my soul the uncreated conscience of my race'. Stephen in *A Portrait of the Artist as a Young Man* speaks of his ancestors throwing off their language and allowing a handful of foreigners to subject them and asks, 'Do you fancy I am going to pay in my own life and person debts they made?' There is a certain danger in stressing the autobiographical elements in the novel, yet Joyce never tried to write outside the framework of his early environment and was obliged, however critical his attitude, to convey its implications. Not until the emergence of people, cultures, ideas and psychological tendencies have been studied with the care and comparative research now given to factual history, will the issues inherent in Joyce's work be clearly defined. For one thing, the early books delineate that subjectivism (so often exploited by colonial and military interests in Ireland) of those for whom friendship often has something of the old fosterhood nearness, and which, by some slight or disillusionment, can quickly turn to hatred. Joyce's chosen prototype was Ulysses, 'the victim of enmity'. 'I do not think that Jim ever forgot a thing—all his life,' said someone who had known him well.

4

Yet by the time *Finnegans Wake* came to be written, Joyce had worked out of himself the bitterness and *agenbite of inwit* of his youth. If Oliver St John Gogarty could call his review of the first edition in 1939 'Roots in Resentment', he must have been digging in his own garden. Yet it is not for nothing that there are so many trial scenes in the work—litigation was a favourite occupation in Ireland long before Norman times—but Joyce was able to define his deepest fears, the darkest possibilities of his nature, and to laugh at his own seriousness.

After 1922 Joyce turned from the daytime realism of *Ulysses* towards the shadowed landscape of Dublin at night. He had come to know the character of physical darkness in a way few people have done. At times a shield had to be worn over an operated eye or coloured glasses used to filter his vision against the sun. He knew its variations from the shuttered rooms of clinics to times when the sound of those hundred-wheeled milk-carts of Paris reached him in the early morning after a bad night. The future of his family had, in a number of ways, become at first disturbing and then tragically destructive of his peace of mind and at times he must have felt there was no solution to it all. Yet on such a morning, a cup of coffee, his post with some amusing comment or criticism of his work, a useful book sent by a friend, and Joyce had caught hold of life again. It is this quality of refusing to be beaten that underlies *Finnegans Wake* and which demands the same patience and resilience from the reader.

Joyce rightly regarded his previous books as a contribution to the social history of a certain period and he wrote of one particular place and its traditions as a means of showing the whole 'comédie humaine'. Yet although he stands behind the work, he uses no part of it to advocate a predominant idea. Vico's view of the cycles of history, eastern religion, esoteric symbolism, the works of Freud and Jung, Levy-Bruhl's studies of the primitive, and the space-time theories of our period, are implied or parodied but never presented as final truths. It is this refusal to make a moral judgment which has irritated certain critics. As a young man Joyce had repudiated Catholicism because he could not accept and would not evade its law of intellectual obedience. 'Joyce was always concerned with religion,' a sister said to me. 'He was obsessed by it.' But Stanislaus Joyce considered this an exaggerated statement. Joyce remained anti-clerical to the end of his life but would defend the logic and psychology of Catholicism against its opponents.[1] He clearly recognized the human need to believe in a father figure, and that dependence on the feminine which takes so many forms, but unlike Tolstoy never pushed himself towards a mysticism which was not part of his temperament. For him 'the sword of certainty' never fell. Although his last and most important work is confessional, Joyce achieved the complete detachment of the artist, who remains 'within or behind or above his handiwork, invisible, refined out of existence, indifferent, paring his finger nails'.

It is probably this aspect which has made Joyce so attractive to the American mind, concerned with absorbing the culture of older civilizations but unable to commit itself wholly to the traditions of Europe. Every period, indeed each stratification of a society, seeks for its own figurations, thus the emphasis given to the parental theme in Joyce is a reflection of that need to find a different road to those territories of wisdom whose contours, always remaining the same, must be continually rediscovered, mapped and surveyed by each succeeding generation. In Ireland itself, after thirty years of peaceful development, the dark and romantic figure of the gunman is now part of the past. However individualistic life may seem on the surface, running through it are those lines of world development, like wires in a sheet of glass, which tend to make a nation strong in itself and yet more dependent on an external economic framework. It is the gaberdine-coated inspector or the specialist, sometimes limited in outlook but on the whole honest and enthusiastic, who walks with authority through the fields or from some Dublin office alters the cities. Now it is the shadow of the exile, thrown by the conflagration of ideas in the outside world, which moves over the small, half-decaying towns, the factories and the cement-improved farms. The disappointed or ambitious, those who would fly by the nets of everyday existence or convention, are always watching the minds of those expatriates who return to Ireland through their work. For the thoughtful they often delineate those issues which face men and women everywhere—war or peace, food production and over-population, the need to understand the forces of destruction both in the group and the individual.

[1] For Stephen Dedalus in *Ulysses*, God was a manifestation of energy, 'a shout in the street'. In *Finnegans Wake*, Our Lord becomes 'Our Loud'.

As Proust reflects in *Remembrance of Things Past*, a work of art must create its own posterity, and the salvaging of correspondence and biographical detail is part of that process:

> The reason for which a work of genius is not easily admired from the first is that the man who has created it is extraordinary, that few other men resemble him. It was Beethoven's Quartets themselves (the 12th, 13th, 14th and 15th) that devoted half a lifetime to forming, fashioning and enlarging a public for Beethoven's Quartets. . . . And so it is essential that the artist, . . . if he wishes his work to be free to follow its own course, shall launch it wherever he may find sufficient depth, confidently outward bound towards the future.[1]

And Joyce, it would seem, has thrown his work forward to land on a stretch of the Vico Road which we have yet to travel.

London, 1956

[1] *Swann's Way*, translated by C. K. Scott Moncrieff.

I

CORK—DUBLIN
1882–1898

The Dublin train leaves Cork through a tunnel as if crossing over the darkness of a river into an entirely different country. In my childhood Glanmire station was the last fortification of the known world, with its embankments of grey young-gull colour stone, and the houses of Summerhill rising high above them. There was something Nibelungian about the start of that journey, the burrowing and chuffing of the engine, the hasty closing of windows and the suddenly imposed night. As we came to see the brown photographs and the crochet trimmings of our carriage, the world outside never settled down into real places, like our home on Bantry Bay. There were the furze-edged fields of north County Cork, the tilled land round Mallow, the huge elephant trunk which watered the trains at Limerick, later a glimpse of Kilcolman where Spenser had lived, and long afterwards the sleepy drive in a 'closed car' along the Dublin quays.

John Stanislaus Joyce probably left Cork for Dublin by the same route many years earlier. His grandfather, according to Herbert Gorman,[1] was related to Daniel O'Connell on his mother's side and lived in Fermoy. Some of the family owned a shop in Great George's Street in Cork where the Liberator is supposed to have made a friendly call from time to time. Several portraits by Comerford and an embroidered hunting waistcoat were preserved by the family and are now in America. In the *James Joyce Yearbook*, 1949, an unnamed journalist describes a visit to John Stanislaus Joyce in his old age which includes a description of his youth in Cork where he had been educated at St Coleman's College, and later studied medicine:

There is not a field in County Cork that I don't know, for I hunted them all

[1] *James Joyce—A Definitive Biography*, 1941.

and I now go through all these hunts and the jollifications that we used to have after them. They were great. I was one of the best men after the harriers. I used to hunt with the Southern Harriers. We had a great pack and I was one of the best on foot. When at college—Queen's in Cork—I took several Exhibitions but I lost the certificates long ago. I put my portmanteau in pawn one time for 10/- with a pawnbroker named Cunningham in Marlborough Street. He was a very decent fellow. There was a set of false teeth in the bag too, but he sold bag, teeth and certificates which were in it.

He claimed to have been related to the well-known Daly family of Cork and through other friends in the industry was appointed secretary at a distillery in Chapelizod, having put £500 into the business and drawing a salary of £300 a year. The interviewer asked him if he knew anything about the quality of the water of the Liffey and was told, 'Not a damn bit, because I never drank it without whisky in it.' There is also an excellent description of how he became secretary of the Liberal Club in Dublin, the election during which he helped to get two candidates into Parliament and the celebrations afterwards. Until the end, as we see by this amusing and authentic-sounding record, he remained an entertaining appraiser of his own past.

James Augustine Joyce, the eldest surviving son, as a small boy accompanied his father to Cork on at least one occasion, but he can have had only a vague memory of the place itself. In 1909 at the age of 27, after a period in Trieste, he went again, with his partners in the Volta Cinema Company, to investigate the possibilities of establishing a cinema there. On this second visit he undoubtedly made notes which enabled him to describe the earlier occasion with such clarity in *A Portrait*.

It is possible that the feeling of boredom and guilt which underlies the description of that excursion in *A Portrait of the Artist as a Young Man* is a transposition into boyhood terms of Joyce's own mood in 1909. In Dublin he had experienced a shock from which he did not easily recover [see page 84] and the matter had not yet been cleared up. Part of the self-accusation and remorse which is defined in the play *Exiles* through the character of Richard Rowan may have been experienced on that business visit to Cork. Then Joyce must also have remembered the frustration felt by a small lad trailing round with his father as he reminisced about the good old days, the search for initials carved on the wooden desks of the anatomy theatre in the college, and the way in which the whole of the boy's morbid curiosity moved back upon him. Into these forms Joyce, as a writer, worked his definition of a particular state of mind, knowing that the elements were the same for the adolescent or the young man moving towards maturity.

In the novel the journey to Cork from Dublin was made by the night mail but Joyce and his partners went down by the early morning train, arrived at 1 p.m. and spent the afternoon there. They may have had a meal at the Victoria Hotel in Patrick Street. The frontage is probably the same with its square apron over the street and the dark comfortable-smelling interior, where nowadays priests sit in brown leatherette chairs and talk to their relatives, or the more prosperous commercial traveller and businessman passes in and out between the tourists.

If there is such a thing as a 'family' voice, traits of timbre and tone shared by a number of people related to one another, it is surely to be found in the Joyces. The writer, to judge from recordings, his brother Stanislaus, and Giorgio Joyce of the next generation, all have something similar in their way of enunciation, traces of the southern 'r' are there, derived very likely from John Stanislaus Joyce who had been brought up in 'the city'. In *A Portrait* Mr Dedalus tells everyone he meets 'that he was an old Corkonian, that he had been trying for 30 years to get rid of his Cork accent up in Dublin and that Peter Pickackafax beside him was his eldest son but that he was only a Dublin jackeen'. In Newcombe's Coffee House (in reality Newsomes near Winthrop Street, I am told) his father's friends said Stephen had a great look of his grandfather 'and Mr Dedalus had agreed that he was an ugly likeness. They had unveiled traces of a Cork accent in his speech and made him admit that the Lee was a much finer river than the Liffey'—a view not to be maintained later.

The reason for John Joyce's visit was the sale of what remained of his Cork property, which may have been Joyce's Court in White Street on the south side of the city. On the suspension bridge between South Mall and Union Quay there was a narrow footpath between the iron girders and in the middle of this sat a blind beggar, a well-known character who had been there for many years. 'He wore a card on his chest', someone reminded me, 'and his fine fat round face and lidded eyes were turned up to heaven under a bowler hat while he shouted for alms and blessed the sighted.' As children coming up from the country we always stopped to talk to him, persuaded that he recognized our voices. Indeed, he was so much part of the river with its gulls and the beautiful grey-white granite of the walls, that one can imagine him, or his predecessor, to have touched his hat to the figure of Mr Joyce and his small son as they passed there to have a look at White Street. At the time there were probably a number of fine residences along the quays and although they have become stores and garages, the interiors often show signs of the older structures into which they have been built. Down White Street there is still a series of houses which suggests the days when Cork had a prosperous society of merchants, professional men, or middle-sized property owners who, like the Joyces, built in the classical style, with pillared entrances and finely moulded ceilings. Cork furniture, for instance, although little known outside Ireland, followed an excellent tradition of craftsmanship, modifying or adapting the style of the Adam brothers or Sheraton.

When searching for Joyce's Court with a photographer friend we were sent to 'O'Shea's the builder', and found that although we entered a doorway as if into a private dwelling, the whole of the interior had been scooped out like an eggshell and there was now a joinery smelling of raw timber and sawdust where electric lathes and machinery of all kinds were buzzing and humming. Along the walls it was possible to trace the partition lines of former rooms. The man who owned the adjacent property said that it was not very clear which site had been Joyce's Court; in fact, until some industrious searcher, probably from overseas, investigates title deeds and other evidence which may remain, no one can be quite sure whether the writer's family actually came from that part of Cork or just owned property there. At the same time, it was interesting to find that Joyce's Court had looked across the old bowling green and that the present owner of the site had taken care of a large half-moon shaped stone with an inscription which dates from 1777. He intends to restore it later to its original position above the entrance arch. He also showed us an ancient house in the corner of his transport yard and described how he had carefully replaced the remains of an old doorway when doing repairs recently.

Beyond it can be seen the top of the Red Tower built by the Normans. On the bowling green, or perhaps the open space surrounding it in those days, it is said that the forces opposed to Catholic emancipation had been drilled, while Daniel O'Connell's supporters came together outside the city. While the ballad of *The Bells of Shandon* by Father Prout is echoed in *Finnegans Wake*, there are also references to a bowling green, but this might have been at the back of the Mullingar Hotel at Chapelizod, mentioned by John Stanislaus Joyce. When alcohol and much talk eventually brought him and his family to the sordidness of their life in Dublin, that sense of aristocracy which is so much a part of Irish life was never altogether rubbed away. And if Joyce's gesture in Paris, when he had a picture of the Lee framed in cork, has been ridiculed by those cleverer than himself, surely it is an amusing reminder of his origins there?

RATHGAR—BRAY

Like the cad met by Earwicker in the Phoenix Park, children in Dublin are always playing the game of asking 'the right time please', and certainly every street clock has its own idea of the speed of the earth round the sun. It is possible to leave home at the hour by Mooney's pub and find Trinity College going its own sedate pace, which is then contradicted by the opposing views of the *Irish Times* and the Ballast Office,—'that piece of Dublin's street furniture' under which James Joyce and J. F. Byrne discussed aesthetics. Yet with all this one can arrive in front of the G.P.O. a few minutes before departure. . . .

In Ireland there is still a sense of *temps*, the present and the past, but little concern with *l'heure*, to use a handy distinction for a stranger wishing to catch a train or make an appointment. A street or surname, lettering on an entrance gate, the Irish or English for a particular field, very often carries some association with the experiences of other generations. In countries with a less disrupted social and economic development, changes have become blurred by acceptance: with industrial and urban conditions dramatization tends to disappear, gossip, newspapers and politics replace story-telling. This is happening everywhere, for time as history has given way to a neurosis based on speed, immediate accomplishment, and Ireland is becoming more and more involved. L. A. G. Strong points out [1] that Shakespeare's work contains many instances of the 'basic intolerance of time' which brings certain characters to disaster. If Joyce was at last able

[1] *The Sacred River*, an Introduction to James Joyce, 1951.

13

to free himself of these and other compulsions—as we must do or bomb everything to pieces—it was through his effort to face the implications of the daytime world and later, in *Finnegans Wake*, to reach a full possession of himself in patience.

Dubliners, like most Irish people, are promenaders. Spend a night in a hotel front-bedroom in Bantry or Sligo, or along the Dublin Quays, and there will be plenty of time to analyse the social, economic and temperamental implications of this trait.

In James Joyce this was accentuated. His books are peregrinations; people are always coming or going, and Dublin landmarks are the lace-pins about which the whole structure is designed. As a young man he spent hours, even whole days, walking through Dublin. On one occasion Mr Dedalus asked Stephen what the hell had brought him out as far as Dolphin's Barn, a considerable distance from his home in Fairview at the time.

With his developing awareness of the personal past, Joyce must have found himself on one occasion before the straight, red-bricked little house where he was born in Brighton Square, Rathgar, in 1882. The hills can be seen from there, cherry-trees show over garden walls; all is very quiet, untrespassed-looking. *Thom's Directory* shows his father, John Stanislaus Joyce, to have been in the Collector General's Office, a good job with the administration of the city. Their neighbours were mostly ladies or 'esquires' with a bank official or two thrown in.

They did not remain long at this address, for Stanislaus Joyce was born at 23 Castlewood Avenue in the same district in 1884; and *Thom's Directory* for 1885 shows that Mr Joyce was the occupant there, although the distinguishing middle name had gone, together with 'Co. gen. office'. Perhaps it was at that time that he 'lost his position through the closing down of his department', as Joyce's brother has put it.[1] 'William Osbourne, A.R.H.A., artist, animal painter, etc.' lived a few doors down, and their immediate neighbour was Mr Jones, Secretary of the Church of Ireland Temperance Society, who probably looked across at the convivial Mr Joyce with some disapproval.

It seems that the family moved to Bray not later than 1888, but it is not until 1891 that John Joyce is shown as being in possession of No. 1,

[1] *Partisan Review*, January–February 1952.

Martello Terrace. The house is still there, next to the baths at the sea end of a short grey terrace made uniform by a continuous wooden paling in Greek key pattern running under the first-floor windows. Some of the doors retain their Victorian leaded glass panels, and the grass around them has that dry and down-trodden look of the seaside. Modest, private, they stand slightly aside from the more popular hotel and boarding-house roads of that part of Bray. Joyce first went to Clongowes Wood from here at just over 'Half past six', as he called himself, and in the College Chapel, thinking of the Christmas holidays, he remembered the tide washing against the sea-wall. The household seems to have been prosperous. There were several servants, heavy metal dish-covers over the Christmas turkey and a nursery where the younger children had their meals. When the small boy in Eton jacket and stiff collar asked his father for sixpence, he was given a shilling.

BLACKROCK

It was not long before the Joyces moved again, this time to Blackrock. At Leoville, 23 Carysfort Avenue, they spent something like eighteen months, as shown by the Directory, during 1892 and 1893. The house stands on the right at a bend above the Protestant church, with fair-sized, well-proportioned rooms. Between the two porticoes sits a rather weather-weary lion, as if watching the comings and goings of its owners. The windows have stained-glass medallions in the corners, and the hall door contains two leaded panels representing a Doge-like man's head, opposite that of a lady, guardians too of the history of the house.

Smelling of very strong tobacco, 'Uncle Charles' in *A Portrait* used to take his great-nephew down to shop in Blackrock, or to the park at Tock Hill, where Stephen puffed out his chest and did a little 'training' under the eye of Mike Flynn. With his father they often went for walks on Sundays through a hinterland of fairly large estates, to Goatstown, Stillorgan and Dundrum. The small, whitewashed house among many rose bushes, on the road to the mountains, where Stephen, after reading *The Count of Monte Cristo*, imagined another Mercedes lived, has probably disappeared into a building estate or sanatorium. Yet milkmen still come from the farms with their horse-drawn carts, and small boys often accompany them. Down on the shore gangs play around the old castle, and bathe at the foot of the Martello Tower at Seapoint, all talking and shouting like a group of starlings, not to return home at night until the lights begin to shine in the comfortable houses. If the servants whispered together in the hall, and his father often stood before the fireplace talking of his troubles, while Uncle Charles begged him to continue his meal, the small boy was only aware of food and bedtime, the next long, school-less day before him, the 'comfort and reverie' of that eternal present of childhood there.

FITZGIBBON STREET

'Dublin was a new and complex experience.'

At the end of O'Connell Street the statue of Parnell points ironically to the slums which bear his name. 'No man has the right to fix the boundary to the march of a nation' declares the gold lettering. 'No man has a right to say "Thus far and no further shalt thou go".' Within smelling distance are the open street markets, rubbish in the gutter, women behind barrows screaming against each other with the long, flat vowel extension of the Dublin accent. The girls are often pretty, with skin white as the bread they eat, the old people bent and distorted by rheumatism like withered potato haulms. Many windows in the eighteenth-century houses are broken, their lace curtains every shape of rags; as Joyce said, 'gaunt, spectral mansions in which the old nobility of Dublin roistered'. Some have been reconditioned by the Corporation, but this is only a flea's bite at the problem.

The area round Mountjoy Square was perhaps less battered fifty years ago. Several more generations of grimy children have 'crawled up the steps before the gaping doors, or squatted like mice upon the thresholds', as Joyce described it. The smell of black-furred mould has increased in the elaborately decorated rooms, the beautiful fanlights are cracked or dismantled, fallen like the system which erected them. FitzGibbon Street is on the slope eastward from the Square, and No. 14, where the Joyces lived for a year (according to *Thom's Directory*, 1894),[1] stands on the left-hand side. In spite of their dignity of style, these three-storied, brown-grey

---

[1] Gorman gives the number as 13, which is now a small shop without living quarters. Joyce also refers to the number in *Ulysses* and *Finnegans Wake*, see p. 224.

houses, each with a little iron balcony to the drawing-room, must have seemed high and shut-in after the seaside atmosphere of Blackrock. 'The rapid down-hill slide to almost abject poverty began when we left Blackrock for Dublin,' Stanislaus Joyce wrote in *Partisan Review*.

It was probably from FitzGibbon Street that James Joyce went out with his mother to visit relations. According to *A Portrait* a sense of bitterness was already setting in, a fear of the squalor and insincerity around him, a feeling of his own helplessness. Dressed up for a party at Harold's Cross, the brothers and sisters had hurried down the steps to take one of the trams with their lank brown horses and jingling bells which served the city and outskirts. It seems there was a considerable pull up to the bridge, so that two extra horses were taken on, children scrambling for the front seats on top to watch their performance.

The next day, in the bare top room there, remembering their journey home with some of the other guests, the boy spent hours trying to put into verse, after Byron, that romantic feminine image which was to follow him through many changes—Eileen in Bray with long cool hands over his eyes, Mercedes imagined in her cottage, the girl in Richmond Street North, Emma Clery and finally, Anna Livia.

At first content with timidly exploring the Square, on growing more used to the city he soon made out a skeleton map of the neighbourhood in his mind. Going down Gardiner Street, James and Stanislaus reached the Custom House, and then, wandering about the quays, watched the ships unloading or taking up cargoes there. 'The spell of arms and voices; the white arms of roads, their promise of close embraces, and the black arms of tall ships that stand against the moon, their tale of distant nations.'

BELVEDERE

Although it is Cranly in *A Portrait* who has the habit of remembering thoughts in connection with places, this had already been developed by Joyce as a child. To remark the name of an inn, a street, some alley way, or a trick of speech, was a consciously played game, a compensation perhaps for that isolation which increased in depth and meaning as he grew older.

One day by chance 'Mr Dedalus' in *A Portrait* ran into the Provincial of the Society of Jesus 'just at the corner of the Square'. From this meeting it was decided that his two eldest sons should go to Belvedere College, ten minutes' walk away. (In reality it was Father Conmee's idea. The Joyces were at the Christian Brothers' School at the time, according to Stanislaus Joyce.) A few days later, on calling at Belvedere House in Great Denmark Street, Mr Joyce was probably shown into the waiting-room on the right of the hall, and brushing his top hat, looked round at its elaborate Georgian decorations. A mantelpiece by the Italian craftsman Bossi, of finely inlaid marble, yellow as a dead rose, the beautifully designed cornices and the painted ceiling, now seem to have no power of protest against the well-kept mahogany furniture, and the framed photographs of the school's Gilbert and Sullivan successes on the walls.

The Belvederean, on art paper thick as a flower catalogue, was started in 1906, and there appears to be no trace of the essays written by James Joyce ten years previously. Nowadays 'A Visit to the Zoo' carries off the essay award. Debates include the motion that 'This house is critical of the Franco Regime', that 'The Cinema is a Social Evil' and that 'Ireland has sacrificed Ideal to Expediency in her National Life'. A poster by one of the boys, some way after Picasso, announces that 'The contribution of the twentieth century to Art is in no way inferior to that of any other century'. At the same time, one would hardly expect to see *Ulysses* or *Finnegans Wake* in the bureau with its heading 'Books by Belvedereans'. This selection includes several religious and Gaelic studies; St John Gogarty's *St Patrick*—not his other work—and some of Austin Clarke's plays.

As the Rector entered, I saw that my enquiries there would be easier than anticipated. A man born to deal with other people in that tricky relationship of teacher and pupil, I thought, as we talked of the house and its projected redecoration. He allowed one to set the pace, to come to the subject of Joyce in easy stages.

'He would have known this.' We entered part of the reception room which runs across the front of the house, partitioned by huge doors. 'It's called the Venus room.' Brown books covered most of the walls, and I noticed the knots in the wood of the floor, rising like knuckles in an old hand. There was the same air of saddened splendour given by the dulled Victorian gilt paint of the hall and stairway. Some of this was now being changed to light blue and cream colours by men working on scaffolding high above us.

'We are going to get rid of that terrible window, too,' said the Rector as we went downstairs again, under the gloomy yellow light transmitted by saints and martyrs.

The 'new building', in that ecclesiastical box-of-bricks style popular in Ireland, stands on the other side of what was once the 'grass plot' mentioned in *A Portrait*. This became a large cemented play-yard when the College took over two neighbouring houses. A photograph taken in what might be called the Joyce period shows part of the fountain in the centre of the flower-beds. 'I remember in my time how boys who became too boisterous were sent to stand over there by the fountain,' the Rector remarked.

It also includes the shed where 'Heron' (Albrecht Connolly) talked to Dedalus in the darkness, beyond the bobbing Chinese lanterns in the garden, visitors passing down the steps on their way to the festive ark of the theatre. In *A Portrait* Joyce skilfully uses the 'flash back' to summarize the previous years of school life, Stephen's sense of intellectual superiority and those leisure hours 'passed in the company of subversive writers whose jibes and violence of speech set up a ferment in his brain, before they passed out of it into his crude writings'. He heard about him 'the din of hollow-sounding voices', the constant voices of his father and his masters, 'urging him to be a gentleman above all things, and to be a good Catholic above all things . . . to be strong and manly and healthy, to be true to his country and raise up her language and tradition', and he was 'only happy when he was far from them, beyond their call, alone or in the company of phantasmal comrades'.

As to Joyce's contemporaries who still live in Dublin, their recollections are usually of a boy like themselves in many ways, yet with some difference they were not able to make out at the time.

'He was the thinnest thing you ever saw,' one man said. 'Not a pick on him. Any day in the summer you'd see him sitting on the rocks along the Bull Wall, in his skimpy bathing toggery. He made an attempt to play football, like a girl, kicking the ball on the top with his heel: I can hear him now cackling over the fact he couldn't do free gymnastics, his legs just wouldn't behave in the ordinary way, no muscles at the hip you see.'

'Of course we knew he was interested in writing. We'd have difficulty in making out a few pages of exercise book for the weekly essay but

Joyce would come along with several sheets closely written over—much of it was above our heads.'

As boys notice everything, it was remarked that Joyce was often called to see the Rector about midday—Stanislaus Joyce promised to give the reason in his own work later—and it was not long before it was rumoured that Joyce was given a meal, a tradition categorically denied by his relatives when questioned. One of Joyce's sisters on reading my manuscript suggested it should be omitted, but as I had also heard the story outside the college from other people, I thought it better to give the matter an airing. Later Stanislaus Joyce pointed out that it was the invention of thwarted curiosity:

> It is difficult to qualify politely a statement so little in accordance with the facts. My brother and I went to Belvedere together, and I remained there after my brother went to the University. It is very strange that though I was nearly three years younger than my brother, I was never included in these meals, nor did any member of the family ever know anything about them. Although secrecy was never his forte, and I shared his life then day by day and hour by hour, now at almost sixty-seven years of age I hear of these things for the first time from Patricia Hutchins. The only breakfast I ever had at Belvedere College was after my first communion together with the other first communicants, and my brother had not even that for he made his first communion at Clongowes.[1]

Father Henry appears to have been a solemn little man, very correct and proper and yet the boys respected him. A story of how he wrote out punishment lines, on being proved wrong over a detail, was not, as I had been informed, due to Joyce's persistence, a mistake corrected by Eugene Sheehy in his book *May it Please the Court*.[2]

Some confusion arises as to the use of the chapel and vestry as temporary dressing-rooms (because of their proximity to the theatre), as described by Joyce in *A Portrait*, with Indian clubs and gym shoes everywhere, the air pungent with the smell of gas-jets and grease-paint, crowded with boy actors and eager masters. We looked through the glass of the old chapel door at the bare walls, now in term time a class-room, where 'the embossed brasses and candle-sticks upon the altar had gleamed like the battleworn mail armour of angels'. A new chapel lies on the right, with

[1] *Partisan Review.*   [2] Dublin, 1951.

*No man has the right
to fix the boundary
to the march of a nation*

Parnell's Monument, Dublin

Joyce's Court, White Street, Cork

John Stanislaus Joyce

Mrs May Joyce?

James Joyce, Paris, c. 1903

Alfred Bergan

windows in the deep-sea blues and greens of Harry Clarke's work, and decorated with the restrained good taste of the College as a whole. In the whitish daylight of the gymnasium there is a corrugated-iron roof with glass along the top, and the long interior, with a floor tilting towards the stage, has that enclosed atmosphere of a place where unpainted wood has dried for years. This smell of school or institution, of empty, rehearsal-echoing theatre—where did Joyce remember it? Perhaps during the preparation of a different kind of play, using associations of sound, odour, circumstance, to get back to that particular evening at Belvedere. Then, as he stood in the wings, thinking of the serious alluring eyes of the girl met two years before at Harold's Cross, 'for one rare moment he seemed to be clothed in the real apparel of boyhood' and 'shared the common mirth amid which the drop scene was hauled upwards by two able-bodied priests with violent jerks, and all awry'. After the success of his mimicry of the Rector, Stephen had hurried out in the hope that the girl might stand talking for a while with his family, and looking down Great Denmark Street, saw that she had gone. Adolescent disappointment has seldom been described so penetratingly.

'Is it true James Joyce was educated without fees here?' I asked the present Rector, as we mounted the steps to re-enter the main building.

'*And* given his breakfast; I think he mentions it somewhere.' The same story again.

'On the whole he acknowledges a debt to the Jesuits——' I was feeling my way. 'The family circumstances . . .'

'Yes, he does.' He stopped and looked at me. 'Do you know what Joyce's father was?'

'A "praiser of his own past"—d'you mean?'

'A *bounder!*' [1]

I examined the word, coming from such an unexpected quarter. His use of it had rather a 'twentyish' flavour, as by one who employed slang rarely and then between inverted commas. John Joyce 'had many many faults and was quite useless as a provider for a large family', as one of them put it, but if he bounced from one money-making scheme to another, it

---

[1] 'My brother's idea was that if he had become a Jesuit he would have run away with the cook!' Stanislaus Joyce's note is in pencil, so the last word might be 'cash'. I doubt if the former would have been very attractive.—P. H.

was without guile and his type, witty, amusing, generous with money owed elsewhere, is not unknown to contemporary Dublin, and maybe other cities.

It had been a mistake, the Rector continued, although well meant at the time, to educate a boy here when his background was so much at variance with the standards of the school, cultural and religious. Far better to have sent him away, to Mungret College in Limerick, as a boarder; anywhere rather than Dublin. After three o'clock or so a boy finished work . . . other influences intervened . . . Joyce had great ability—genius; he might have done much in the Church. . . .

Joyce has defined Stephen's 'equivocal position in Belvedere' as a boy taken free and 'a leader afraid of his own authority, proud and sensitive and suspicious, battling against the squalor of his life and against the riot of his mind'. Behind these factors again, only defined and fully known when Joyce came into touch with the work of Freud and others, were the forces, physical and emotional, which carried him down the hill, past Mountjoy Square and Gardiner Street, to the maze of narrow and dirty streets 'where yellow lamps would light up, here and there, the squalid quarter of the brothels'.

'Has there been no study of Joyce, from a Jesuit, Catholic point of view?' I asked. 'A serious estimate of the religious and psychological factors involved.'

'No,' he said, half smiling. 'He has just been looked upon as one of the bad boys.' [1]

Yet I saw he would have backed James against his father, the sensitive rather than the flamboyant character, and perhaps dealt with the situation more wisely had it arisen in his time.

DRUMCONDRA

Following the same pavement from Belvedere over which Joyce had played the game of stepping within the lines, reading the fate of his weekly essay ' in incident of the way', or with Lamb's *Adventures of Ulysses* in mind, one can turn left into Upper Gardiner Street. Across the road is the Church of St Francis Xavier, with the priests' house beside it. This is brick-

[1] See Niall Montgomery, *New Mexico Quarterly*, 1953, for an illuminating article.

faced, not grey as described by Joyce, returning there in mind from some room in Trieste to remember how he glanced at its windows wondering which would be his if he joined the Jesuit order. During Joyce's years at Belvedere the family moved into various houses. Among them was 17 Richmond Street North, a cul-de-sac near the present-day Christian Brothers' School. The house is depicted in the story in *Dubliners* called 'Araby', in which the young boy waits all the evening for his uncle's return, to obtain money so as to go to the fairground and meet a girl who lives nearby.

A Portrait describes how, between Jones's Road and Clonliffe Road, Stephen was beaten up by Heron and another, with a cane and a cabbage stump. An interesting account of this or a similar incident is given by one of his school-fellows who was with James Joyce and Albrecht Connolly at the time. They had all been at Joyce's home, in Drumcondra then, and on leaving he must have intended to accompany them for a bit. An argument arose as to the merits of two poets, Byron was one and Tennyson perhaps the other. Connolly, a much stockier lad, gripped Joyce's thin arm in a twisted position and marched him all the length of the way down to his own home in Russell Place on the North Circular Road, a full mile. Joyce would not admit he was wrong and the nonplussed Connolly was obliged to let him go, in case his mother should look out of the window and see them! 'The released Joyce turned right about and went away without even a nod for me because I'm sure there were bitter tears in his eyes,' my informant added. 'He felt he had been bullied.' [1] The incident is related to the protest of the small boy at Clongowes against unjust punishment, the scholar and later writer who was prepared to stand by his ideas, even into eternity.

Mr Joyce and his family were living in Holywell Villas about 1894–5, according to Stanislaus Joyce, though the houses do not appear in *Thom's Directory* until 1897, with the names of Thomas Morrow and William Cox as ratepayers. They were probably built as a speculation in an undeveloped area. To reach this from Jones's Road, one must pass the high walls of

[1] 'I remember it distinctly,' notes Stanislaus Joyce. 'Even a man could only with great difficulty "march" a struggling boy of thirteen or fourteen a "full mile" without assistance. I had a fight with Connolly and though I got the worst of it (I was some years younger) I know he was no Hercules.' Allowances should be made here for the story-teller's art.—P. H.

Clonliffe College, which Stephen, when at the University, visited with a former Clongowes boy training for the priesthood and re-entered again in thought 'the seminarist life which he had led for so many years, to the understanding of the narrow activities of which he could now in a moment bring the spirit of an acute sympathetic alien'.

Going over the hump of Drumcondra Road one passes the well-kept, armorial gate to the Archbishop's House, as Joyce must have done, hearing again the voice that urged him to take up the proud claims of the Church, the mystery and power of the priestly office. But his destiny was to be 'elusive of social and religious orders . . . to learn his own wisdom apart from others or to learn the wisdom of others himself wandering among the snares of the world'.

On the left, just before the bridge over the Tolka river, is the 'ham-shaped encampment of poor cottages' where Stephen 'turned his eyes coldly for an instant towards the faded blue shrine of the Blessed Virgin which stood fowlwise on a pole'. When I first went there Tolka cottages were being demolished and boys and men played cards among the ruins of old mud and straw-built walls. The statue had not yet been removed but still stood there with its faded blue mantle, almost featureless, hands outspread in a mild gesture of acceptance.

'Isn't she lovely?' said a woman from one of the remaining houses. 'Been there a hundred years: the floods were terrible at one time. They put Her up on that account, they say, to help, don't you know.'

When Stephen had crossed the bridge he turned left by a lane leading through what was practically country then. There were two dairies and a gardener's cottage in Millbourne Avenue. Holywell Villas stood at the corner of Goosegreen Avenue, a name, disappeared now, suggesting the old character of the place. It was on the patchy ground there that a friend remembers Joyce attempting to play football. The two semi-detached houses, he said, had a 'weird appearance' standing there alone. *A Portrait* records that from the back the family could see the solitary farmhand in the kitchen gardens and nicknamed him The Man with the Hat. Before he began work he always considered in turn the four points of the sky and then regretfully plunged his spade in the earth.

Joyce has caught the atmosphere of certain Dublin evenings in describing how in the quiet glow the children used to sing in the kitchen there while he listened with pain of spirit 'to the overtone of weariness behind their frail fresh innocent voices'. 'Even before they set out on life's journey they seemed weary of the way.' He remembered how Newman had heard this note in Virgil, 'giving utterance like the voice of nature herself, to that pain and weariness yet hope of better things which has been the experience of her children in every time'. Most writers have done better when writing about hell than describing heaven, except Swedenborg perhaps. Joyce emphasizes shadow rather than light. For instance his mother, I am told by one of her children, was quite a cheerful person, often singing to them or about the house.[1]

The villas now stand amongst a corporation housing estate, and one of them, as if to assert its difference, has been painted in that white-and-green raised squares design in which Osbert Lancaster sees the Irish love of abstract forms. The tangle of sally and willow along the river, where the younger ones must have played, has gone, the Tolka running between cement walls and restrained by little weirs to pass through the tidy grass and young trees of Griffith Park, a name standing for another period of Irish history. There is also a public library, where Joyce's work is certainly not available. Further westward the round-tower of O'Connell's monument rises like 'an overgrown pencil' above the dead at Glasnevin.

[1] Bernard Murray, Joyce's cousin, said they used to take ass and cart, tent, provisions and picnic along the Liffey. The Joyces may have joined them, as suggested by the 'Strawberry Beds' theme in *Finnegans Wake*.

II

UNIVERSITY COLLEGE
1899–1902

During 1898–9 the Joyce family moved again, for No. 1 Holywell Villas is vacant and Mr F. N. Binks has taken over No. 2. As his son remarks, Mr Dedalus had no acute sense of the rights of private property and he paid rent very rarely. 'To demand money for eatables seemed to him just but to expect people to pay for shelter the exorbitant sums which are demanded annually by houseowners in Dublin seemed to him unjust.'

At the time when the Joyces were living in FitzGibbon Street, the Irish Local Government Act came into being and John Joyce's job in the office of the Collector General of Rates was terminated. He carried on occasional work for his former employers and acted as election agent before the revising barrister for parliamentary returns. From Drumcondra the Joyces probably moved to Windsor Terrace, where the landlord was the Rev. Mr Love (according to a note by Stanislaus Joyce) who figures in *Ulysses*. During that period the question of James's future became important. His father thought he was 'cut out' for the law, while at Belvedere they had hopes of getting him a clerkship in Guinness's brewery. In the end it was decided that he should graduate at University College.

By 1901 the name of John Joyce again appears in *Thom's Directory*, as occupier of No. 8 Royal Terrace, Fairview. This address probably coincided with the end of Joyce's first year at University College. The immediate vicinity was once a little Scottish colony, it seems, built by the founder of a neighbouring firm and perhaps accommodating families connected with the distillery on the river. Bright red brick and rather nonconformist-looking, the tidy roads bear the names Melrose, Lomond, Waverley. No. 8 Inverness Road, once Royal Terrace when crowns were popular, is one of a row of grey-plastered, ordinary-looking houses, with its semi-basement and a door, inset with frosted green glass panels, reached by a number of steps. The large letter-box flap once received John Joyce's bills, and, surprisingly enough, a communication from a friend of Ibsen.[1] Round the back the real character of the place reveals itself, as though the fronts of the houses wore their Sunday clothes. There are narrow strips of garden or yard, with a few bushes and clothes-lines, and the sound of gramophone or wireless from backdoors open in warm weather. In *A Portrait* Joyce suggests the disorder of the household, the hasty wash and breakfast, the querulous voice of Simon Dedalus upstairs, his mother telling him to slip out by the back. In actual fact it was probably not much worse than many others.

The narrow lane which Joyce described is still there, running behind the houses, grass growing up through the heaps of rubbish. This was damp and muddy on the day Stephen remembered so clearly, as much a part of his depression and despair as the scream of the mad nun in the female lunatic asylum, whose grey-slated roofs rise on the other side of high, barbed-wired walls. His heart was 'already bitten by an ache of loathing and bitterness' at so much that offended and threatened the pride of his youth . . . but as he walked down the avenue and felt the grey morning light falling about him through the dripping trees and smelt the strange wild smell of wet leaves and bark, his soul was loosed of her miseries.[2]

---

[1] This was William Archer. A contemporary said to me, 'The first inkling the crowd here got of Joyce's unusual literary talent was when Ibsen wrote thanking him for his criticism of one of his plays.' Surely a prophet has no honour until it comes back to him from another country.

[2] 'Sometimes things went very well and sometimes things were very bad,' one of Joyce's sisters said. Her father had been a man of great charm and they were very fond of him, but he was hardly the person to bring up a big family. It is interesting to note that in *Stephen Hero* the sordid effect is less dramatized and perhaps this earlier draft comes nearer to his own life than *A Portrait*. It is typical of the curious effect which the use of partly autobiographical material had upon Dubliners who recognized people and places within Joyce's work, that someone should say to me that they had 'given Joyce something for his hair'. It was no wonder that the younger members of the family suffered from the reactions to Joyce's books. 'It gave me quite a feeling of inferiority, up to the time I got married,' one of them said. 'It left a scar.' The younger generation, on the other hand, have had a certain prestige at College and elsewhere, as relatives of the famous man.

It was with some diffidence that I pointed out to Stanislaus Joyce that although lice are mentioned in *A Portrait* no reference was made in an earlier draft, suggesting that Joyce's experience of them might have been abroad. 'No—definitely Dublin. In Liverpool they call

If the trees which always evoked memories of the girls and women in the plays of Gerhart Hauptmann have gone, now young ones grow along Fairview Strand. The sloblands, beside which Joyce began his morning walk across the city thinking of the 'cloistral silver-veined prose of Newman', have been walled in from the sea and become a wide green park. Some of the same pubs and provision shops mentioned in the Wandering Rocks episode of *Ulysses* are still there in North Strand Road with their heavy Victorian mouldings and gilt lettering. There 'he would recall the dry humour of Cavalcanti and smile'. Baird's stone-cutting works in Talbot Place, 'where the spirit of Ibsen would blow through him like a keen wind', have disappeared, and with them the marine store which, for some odd reason, had been associated with a lyric of Ben Jonson.

In *Stephen Hero* Joyce describes how at other times he took the tram as far as Amiens Street station, sitting in the front seat on top with his face to the wind. He would get off there instead of continuing to the Pillar 'because he wished to partake of the morning life of the city. This morning walk was pleasant to him and there was no face that passed him on its way to its commercial prison but he strove to pierce to the motive centre of its ugliness'. Sometimes he would not go to the College at all but followed some trivial indication of city life, often walking by himself for seven or eight hours without fatigue in the damp Dublin autumn and winter. 'He had his ears and eyes ever prompt to receive impressions. It was not only in Skeat that he found words for his treasure house, he found them at hazard in the shops, in advertisements, in the mouths of the plodding public. He kept repeating them to himself until they lost all instantaneous meaning for him and became wonderful vocables.'

---

lice "biddies". The girls or women of the (Joyce) family try to conceal as much as possible. The fact is the house and family were too much for my mother, a frail woman in bad health who was to die within a year. A family of (then) nine children and a husband who came home drunk four or five times a week, was noisy and quarrelsome and had a tireless Cork tongue—the burden crushed her.

'As for the Dublin reader, he does not like to be confronted with the details of the squalor to which Irish "flamboyance" (if I may coin a word) had reduced a family which did not belong to the lower class. And as for my brother, he liberated his soul from that memory by recording it dispassionately. In a manner, it was "passing the buck"! If he had written in bitterness, the memory would still have rankled.'

The large industrial towns have brought about a self-conscious conformity, a fear of admitting poverty or appearing different from the average, which has not yet reached southern Ireland. Dublin streets and each neighbourhood have their own set of public characters, the more or less permanent elements among the shopping, lounging, or hurrying crowds. They are seen every day at certain times or in relation to particular places: beggars with their distinctive equipment such as that of 'Forty Coats', who often appeared to be cooking a meal under his tent-like garments, others carrying a child which remains the same stunted age, or a Darby and Joan couple, with the air of having known the old gentry, who play a large gilt harp in the vicinity of Grafton Street. There are also students, literary and artistic promenaders who gain a certain satisfaction from being known to many, and their odd clothes or behaviour enters into the conversation and anecdotes of pubs and restaurants, in suburban homes or chance meetings along the way.

Some of those who figure in Joyce's work are still part of the scene and, even if the reference was uncomplimentary, are glad to have been included. A side-line of the tourist industry is the pub-talkers with stories about the writer, part of a curious folk-lore as inaccurate as it is affectionate. Others in the streets repeat the pattern Joyce knew in the material of another generation—a Gerty MacDowell with pretty hair and a sex-conscious limp, out from an office near Merrion Row at lunch time, or Blazes Boylan who wears a bright green tweed jacket and goes in for cars. . . .

If the open-topped trams with their symbols for the illiterate, and then their enclosed successors, have now been replaced by a modern bus service, there are still one or two dusty black cabs, which perhaps carried Gogarty and his medical friends, waiting at Westland Row. The cobbles which gave back the continual rattle of wheels and the 'jaunted jingling' of a viceregal cavalcade only bother the cyclist in out-of-the-way places. Sackville Street and its D.B.C. have gone, but the 'great-cloaked Liberator' survived the ruins of 1916 and now guards his own-named thoroughfare, surrounded by the plump ladies, with wings incapable of flight, whose arms and breasts are bullet-holed. The Empire and Dan Lowry's Music Hall and the Ship have disappeared. If Davy Byrne's 'moral pub' is glass and chromium, many of the smaller houses retain their Victorian gilt and heavy paintwork. Bookshops on the quays continue to stock the 'sweets of sin'—and more serious literature.

From Butt Bridge the cranes and masts of the docks are distanced by the open sea, and up-river the soft distemper colours of the houses pleat into one another across the water. The Metal Bridge is like a piece of crochet-work, held from side to side, with the dome of the Law Courts beyond, and down below the gulls flap strongly, 'wheeling between the gaunt grey walls'.

ST STEPHEN'S GREEN

When Joyce crossed the Green—'St Stephen's, my Green'—the high equestrian figure of George II dominated its ponds and flower-beds. This was blown up a good deal later. If the nursemaids are no longer a distinct category and there are no top-hats and parasols, children still feed the ducks, play over the grass, scream and laugh along the paths. Other days in the 'misty Irish spring' or in the damp, sharp-edged winter mornings, the gardens are almost empty and the air webbed with water vapours as he had known it.

One of the smaller gates leads on to 'the footpath inside the chains where Stephen had so often walked at night with his friends': some of the lamp standards remain, but the chains themselves became weapons, in World War One probably. Opposite are the granite-faced, eighteenth-century buildings, Nos. 85 and 86, which are used as the Students' Union, while the main body of University College is now in Earlsfort Terrace. These houses had seen the landed families give place to other owners, and eventually became part of the Royal University of Ireland. As a reorganization of the Arts and Sciences faculties of the Catholic University founded by Cardinal Newman, it symbolized the achievement of that struggle for an adequate, and separate, education for the Catholic majority. The College was conducted from 1883 to 1911 by the Society of Jesus.

In the hall are the old stone flags and black tiles, cracked and worn, over which the life of the College had passed for nearly twenty years before Joyce's time. It was here that Francis Skeffington, the 'serious young feminist with cavalier beard and shooting suit', hung the Tzar's peace manifesto and asked Joyce to sign it. Father Darlington, who figures as

Father Butt and the dean of studies in *Stephen Hero* and *A Portrait*, used to stand at the bottom of the main staircase. According to J. M. Hone, he had known Gerard Manley Hopkins well. Described by Joyce as 'an elderly greyhound of a man' in a chalky soutane, it seems that he had been an Anglican clergyman and a later convert of Newman. Perhaps he came of a printing or publishing family in Birmingham, for he knew a good deal about the subject and played a prominent part in the activities of the Catholic Truth Society. In his book of reminiscences, *Silent Years*, published in New York in 1953, J. F. Byrne gives a sympathetic portrait of Father Darlington and shows him to have been active about the college, often doing jobs which others would have found humiliating. It was on the side stairs that turn upwards to what were then the sleeping quarters of the Jesuits and a few resident students that Joyce first saw George Clancy's 'rustic face' and realized the simplicity and honesty of the boy, using him as model for Davin in *A Portrait*. He died for his nationalist principles, shot by the Black and Tans when Mayor of Limerick.

Recently the fine ceilings and plasterwork of the halls have been restored and repainted. The place smells of floor polish and good linoleum; there are thick carpets and period furniture in the main rooms. Across a landing from the salon in No. 85, a chapel in Joyce's day, is the room once known as the Physics Theatre, although there was little or no apparatus there. With grey cobwebbed walls, its bare floors were noisy as classes came in and out, and a series of raised benches ran across the three high, gothic-arched windows. It is now quietly elegant, and a bookcase has been placed over the large fireplace to the right, where the dean of studies bent to supervise the fire and talked at cross-purposes with Stephen as to the good and the beautiful.

'Father Darlington would have spoken just like that,' our guide said. 'I can hear him—Ah! Joyce reproduced conversations with great accuracy.' [1]

'And the President, Father Delaney?' I asked as we went out of doors. 'You remember how in *Stephen Hero* he was saying his office in the garden and Stephen went to ask why his paper on Drama and Life for the debating society had been censored?'

'That discussion took place near the ball alley, which has gone.' We

[1] J. F. Byrne claims to have told Joyce the story from which the incident was written.

31

were pointed out the place, built over some time ago by classrooms. Students now have access to the gardens of Iveagh House, passing down a path between two lawns which are part of the area mentioned by Joyce. It was here that the President and members of the staff, Joyce, J. F. Byrne, George Clancy, Felix Hackett, and C. P. Curran, were photographed together.

Thus with University College and his student life there, Joyce becomes part of a clearly marked period. One can turn from his own work to look for other evidence, facts, and opinions and to see him against the general background. *A Page of Irish History*, edited by the Society of Jesus and published in 1930, gives the official view. A former student declares that the Gaelic League 'was beginning to get into its stride and nowhere was the new movement accepted with more enthusiasm than among the students of University College . . . and by giving us students an ideal raised the tone of our lives, and an exceptionally high moral standard prevailed among us'. A footnote follows: 'Readers of Mr James Joyce will get a different impression, but this is the actual fact. Among the students of the College about this time were P. H. Pearse, T. M. Kettle, F. Sheehy-Skeffington (prominent Nationalists). Joyce is true as far as he goes, but confining himself to a small knot of medical students he gives a wrong impression of the whole.'

'Though still in his first year,' Joyce wrote of Stephen, 'he was considered a person and there were even many who thought that though his theories were a trifle ardent they were not without meaning. Stephen came seldom to lectures, prepared nothing, and absented himself from term examinations, and not merely was no remark passed on these extraordinary vagaries but it was supposed probably that he represented the artistic type and that he was, after the fashion of that little-known tribe, educating himself.' *A Page of Irish History* declares that 'during his student days James Joyce was not taken seriously. It was understood that he had a weird sort of talent, but no one in the college seems to have guessed that he was destined to achieve almost world-wide celebrity.'

Time has spread a pleasant glow over this period for many of those who took part in the day-by-day ordinariness of it all. At first it seems as if Joyce's descriptions have swung to the other extreme, delineating the crudity of this small society, as though exile had emphasized a sense of bitterness, that it had in fact rejected him. Joyce selected those emotions which he could re-experience, as it were, those most likely to serve his narrative. Stanislaus Joyce does not agree with me here and declares that in writing *A Portrait* 'he felt exultant', but surely there soaked into the work something of that hard struggle to live, Joyce's lack of a publisher for *Dubliners*, which at the same time enabled him to understand and thus delineate his earlier self? That Joyce often enjoyed himself during his college days is suggested more clearly by the surviving fragment of *Stephen Hero* where Dedalus was 'equipped with a vision the angle of which would never adjust itself for the reception of hallucinations and with an intelligence which was as much in love with laughter as with combat'.

St Stephen's, the student publication started in 1901, provides an un-self-conscious expression of facts and opinions about College life, written without regard to the future. Here and there we see Joyce as he appeared to his contemporaries, undistorted by fame, by friendly or resentful reminiscences made in later years. At one moment he is the 'mystic Joacax', at another 'the dreaming one of Nola' or 'the Mad Hatter'. There is no blunting of the pencil-point sharpness of these little sketches, margin-doodled, as it were, for the amusement of that small, self-critical world of the College.

If Joyce's account does not correspond in detail with the early numbers of the magazine, the articles mentioned are selected from various issues. He saw it as inspired by the College authorities, but was glad enough to have a means of seeing himself in print. Arthur Clery, writing in *Dublin Essays*, 1919, regarded *St Stephen's* as one of the most important features of College life. 'It was conducted by a students' committee, but Professor Henry Browne, S.J., turning aside from Grammarial and Homeric studies, had not a little to say in the conduct of it.' Besides contributions by members of the staff, and essays in Irish, there were reports from the medical school, the Sodality, the Academy of St Thomas Aquinas, and other notes. 'Stability was secured by the remarkable principle that there should always be *two dull articles*.' In the second number there appeared a column headed 'Parvula Blandula' and signed 'Chanel'; the significance of the name was to emerge later. Arthur Clery, a year or two older than Joyce, was one of those people to be found in and out of college long after their own university days. Always a keen nationalist, his youthful wit tended to earnestness in middle age, but at that time *The Leader* declared: 'The humour of the lighter contributions of *St Stephen's* is very sportive and even a rank outsider might find many of the touches irresistible.'

A former student, with what he describes as a 'hardened ranchman's heart', wrote from Brazil:

> In those parts of the paper which are obviously intended to be in 'lighter vein', I notice the tendency to become 'self-centred' which in this case is merely a polite way of saying 'unintelligible'.
>
> For instance, take those effusions which appear over the signature 'Chanel'. He is evidently the wit of your staff but his jokes are utterly incomprehensible to me. They are quite archaically classical, and have the appearance of having been faked up out of tag-ends of old law books or the appendix columns of literary primers.
>
> By the way, has the title 'Chanel' any particular signification? Thinking that I might throw some light on the subject for myself, I tried to hunt up its meaning last night. The only information I obtained was that 'chanel' is the Middle-English term for 'Gutter'. Without intending to be uncomplimentary, I think you might substitute the word Chanel for Parvula Blandula at the *top* of the page in question.

As a matter of fact, Chanel was Clery's middle name, after the French missionary and first martyr of Oceania. Chanel is always going off on trips to Homburg, with Madam; at another time the column is signed by his executors and much of it suggests the various tendencies, a love of unusual words, puns, tricks, and parodies of newspaper and novelette styles, the use of nicknames and the topography of Dublin, which Joyce was to develop in *Ulysses* and *Finnegans Wake*. Without pushing the point too far, could this have been a case of deliberate, or quite unconscious, cold storage on his part, an absorption of material to be used years later in his own very much more sophisticated way? Stanislaus Joyce cannot see any connection, pointing out that this is the usual chaff of a students' magazine. He may well be right but we do not yet know enough of how those curious jumps of style between Joyce's different books came about. The parody is very much part of Irish life; ballads, ranns, popular songs, are always being made to twist and turn facts and impressions inside out; and these are the voices of the older, Catholic and perhaps one should say Gaelic-influenced majority.

Various aspects of College life emerge from Arthur Clery's notes. For instance, a reading room in the College with daily papers and periodicals had been suggested. 'The National Library is an excellent place for talking . . . but Mr Lyster sometimes grows tired of the self-imposed task of providing matriculation men with variorum editions of Shakespeare and undertakes a crusade again in the interest of silence. Even an assistant librarian may prove cranky if the day's sporting has been unfavourable. Chess, at any rate can only be carried on under difficulties.' The College was without adequate premises.

> Our University, though not a mere creature of the mind, as some would have it, still suffers from the defect of being rather sporadic. University College teaches us. The Royal University examines us. Mr Lyster presides over the College Library and Philosophical Society whilst the University dining hall is at present under the control of the Dublin Bread Company. Here you may see the opulent professor devouring roast beef and tomatoes; the lady student indulging in cream cakes; the impoverished student paying fourpence for a commons of tea and unprocurable Vienna bread, whilst at intervals the University orchestra pours forth West British strains. All is ours. Truly it may be said, we have made the pond in Stephen's Green a University College lake.

When *Countess Cathleen* by W. B. Yeats was performed by the Irish Literary Theatre in 1899, in Lady Gregory's words, 'Young men from the Catholic University were roused to come and make a protest against "this insult to their faith".' Soon afterwards a manifesto was drawn up among the students, but Joyce, who took a great interest in the theatre and went frequently to the gods, refused to sign it.

In April 1900 the *Fortnightly Review* published an article on Ibsen by Joyce. People still remember the stir it created, even among members of the staff; for instance, Professor Semple, who taught Latin but knew Joyce only as one student among many, mentioned this fact in particular. A librarian in the National Library, a boy at the time, speaks of 'Mr Joyce' coming up to the counter and asking for the *Review*. The copy there now is probably the same. Somewhat grubby, it looks as if it had been folded in two at one time: perhaps 'pocketed' for a while to read on the steps or to show someone. The pages open, as if from habit, at the particular number on which the article appears. At the end someone has pencilled in rather childish characters 'Aetat 19'. It would need psychic powers to draw from this ordinary, even dull-looking volume, the pride, the sense that 'this then is the beginning' and '*they* recognize me' with which Joyce handled the magazine, or those other half-envious, somewhat bewildered impressions of boys from farms and the smaller Irish towns, professional families in Dublin or the suburbs, destined for parish presbyteries, the law, medicine, or some office building in America.

John Joyce, who took a great pride in his eldest son, often to the detriment of the other children, was delighted and sure 'that they had struck oil', a favourite expression according to one of his daughters. Father and son went off to London to interview the editor, but as no important post was offered to the young man he returned to his studies.

At home, as *Stephen Hero* suggests, the family were again in difficulties. As the rent had not been paid, Mr Dedalus received notice to leave their house in Fairview, but owing to a legal flaw in the writ they had been able to prolong their stay. The time was running out and it seemed that they would have nowhere to stay. At the eleventh hour a friend offered to let them use some of the rooms in a large and dilapidated house in the neighbourhood. The Dedalus family moved by a process familiar to Dublin, the little furniture which remained being carried on a float, while Stephen and his mother took charge of the ancestral portraits as the draymen were tipsy. As they passed along the sea-wall,[1] even Mrs Dedalus felt more cheerful at their successful evacuation. Ahead of them was Simon, his voice 'like a muffled flute singing a love song'. The house which sheltered them is described in such detail in the draft novel that the incident may have been experienced by the Joyces or happened to the writer himself at a later period.[2] One of Joyce's sisters can remember running about in the grounds of such a house. 'Yes, yes,' she said, 'Jim used to play the piano for hours, I well remember it, while our brother George was dying upstairs.' Bernard Murray thought Rudy in *Ulysses* was based on him and Stephen plays to his mother in much the same way.

[1] Owing to the redemption of the sloblands, this area is no longer upon the seafront at high tide.

[2] *Thom's Directory* for 1903 shows John Joyce at 32 Glengarrif Parade. As Richard Ellmann points out in 'The Backgrounds of Ulysses', *Kenyon Review*, 1954, the painfulness of recounting the death of George, of whom Joyce was extremely fond, was relieved by the change of name. His own son was called after the boy.

St Stephen's my Green

Paris
Only a fadograph of a yestern scene

Glendalough

The Vico Road
where terms begin to meet

In Dublin the following year the project of an Irish National Theatre was being discussed. Players, actors, even financial support had in some miraculous way come together. Joyce was not satisfied; he wanted them to perform continental plays, Ibsen in particular, following the original pro-gramme. An article expressing his views was discussed with the editors of *St Stephen's* and commissioned by them. When this was presented, under the somewhat startling title of 'The Day of Rabblement', if the editorial committee might have enjoyed the fireworks, the guardian angels flapped their wings and pronounced a decided *no*!

Francis Skeffington, former student and first registrar of the College, at £100 a year, met with the same refusal. One of the most notable College personalities at the time, he was regarded with affectionate amusement by the students and side-long glances by the more conservative members of the staff. The character of McCann or 'Knickerbockers' in *A Portrait* and *Stephen Hero* shows a considerable but not wholly accurate resem-blance to him. 'With a beard, a cycle suit and a golden fount of words,' Clery says, 'it was he who canvassed, collected subscriptions for the debat-ing society and got signatures for the Tzar's peace manifesto.' At one moment Gaelic dress is designed for him by one of the Irish students, at another he is called 'Mr Chaffington' or 'the irrepressible one' demanding the downfall of an incompetent committee. A nationalist who could not believe in insularity, he did not support the language movement and later left the Catholic Church, so that certain remarks in *Stephen Hero* are not true to his character and outlook. There Joyce reserved the role of interesting rebel for himself alone.[1]

A champion of the freedom and education of women, he spoke of their rights on every possible occasion; on marrying a fellow student, Hanna Sheehy, one of the daughters of the 'Daniels' household described

[1] 'At the time when they were students together, Skeffington had shelved the religious question, and declared his intention of devoting a year to its solution later on. He was a methodical man,' says Stanislaus Joyce.

In a letter written in September 1950 concerning this present work on Joyce, Professor Owen Sheehy-Skeffington remarked: 'You have not felt it necessary to do what Zola reproached Dumas for doing to Richelieu: removing those black spots from his character which are the shadows necessarily cast by the great qualities of the man. I was personally very pleased, I should like you to know, by your references to my father. Curiously, I feel that Joyce would have liked them too. I thought I could hear his quick laugh when I read your observation that he tended to reserve the role of interesting rebel for himself alone!'

in *Stephen Hero*, he combined her name with his own. Some of these ideas on feminism were brought together in an article, 'A Forgotten Aspect of the University Question'. This too was unpopular with the hierarchy. The policy of the University College was to allow women only to certain of its functions, and in view of the Royal Commission of Enquiry in the offing, the campaigns of Francis Sheehy-Skeffington proved embarrassing. Later he resigned his position on this account. Ahead of him lay a comparatively short life, as free-lance journalist and editor, member of the Independent Labour Party and campaigner against conscription, sympathetic to the independence movement but averse to physical force. As sometimes occurs to those who have a certain disinterestedness about them, as Gandhi perhaps, Francis Sheehy-Skeffington, the pacifist, was shot by a British officer (declared insane, but released later) during the rising of 1916.

The refusal of his essay brought Joyce into closer touch with Sheehy-Skeffington and they decided to publish their work together. A printer called Gerrard was found. Francis Sheehy-Skeffington probably provided the funds, and eventually a pink-ice-cream-coloured pamphlet was produced, priced 2*d*. The following comment concerning Joyce's part appeared in the next number of *St Stephen's*:

> The opening sentence describes his attitude towards the subject which he treats, the Irish Literary Theatre. . . . 'No man', says the Nolan, 'can be a lover of the good and the true unless he abhors the multitude.' In deference to the multitude, or, as Mr Joyce prefers to say, the rabblement of which the Irish Literary Theatre must now be considered the property, the directors have refrained from presenting Ibsen, Tolstoy, Hauptmann, Sudermann, Bjornsen and Giacosa, 'even where *Countess Cathleen* is pronounced vicious and damnable'. Now as we understood the Literary Theatre, its object was to *educate* a vulgarized public, in a word, to rescue the rabblement from the influences which, from the point of view of the artist, were working havoc. But this rabblement clung to a standard of morality, the tradition of the Catholic Church, the ethical teaching of Christendom. For a spiritual life based thereon it had sacrificed material prosperity and well-being, and it now showed itself willing, in the same interest, to forgo all that art might add to the surroundings of life. So it happened that when this rabblement protested against *Countess Cathleen*, our fellow students approved and supported the protest. Mr Joyce alone, to our knowledge, stood aloof.

Prophetically enough the writer continues:

> If Mr Joyce thinks the writer must stand apart from the multitude, and means that he must also sever himself from the moral and religious teachings which have, under Divine guidance, moulded its spiritual character, we join with him, and we prophesy but ill-successful any school which offers an Irish public art based on such a principle.

In the same number Chanel published an extract from a State Paper, Aet. Eliz., furnished by Mr P. W. Kent of the Record Office:

> And we also call to your Lordship's notice that there beth a certayne unlicensed press, owned by one Gerrard, a printer, wherefrom there doe issue sundrye riotous and sedytious publications under the names of one Skeffington and one Joyce, whom we believe to be a rebell, the which are most like to ruine the good manners of this our citie, for whereas the latter, corrupted, as we do verily believe by the learning of Italy or othere foreigne parts, hath no care for Holy Religion, but is fain to mislead our players, so that they doe perform evill workes; the former doth distracte our young maydes, who doe quit the distaff and would lief invade our schules and have it out with the lads as being their equals, so will they cease their fooling till they be whipt, the which we do submit to your graces were mete punishment for they that do mislead them.

As a matter of fact it is unlikely that 'one Gerrard, a printer' would have undertaken the work if he had realized its character. The firm, now Messrs Gerrard and Hughes in Merrion Row, undertook a good deal of work for the Jesuits and had supplied Newman at one time with stationery. Bernard Shaw had visiting cards printed there; George Moore came in and out from Ely Place nearby; the Yeats family were well known to them. Mr R. J. Gerrard, a son of the owner at the time, remembers Mr Skeffington coming in about the job but does not recollect seeing Joyce. He set up the pamphlets by hand but does not recall the size of the issue, which would not have cost much in those days.

It was probably later that Joyce prepared his paper on *Drama and Life* for the Literary and Historical Society. Many of the minutes remain and are of particular interest to Joyce's contemporaries. The Society brought together both students and certain members of the staff. Father Darlington, who figures as Father Butt and the dean of studies in *Stephen Hero* and *A Portrait*, took a particular interest in its debates.

Ireland is a wonderful place for meetings, for most people can talk well, if not think very clearly. The herrings introduced are of all shapes and colours; the starting point is only reached again by a considerable effort on the part of the chairman, who, most of the time, has been preparing his concluding joke. There is usually the nationalist, the rationalist, and the man who talks about afforestation or a vast co-operative cultural scheme. Yet one often has the stimulating sense of all being actors in a play, evolving into some sort of higgledy-piggledy pattern of Irish life. Nor was it very different in James Joyce's time. A contributor to *St Stephen's* described 'the sea of troubles' to be faced by the organizers 'before the finished whole is placed before the world'. There were 'the ceaseless committee meetings held in the professors' room, in the street, at Choral Union concerts, or in the mysterious mazes of newspaper offices, and the struggles with speakers who decline to speak, or worse encounters with orators whose anxiety to address the public outweighs the desire of the public to listen to them'.

At one time James Joyce appears to have been proposed for the auditorship against Hugh Kennedy. But as someone remarked to me, 'The Hatter never wore that particular crown.' The subjects debated varied from The Adoption of National Dress to Compulsory Land Purchase, The Position of Women, The Temperance Movement, and Compulsory Irish in Schools. On one occasion Mr Kinahan read a paper on 'a mysterious subject entitled "The Social Problem" . . . "The wrongs of the Proletariate!" and their remedy formed his theme. . . . Had Mr Churchill been present that night (having mistaken, we will suppose, the College for the Shelbourne) he would soon have imagined himself in the House of Commons. The orators who thundered forth that there was no occasion for party politics but that for their part . . . *a nation rightly struggling to be free* (applause) would have made him feel quite at home.' There followed a great deal of varied and noisy discussion:

> Not that these questions are contentious for us . . . Even the *Irish Times* reporter contented himself with a blank notebook and a sarcastic smile. A disturber who answered the orator's question, 'Why are there no anarchists in Ireland?' 'Because there is no King,' certainly scored a point. Moreover, we felt individualism had received a severe blow at the hands of collectivism, when an interrupter was expelled. We would certainly like to

have heard more from the rearguard socialists, while *dreaming Jimmy* and J. F. Byrne, standing on a window-sill, looked as if they could say things unutterable. . . .

Mr Taylor spoke of the miseries of the poor and the cruelties of the compulsory individualism of the Saxon . . . with a style that reminded one of our Joyce at his best, he has a broadness of sympathy that the latter has yet to acquire.

In one number of *St Stephen's* John Kennedy wrote a skit entitled 'Alice at a Debate' in which Joyce figures as the Mad Hatter and J. F. Byrne becomes the White Bishop:

'There's to be a debate in the Physics Theatre', said the Red Queen to Alice, 'so let's go now, for I've to take the chair.'

'If you do what will they sit on?' asked Alice as the Red Queen dragged her upstairs.

'Oh! all the old members sit on the new, and the Chairman sits on them in turn'.

Before Alice could say another word, she found herself in a large room. The Red Queen sat down between the March Hare and the Dormouse at a table with a candlestick and writing materials on it. Alice saw her old friend, the Hatter, sitting far back in a corner, raving but thinking beautiful thoughts, produced evidently by the remarks of the White Bishop (of the Cistercian Order) who sat near him.

'Who is the old woman over there eating feathers and whispering jokes to Tweedle-Dum and Tweedle-Dee?' asked Alice.

'Hush!' said the Red Queen, 'that's not an old woman, that's Chanel, *St Stephen's* Chanel'.

'Anything to St George's Channel?' asked Alice, remembering her geography.

'Silence! child, you are a West Briton!'

'But what's the debate about?' asked Alice.

'The Irish Revival, of course,' said the March Hare. 'What else *could it be on*? But you are allowed to discuss any matter you wish'.

'I will call upon the Hatter to open the debate,' said the Red Queen.

The Hatter, as usual, was dreaming beautiful dreams; but the sharp prod of a needle awoke him. He stood and commenced.

Alice, being only human, could not understand but supposed it was all right, although there was much mention of Ibsen, Hauptmann, Bjornsen, and Giacosa.

Everyone said it was divine, but no one seemed to know what it meant.

Eugene Sheehy records in his memoirs Seamus Clandillon's remark to Joyce, 'That was magnificent but you're raving mad'. As Stephen said in *Stephen Hero*, 'No one would listen to his theories, no one was interested in art.'

Yet there were times when Joyce was taken seriously. His paper on Mangan may have something of the ornateness of the period, a youthful flamboyance, but it shows exceptional ability in a young man just over twenty. How did it strike his contemporaries?

The 'Hatter's' paper proved highly interesting. Everyone went home feeling that he knew a great deal more about Mangan's purpose and aims than he had known when he entered the theatre. The most interesting part of the evening was the boy-orator's rentrée. Filled (doubtless by reason of his golden spoils in the past) with a confidence and daring that the poor ordinary member could never attain to, he made a bold frontal attack on Mr Joyce and the Nolan. The rabblement, whom the mention of Giacosa and Paracelsus customarily appals, rallied with 'timid courage' to the side of the newly-found champion. The idealistic cat was belled, and ignorance had a *field-day* for the nonce.

Yet notwithstanding the Philistinism of young Ulster, Mr Joyce certainly read a paper which displayed exceptional qualities both of thought and style. If Mr Magennis alone could understand what was meant by the 'retreating footsteps of the gods' [was this the retiring Committee?] and even he did not seem to be a thick and thin supporter of the doctrine that death is the highest form of life; still, apart from the mist which over-hung the writer's closing remarks, the *exposé* and appreciation of Mangan's life and writings was almost perfect. In parts the paper itself rose to no mean height of eloquence. Mr Magennis's summing-up on this occasion was perhaps the best we have heard for years in the society and made one regret indeed that the other professors do not take a larger part in the Society.

One who was present at this debate mentions that Professor Magennis, who had a good memory, quoted the poet at some length and added, rather slyly, 'It was supposed to be extempory but I rather think he had done a little preparation first!'

As the final examinations drew nearer, the notes in *St Stephen's* reflect the uneasy sense of the future which overhung those students who had almost completed their time at University College. In the summer of 1903 *St Stephen's* includes a note by Felix Hackett on:

THE COMING HOLOCAUST AT THE ROYAL

The Royal Examinations are close at hand, and the slaughter of the Innocents will be over before our next appearance. A brief sketch of students likely to pass through the dangerous crisis in safety, and perhaps brilliantly, will not be out of place. . . .

The B.A. class this year is a record one for many years past. Modern Literature should scarcely have its usual appearance of a reserve after the combined attack which is being made by Clandillon, Clancy, Kelly, Curran, and Joyce. By the way, we hope to see one of these carry off the Irish studentship in 1903.

According to *Stephen Hero*, Cranly had a plan for reading the course in five days, 'founded on an intimate knowledge of examiners and examination papers . . . which neither succeeded nor failed for the very good reason that it was never followed'. They sat on the Library steps, gazed up into the tranquil sky and discussed how it was possible to live with the least amount of labour. 'Cranly suggested bees. . . . Stephen said it would be a good arrangement if Cranly were to live on the labour of the bees and allow him [Stephen] to live on the united labours of the bees and their keeper.'

By the November issue the worst was over. Joyce had passed and an article in the College magazine dealt with 'The Conferring':

. . . The Chancellor puts forth golden sprays, the Senate springs into bloom, the Fellows don their brightest tints, the Undergraduates burst into song, all nature is clothed in a brilliant mantle. . . .

It was early evident that something was up in Earlsfort Terrace. Sir James and Mr Kane hurried in with a worried and expectant air. Candidates began to crowd in about eleven. The University officials entrenched themselves behind a zareba of examination desks, and Mr Kane gallantly took his stand in the pass and kept back the infuriated competitors, thereby at the peril of his life, protecting the secretaries who were announcing the results in the rear.

43

When a gown has been procured and lunch is over, photographs are taken:

> The initial ceremonies of graduation are somewhat elaborate. The proceedings opened with a paean or healing tune,[1] capably rendered by the M. B.'s. Certain of a livelihood in the immediate future, these young men displayed a becoming gaiety that distinguished them from the grim-visaged lawyer, philosopher and mathematician who surrounded them.
>
> The second stage of the initiation [possibly of Northern derivation] consists of stair-climbing. The ladies now appear on the scene, carefully chaperoned by the officials, who prevent them from mingling with the throng of bachelors. Having passed through the ordeal we are permitted to view the Fellows in their magnificence.

The Chancellor's address is, of course, always the pleasantest feature of the meetings. Lord Dufferin was so successful—he had the useful qualification of being stone deaf—that there was some difficulty in finding a successor. . . .

> At present the ceremony is too long. A concert, an address, a conferring, it is all interminable. Might they not all be combined into one? Drs Foye and Smith might learn the 'Marseillaise', 'A Nation Once Again', and even (if absolutely necessary) 'Dolly Grey' or 'Two Little Girls in Blue'. These they would perform in pleasant concord with the choral students in the gallery. Meanwhile the Chancellor, reciting to music, would be reading his address to the Senators and the Press, and pro-Vice-Chancellors would simultaneously be conferring the degrees. Thus all would pass off in pleasant harmony and concord, and the ceremony be shortened by half. It is the result of our meditation on the day's experiences. We recommend the suggestion to the University Commission. (*Victim*, November 1903.)

Yet the matter was not to rest there. In December the editor is supposed to have received a document, whose author desired to remain unknown. 'The Government notepaper he employed seemed at first to provide a clue; but we learn on investigation that nine-tenths of the private correspondence of young Dublin is conducted in this economical fashion.' It consisted of two cuttings from Dublin papers, and it is interesting to

[1] Eugene Sheehy mentions that the nationalists had protested against 'God save the King' and trouble was anticipated.

note the use of newspaper headings and a parody of journalistic styles which Joyce used later in *Ulysses*.

The first was by '*Alflox*':

ROYAL UNIVERSITY OF IRELAND
CONFERRING OF DEGREES
IMPRESSIVE SCENE
DISGRACEFUL ROWDYISM OF STUDENTS

In order to prevent trouble 'a strong force of police were drafted within the Academic walls', but eventually, the outcome of the day's proceedings was 'a signal triumph for the forces of authority in this country, and all right thinking persons will, we have no doubt, feel glad that so firm and resolute a stand against insignificant and unrepresentative self-speakers was made by the executive'.

'We hear on good authority that the Degree of Laws will shortly be conferred *Honoris Causa* on Inspector Larrisey, D.M.P. The degree will be conferred at a "special Conferring".'

'From the *Simplideplorable*'

ROYAL UNIVERSITY OF IRELAND
FREE SPEECH VINDICATED
GREAT UNDERGRADUATE TRIUMPH
POLICE OUTWITTED

'Once again the graduates of the Royal University have shown the civilized world what they are prepared to do for the principles they hold dear.'

After describing interruptions and confusion, the report continues:

THE POLICE ENTER THE HALL

and a scene of indescribable confusion ensued. The leaders of the student party, anxious to avoid bloodshed, warned their supporters not to come into collision with the officials of the law. . . . The ceremony ended with the playing of *God Save the King*, which was heartily hissed.

On leaving the hall, the students formed round Mr Joyce, who was proceeding to address them, when the

MEETING WAS CHARGED BY THE POLICE

and Mr Joyce and some friends were forced to take refuge on an outside car.

Later he addressed a 'large and excited gathering' and the scene at this moment was

He defended their right to 'make as much noise as they liked'. A voice—'Sunny Jim's too fond of force.' (A reference to a rather unpopular official.)

'And how could we die better
Than facing fearful odds
For the rights of Undergraduates
And the Freedom of "the Gods"?'

BELVEDERE PLACE

It was in the evening that we went to find the house in Belvedere Place, cornering Mountjoy Square, which Joyce used to visit as a young man. We walked up the broad, dark funnel of Great George's Street North, where an old tower rises among the bulk of eighteenth-century buildings like a piece of opera scenery. The whole neighbourhood seemed theatrical. On the steps of the house where we had once seen and photographed a cat sitting in the broken fanlight, a group of shawled women sat talking in the dark, figures from *The Plough and the Stars*.

A choir was practising part-songs in one of the mansions, now headquarters for unions and football clubs, a few youths and girls listening outside. The sound followed us down the long dark streets, where an occasional ornate lamp-standard still remains. Many of the rooms above us were lit by the dim, undersea greenness of gaslight, thrown on the elaborate ceilings of the old drawing-rooms and showing some of their oddly assorted furniture through thin, web-like curtains. Several of the fanlights over the doorways had the same other-period luminousness, setting off their full beauty, lace-designed, feminine, like the flounced and embroidered dresses that had once swept over the polished floors.

Vincent Clarke, who had been at school with Joyce, had been talking of Parnell and I thought of how he was taken as a boy to hear him at the Leinster Hall. They had edged in through the crowd almost up against him. It was the time of the split when excitement was intense, and the benches with their wooden back rests were crowded. Every now and then there would be a crash when some of those who stood or squatted upon them fell off, which must have been trying for the speakers. Dublin, he said, was 'pro-Parnell', 'every hat went off to him there'. Later he had seen the start of Parnell's funeral, the G.A.A. making a line with hurley sticks to keep back the crowds, and 'the pick of the men of Ireland were there'. Another incident which had stayed in his mind was the unveiling of the O'Connell monument, when he had been very taken with the bands and banners.

Now we were passing down the street where Mr Clarke remembered so clearly the policemen walking up and down as they guarded the house where Maurice Healy lived, turning over in their minds maybe the strange details of that tangle. Then we came upon Belvedere Place, just off Mountjoy Square, which is still quiet and circumspect. It was there that David Sheehy had lived with his wife and lively family of two boys and four girls. A member of the Irish Parliamentary Party which had stood for gentlemanly home rule, friendliness to England, and cultural regionalism, he had been anti-Parnell. Next door, I believe, was old T. D. Sullivan, one of the Bantry Band and author of the ballad 'God Save Ireland'.

For a number of years this tall, comfortable-looking house with its high granite steps, pillared door, and balcony on the first floor, was the meeting place for much of that middle stratum of Irish society which stood somewhere between the landed gentry, colonist and conqueror in outlook for the most part, and the growing body of extreme nationalists, some of whom were later to become revolutionaries. The picture of the Daniels' household given in *Stephen Hero* corresponds in many details to this milieu, but it is presented through a mood of critical superiority, reflecting a time when Stephen Dedalus could find nothing good to say about Dublin. In Joyce's case this may have arisen as a reaction to the disapproval shown by these and other friends to his behaviour during what might be called the 'Martello Tower period', and his subsequent elopement.

I was told that Joyce was often given a shakedown in the drawing-room after a party at Belvedere Place, and on occasions Mrs Sheehy even mended his socks and had his shirt washed, lending him one of her son's in the meantime. But as Joyce's brother pointed out in *Partisan Review*, the Joyces lived 'at about ten minutes' easy walking from the house of Mr Sheehy, and sometimes we used to go there—for I was bracketed in the invitation—on Sunday evenings, as all the members of the family had their several engagements during the week. Why in the world should my brother sleep there? And is it usual for wives of members of Parliament in Ireland to darn socks and have shirts washed on Sunday evenings when they have guests? Could the inventor of this story not manage to give it a greater air of probability?' This was another instance, I should say, of the effect of Joyce's work and that half-unconscious wish by those concerned to dramatize their discomfort away.[1]

'The attraction of the Sheehy household,' I have been told, 'for Joyce as for the other thirty or forty of us, was its genuine homeliness. Old David and Mrs Sheehy were open-hearted and had an old-style Irish welcome for everybody, young and old, rich and less rich. Joyce readily appreciated it just as we did. In fact, at Sheehy's house, and maybe nowhere else, Joyce became a normal young man in his early twenties and freely entered into whatever amusement was going. As for the politicians, the house was a rendezvous for many provincial nationalist M.P.s whenever they were spending a night in Dublin. So it was there several of us picked up our political and secular education. Father Eugene Sheehy, a brother of our host, from Limerick, was a great old "Land League" priest, who went to gaol on account of his speeches in the eighties, often to be met there.'[2]

'Ah . . .' he continued, 'The Sheehy's back parlour! I think all the so-called modern games originated there. "Information Please", "Question Time", and all the rest. In those days we invented our own amusements and there was no lack of imagination.'

Later on I met one of the daughters of this family. They had all been handsome, vivacious, sharing that pleasant-sounding, half-humorous intonation, the accent of the Ireland-educated gentlemen and gentlewomen

[1] 'The only house where my brother was given a shakedown for a night or two was that of the poet Cousins, darning and washing not included,' Stanislaus Joyce remarks. Mention will be made later of J. H. Cousins and his friendship with Joyce.

[2] From another source I was told that he was E. F. Sheehy, parish priest of Bruree, Limerick, and had been anti-Parnell. During the Fenian movement he was reproved by his Bishop and took the case to Rome and won it, but was shocked by the luxury there and on his return preached a sermon describing it. None of his parishioners gave Peter's Pence. This would, of course, need to be checked. Stephen Hero meets Emma in a room with a horse-hair sofa and this unprepossessing piece of furniture is mentioned in *Ulysses* and *Finnegans Wake*, as if to remind Joyce of a particular moment.

of another generation. Bernard Shaw, for instance, had the same way of talking, which has almost disappeared now.

'Joyce—Jim as we used to call him?' She stopped to see the young man more clearly. 'With dark hair and very light blue eyes, which kind of hit you, agate-coloured. Oh terrible serious. . . . There was something about him, *farouche* is perhaps the word, something. . . .' She laughed, unable to define her memory. 'He—he was in on himself.

'In those days people were very prim and proper; I remember being a bit shocked when he sang "Sally in Our Alley" at the mention of "bed"!' A point noted in *Stephen Hero*, which, being banned in Ireland, had not reached her.

On Sunday evenings at Belvedere Place, while the older people gossiped or talked politics, the younger generation played 'sharaydes'— she used the old pronunciation. As stage manager she often hooked James into long dresses and provided an ample bosom. The time he did Carmen she remembers in particular: in velvet bolero and flowered gown, with tambourine, a flower behind his ear. 'With hand on his hip he took off the singers and danced awfully well. I remember him singing, such a lovely voice he had, "L'amour est l'enfant de Bohème . . ."'

On another occasion, Joyce with Dick Sheehy, as lion and leopard at the Zoo, set upon a timid young man—perhaps Charlie Murray—just entering the room, and, although an admirer of one of the girls, he turned tail and was never seen there again. One evening, to the astonishment of some English converts in the audience, the theme was the election of a new Pope. James as a cardinal was bribing the others for votes, and when asked for his blessing on election, declared, 'Oh he'd left it with his luggage somewhere.' The guests were extremely shocked.

Once he played in a version of *Hamlet*, lamenting over Ophelia in the best of Moore Street accents. Again, as a stoic, told of house and family burnt, Joyce remarked, 'And how's the dog?' Another game was a play on place names—'What Chapel is it?' 'I wasn't Lucan' (lookin) or 'Harold's Cross because Terenuhe'—(Terry knew her). It is as though Joyce was preparing all his life for the dream of *Finnegans Wake*. During Margaret Sheehy's little play, *Cupid's Confidant*, done by the Dramatic and Literary Society, he acted the part of Geoffrey Fortescue, a man-about-town. Improvising now and then, he scored a particular hit, at a time 'when Sinn

Fein was at the back of everything', with his remark, 'Damn these Irish matches!'

Listening to the soft voice, humorous, half regretful, one seemed to share in her seeing of Joyce again. When Michael Davitt came to the Mangan centenary, she asked Joyce what poems to choose, and later the old patriot of Land League days congratulated her. Without the affectation of the elocutionist, simply, she spoke the lines from 'The Nameless One' as that audience and James Joyce had once heard them :

> 'And tell how, now, amid wreck and sorrow
> And want, and sickness, and houseless nights
> He bides in calmness the silent morrow,
> That no ray lights. . . .
> Him grant a grave to, ye pitying noble,
> Deep in your bosoms! There let him dwell!
> He, too, had tears for all souls in trouble,
> Here, and in hell.'

KILDARE STREET

James Joyce perhaps used the National Library in Kildare Street from the time he was at Belvedere until he decided to leave Dublin in 1904. In *Ulysses*, Bloom considers the 'handsome building Sir Thomas Deane designed' and to avoid Blazes Boylan he admires 'the cream curves of stone'. Built in 1890, it reflects the weight of words packed into solid Victorian volumes, the certainty that man was proceeding towards a larger, more expensively ornamented world. The portico with sandstone pillars surrounds the ground floor, and the mosaic of the hall contains two well-nourished serpents, each climbing a branch of knowledge, with *Sapientia* inscribed below. Between the 'curving balustrade' of green marble, the wide stairs are worn lip-thin in places by those seeking knowledge—or a look at a directory for an address. Leonardo da Vinci and Michelangelo gaze across from the yellowy-green of a stained-glass window to the stairhead where James Joyce stood for hours talking to J. F. Byrne or another. Opposite the bench which is there now is a plaque to Thomas William Lyster, 'for 25 years the able and enlightened librarian of this library'. William Magee suggests that as he wore a broad-brimmed black hat to cover a big bald head, Joyce may have had this in mind when calling him 'The Quaker Librarian'. To our generation he is only a name, but mention it to the senior Library assistants at the wide counter in 'the constant readers' room', as James Joyce called it, and they immediately see the man again. Something of his interest and enthusiasm reaches one through those he trained; in consultations over an unusual reference or when there is some query about Dublin to be cleared up, an obscure pamphlet traced. In those days when a special point was raised, Mr Lyster himself would often undertake its solution.

'He'd rush out with an armful of books,' one man said, 'indeed, at times he'd weary the man with books.'

'He was a real literary man,' added another, 'and didn't care for special editions worth thousands but liked people to *read*. He'd come in the morning with cuttings from the day's *Irish Times*, and have a typed list of titles on subjects of current interest pinned up; there, below that lamp.'

When there was a question of forbidding students to stand and talk on the steps outside, he declared that it was their library, and he was delighted when George Moore remarked that everyone seemed happy there. Very keen on fresh air, and cycling, he had the windows wide open, and in-sisted that the Corporation car should clean Kildare Street particularly well to keep the dust from the books. Now and then he would take a day's rest in bed and return 'full of vigour and run around'. When things were not going well, Mr Lyster would put his head in his hands—'Ah! The world is too much for me!'—a gesture remembered with a laugh by one of his secretaries.

The high curved roof of the main reading-room, a reminder of Crystal Palace achievements, is glass along the centre; fat pigeons and gulls from Dublin Bay squabble and mate outside, suggesting another dimension. The beige and green walls have a frieze of plump, Neaves-fed cupids, more than child-size; there is a balcony across one end, with four high brass lamps on each side of a square mahogany-embedded clock. Doors and windows are heavily hooded with this brown-leather polished ornamentation, in which dragons obligingly uphold garlands in their mouths. At one time readers entered by a turnstile, mentioned in *Ulysses* and removed some time ago. Desks were foursquare, as shown by a photograph taken in 1897, and sketches in *St Stephen's*. This arrangement, which encouraged both talk and flirtation, was changed later.

'Each desk was supplied with a pewter ink pot, blotting paper and quill pens, and my job as a boy was to go round looking after them,' I was told. 'When there was too much talking going on, Mr Lyster would send one of us over to put a "Silence" notice on the desk before the offender.'

It seems that Joyce used to sit on the right-hand side, as one faces the counter, up near the entrance. William Magee mentioned that at one time he always asked for the *Illustrated London News* and pored over it, probably for the articles by Chesterton and Lang which it contained, Stanislaus Joyce suggests. 'Jim no doubt read them for their rich-Philistine aroma.'

The 'discreet vaulted cell' where the discussion in *Ulysses* takes place may have been based on the room used by Mr Lyster and Dr Best which lies behind the counter and was only lit by a roof light at the time. In the passage is the old bell-push which signalled to the engineer in charge to turn on the electric light. This made a curious hissing noise in those days, a point mentioned in *A Portrait*.

On the library steps Joyce watched the students shelter from the rain, or followed the flight of birds about the buildings in Kildare Street, hoping that a certain girl would come there. In *Stephen Hero* there is a description of how one evening Stephen met Emma Clery as she was about to leave, her soft white boa about her dark face, and walked with her up Stephen's Green, past the chains bearing their 'nightly load of amorousness'. The trees where they may have stood together near Charlemont Mall, which Joyce remembered in *Finnegans Wake*, have gone, and much of the shady canal walk is bare and open. Yet in some places the flat, villa-reflecting water is still flagged and weed-bordered, children fish tiddlers into jam-jars and lovers sit on the stumps of oaks and elms which gave shelter to their parents' love-making.

CABRA

Thackeray remarked the way parts of Dublin can suddenly become country. 'After number 46 Eccles Street', he wrote in *The Irish Sketch-book*, 'potatoes begin at once. You are on a wide green plain, diversified by occasional cabbage plots, by drying grounds white with chemises, and in the midst of which the chartered wind is revelling; and though in the map some fanciful engineer has laid down streets and squares, they exist but on paper; nor, indeed, can there be any need of them at present, in a quarter where houses are not wanted so much as people to dwell in the same.' Now these streets have become a reality, as Dublin has continued to grow. Going up past the Mater Hospital one is soon in Cabra, on higher ground, where it is still windy and the mountains can be clearly seen. With lines of small brick villas, much of the district suggests work-a-day respectability. There is less graceful decay than round Mountjoy Square and Gardiner Street; life is more hidden away.

St Peter's Church stands high and spiky in outline, between branch roads. As we passed, a large notice declared 'Hour of Prayer', and a few dark-clothed women went in and out. After some enquiry we found the old name plaque of what was once St Peter's Terrace. No. 7 is exactly like its neighbours, grimy brick, three-windowed, with a small patch of earth in front of the parlour. The Joyces moved there towards the end of James's period at University College, having purchased the house, I am told.

On October 31st, 1902, according to Gorman, Joyce received his degree of Bachelor of Arts. Soon the following note appeared in *St Stephen's*: 'Much pleasure was occasioned at the school when it became known (for how could it have been unknown when it was a secret?) that Messrs J. F. Byrne, Seamus Kelly, and Joyce intend to join the ranks of Cecilia Street. The veterans who are now in the last lap of their course, look forward to their keeping the old flag flying during their time at the [medical] school.' J. F. Byrne states that in the autumn of 1902–3 Joyce did attend a few first-medical lectures in University College, including biology by Professor Sigerson, chemistry and physics by Professors Ryan and McClelland. 'He only fiddled at medicine! He wanted to be a writer,' said a contemporary. A copy of a letter written by Joyce to Lady Gregory in November 1902 shows that he regarded medicine as a means of obtaining economic security so that he might dedicate himself to his own work. Whereas *Stephen Hero* suggests that the young man was offered work by the Jesuits and refused, Joyce protests that the authorities would not give him coaching and other work to help him pay his medical fees. Therefore he would go abroad and measure himself against the powers of the world, and he concludes, 'I know no one with a faith like mine.'

Joyce was determined to get to Europe, where a new life seemed to be stirring. The direct experience of the Continent was the privilege of such people as George Moore, Yeats, or Lady Gregory. They had only to buy a ticket at Cooks to reach Paris, Vienna or Florence. They knew the ropes and handrails of literary and artistic interchange, the places to stay, the people to meet. With this inherited sophistication behind them, their need was not the social, revolutionary drama of Ibsen but the exploration of country and village life at home. They found a rich seam of verbal and visual ore and worked it well, subject to the limitations of their equipment. This could only be valuable for a time, as the subsequent history of the Abbey Theatre has shown. The scientific recording and documentation of folklore in Ireland and England undertaken during the past twenty years represents an entirely different approach to much the same material.

Until this literary movement, but for the good-natured ridicule of Lover, the patronage of Moore, and the incidental sympathy of Maria Edgeworth, the majority, Catholic and Gaelic in background, had been ignored. 'We, different as we are, believe in you,' was the apologetic attitude of the Protestant nationalist. They accepted the defects of the enthusiasts, the crudity and self-seeking which goes with all idealism, in asking forgiveness for their own advantages. Anglo-Irish literature owes much to that admission of strangeness, love never quite sure of being requited. This approach was impossible for Joyce; like Richard Rowan in *Exiles*, his own doubts had placed him outside. Later he was to prove himself the first major writer to arise from the Ireland to which they could not wholly belong. In *A Portrait*:

> He stared angrily back at the softly lit drawing-room of the hotel in which he imagined the sleek lives of the patricians of Ireland housed in calm. They thought of army commissions and land agents; peasants greeted them along the roads in the country: they knew the names of certain French dishes and gave orders to jarvies in high pitched provincial voices which pierced through their skintight accents.
>
> How could he hit their conscience or how cast his shadow over the imaginations of their daughters, before their sires begat upon them, that they might breed a race less ignoble than their own? And under the deepened

dusk he felt the thoughts and desires of the race to which he belonged flitting like bats, across the dark country lanes, under trees by the edges of streams and near the pool mottled bogs.

This, of course, is an overstatement, for Joyce's family on both sides had been town dwellers and fairly prosperous for several generations and were brought up to think continually of being 'ladies' or 'gentlemen', a preoccupation which ran down through society until it met those who were proud of 'knowing their place'. If his father still spoke with a Cork accent, his son was a Dubliner, something rather different from people in other parts of Ireland. Yeats wrote of the writer's need for detachment from his caste and the limitations of his background. With his father to prepare him, even as a young man he had realized that 'style and person-ality—deliberately adopted and therefore a mask, is the only escape from the hotfaced bargainers and the money changers'. Although *Stephen Hero* shows Joyce schooling himself to a certain reserve (often commented upon later), his work contains a very subtle analysis of that sense of inferiority underlying so much of Irish life. Emotionally an Irishman, in mind he was much more a descendant of Robert Boyle, who, for all his initiation of scientific method, wrote copiously on religion and concerned himself with ghosts. Shaw went to England as by right, but Joyce, as so many from the Gaelic world had done, turned to the Continent. If his voice kept at bay the words of the English language, 'so familiar and so foreign', he was not only to accept but remake them, as Gaelic and the Irish countryside had once claimed and changed its conquerors.

The letter to Lady Gregory suggests that she was more friendly to Joyce than has generally been supposed. Indeed she may have written to W. B. Yeats on his behalf, for Gorman mentions that when Joyce left for London, not immediately after graduation as he states but late in 1902, the poet met him early in the morning at Euston and bought him break-fast. On December 4th, 1902, he wrote to Lady Gregory, 'I have had Joyce with me for a day. He was unexpectedly amiable and did not knock on the door with his old Ibsenite fury.' [1] Later he introduced him to Arthur Symons and one or two other people and it was with hopes of contributing articles and reviews to one or two English periodicals that Joyce took the Newhaven–Dieppe boat for Paris.

[1] *The Letters of W. B. Yeats*, 1954.

III

PARIS—SANDYCOVE
1902–1904

It may have been Thackeray who suggested where Joyce should stay in the Latin Quarter, for he wrote in his *Paris Notebook*, published in 1840: 'If you are a student come to study the humanities or the pleasant art of amputation, cross the water forthwith, and proceed to the Hôtel Corneille near the Odéon or others of its species; there are many where you can live royally (until you economize by going into lodgings) on four francs a day.' On the other hand, W. B. Yeats might have given him the address, for he had stayed there in 1896, perhaps with Arthur Symons. J. M. Synge first met the poet in the hotel, where, according to Gorman, Joyce also entertained 'that dark tramper of a man'.

By chance I spent a night there myself before the hotel was destroyed by a bomb during the Second World War, after a rather late showing of the films of Jean Painlévé, when I was locked out of a hostel in the Boulevard St Michel. With disapproving eyes the night porter rose slowly to the clinking of keys and, with the smooth, sinister movements of his kind, led me across the narrow, paved hall. We passed some weary, long-leaved plants and mounted an old curved staircase of bare wood which turned up into the darkness. Everything was enclosed, waiting within itself. The room where I slept had linen-covered walls and old furniture as if all had remained unchanged for a hundred years. Across the way was the great dark bulk of the Odéon Theatre and in the early morning I was woken by street sellers who congregated noisily below the windows. During the winter of 1903 Joyce rented a top room, with a patched length of carpet maybe, the hard roll for a pillow and families of mice behind the cracked skirtings. There, on a spirit stove, he cooked in one saucepan which was rarely washed out.

HÔTEL CORNEILLE

It was from this quarter, where Latin had been spoken up to the time
of the Revolution, that Joyce first came to know Paris. Under the arches
of the Odéon Theatre, with their lamps of classical design, were the book-
stalls of battered wood, selling music and old magazines, which must have
been there throughout the lifetime of several generations of loiterers and
passers-by. Gradually Joyce had come to work out the pattern of the
district, the lines of streets which fan out from the Place de l'Odéon to
meet the Boulevards of St Germain and St Michel. When he could afford
the luxury of going to a restaurant he sometimes patronized Le Polidor
in the rue Monsieur le Prince, which is still there. Behind his hotel lie the
gardens of the Luxembourg. The artificial levels of its terraces, the statues
and formal beds, high, compressed groups of chestnuts—perhaps the
shadow of Proust playing with his Gilberte—all combine to give it a
peculiar suggestion of eroticism. Here Joyce must have sat until the time
when the nurses and mothers gather their children together, and only the
couples remain, so still that they take on the shape of the trees. 'Paris', as
Joyce wrote, 'is a lamp for lovers lit in the wood of the world.'

Recollections of Kevin Egan (Joe Casey in reality) and his talk of
Fenian days, scraps of conversation, oddments from Joyce's first stay in
Paris, are worked into *Ulysses*, with jokes heard maybe at a later date; for
instance, the waitress who mistook 'Irlandais' for a Dutch cheese. To
reach the rue Cuvier, where it seems Joyce attended at least one class in
the first year of medicine—'P.C.N., you know, *physiques, chimiques et
naturelles*'—he would either have taken the horse bus which probably
followed the Boulevard St Germain or, more characteristically, struck
across country, if the expression can be used of areas built and rebuilt
over for more than a thousand years. At first Joyce's impressions would
refer back to Dublin—the great classical pillars of the Panthéon and the
frontages of College Green, the curious, barn-like atmosphere in the
Bibliothèque St Geneviève where he read Aristotle and Ben Jonson, as
contrasted with the nineteenth-century comfortableness of the National
Library in Kildare Street. If everything at home seemed on a small scale,
Joyce never lost that habit of linking one manifestation of a form or
tendency with another. Some instinct protected him from becoming a

57

cosmopolitan; in *Finnegans Wake* his familiarity with much of west Europe and its languages, his gathering together of the ideas of the world, is presented through the dream of an Irish publican.

In 1902 the authorities of the Collège de Médicine would not recognize Joyce's Dublin degree, but this difficulty might have been surmounted but for the fact that fees had to be paid in advance. This he was unable to do, and hopes of giving lessons and writing articles for journals in London also came to nothing. He hung on in Paris, waiting, often on an empty stomach, for small sums sent from Dublin. A sister has pointed out that he was made an allowance of £1 a week, but even then this was inadequate. 'God, we simply must dress the part', Stephen Dedalus remembers in *Ulysses,* and a photograph taken at that time shows Joyce in a large Latin-quarter hat and long overcoat, which makes him rather like an advertisement for a famous brand of port.

If Joyce had been able to qualify as a doctor, the future would certainly have been easier. For one thing, the trouble with his teeth which appears to have affected his eyesight might have been avoided. Would he have turned towards the new developments in psychology and shown his knowledge of himself and other people through the textbook or the essay rather than the novel? After all, the present is often like a car travelling an unmarked plain; only on looking back does the road seem to shape itself from all the possibilities behind us.

ST PETER'S TERRACE

Gorman mentions that Joyce returned home for the Christmas and New Year holidays and it may have been on the journey that he read *Les Lauriers Sont Coupés* by Edouard Dujardin, as suggested by a remark to the French writer by Joyce many years later. He went back to France, and in the spring of 1903 it seems that on Good Friday he attended the services at Notre Dame, then, having nothing to do and being penniless, he followed his Dublin habit of walking through the streets of the city, murmuring the wonderful vocables of his poems. Late that night he returned to the Hôtel Corneille to find a telegram from his father. Mrs Joyce was dying. A pupil lent him some money and the following morning Joyce set out for Dublin.

May Joyce was indeed very ill, with no hope of recovery. Her sister, Mrs Murray, left her own family of young children to look after the Joyce household at Cabra, for some months as it turned out. During the fine spring and summer weather they waited for the end. Each time Joyce closed the door on his mother's suffering, he faced the presbytery and church at the end of the road, which stood for the beliefs he repudiated but could not forget, and that pathetic appeal that he should return to them. Indeed, it was from her he had inherited his intransigence. In *Ulysses* Stephen is shown as refusing to kneel with the family assembled round the dying woman, but Stanislaus Joyce shows the actual situation to have been less dramatic. 'The order [to kneel and pray] was given in a peremptory manner by an uncle, and it was not obeyed: Joyce's mother by then was no longer conscious.' [1]

Down in the city, with too much talk perhaps, and in too many pubs, he tried to escape from the details of those months. W. R. Rodgers recorded the remark that Joyce was not a drinker but he 'went the pace all right between his mother's death and his departure . . .' He certainly made an attempt to find a means of staying in Ireland. For a time he did some teaching, experience to be useful later. William Magee remembers how one day Edward Dowden told him that 'an extraordinary young man had been to see him, with a request for a job in the Library—quite unsuitable'. Writing as John Eglinton in *Irish Literary Portraits*, he has given an excellent sketch of Joyce at that time. 'A pair of burning dark blue eyes, serious and questioning, is fixed on one from under the peak of a nautical cap, the face is long, with a slight flush suggestive of dissipation, and an incipient beard is permitted to straggle over a very pronounced chin, under which the open shirt collar leaves bare a full womanish throat. The figure is fairly tall and very erect and gives an impression of seedy hauteur. . . .'

One of Joyce's youngest sisters can remember a time when he was asked to a dinner or reception by Lady Gregory and she was given her tram fare to meet Gogarty at Findlater's Church and bring home a dress-suit borrowed from him. 'But the suit was unparcelled over his arm, the striped lining showing. I refused to carry it home and made him come all the way back with me! It wouldn't have seemed respectable in those

[1] *Recollections of James Joyce, by his brother.* The James Joyce Society, New York.

days.' 'And Gogarty did, which shows that he could be a very decent fellow,' commented Stanislaus Joyce.

It was during this period, after the comparative security of College life was over and Joyce's struggle to exist in Paris had shown him the difficulties of trying to live by literary journalism, or the lack of it rather, that many of the psychological patterns of *A Portrait* and *Ulysses* were to shape themselves. For Gogarty he was 'a medical students' pal' with his 'astringent joy and his delight in the incongruous', and 'a hell of a knowledge about literature, mediaeval and the rest of it', who liked 'to deal out the pearls of the poets to the most unreceptive people'. Whereas George Moore noted in a letter that Gogarty 'was very kind to me in the tram, refraining from quoting too many sonnets'.

Joyce had no use for the enthusiasm of his own people, religious or political, and his Jesuitical and Thomist training alienated him from the Protestant, cultured, and what we might now call 'left-wingish' followers of A.E. Their ideas were expressed in *Dana*, 'a magazine of independent thought'. Joyce might agree with the first part of such statements as 'the life of a country is in its heretics, its doubters of all accepted faiths and formulas', but would have given his odd guffaw on reading 'and yet have faith in an ideal. . . .' 'The Irish question would be more than half solved if some of the effort which is being squandered in belabouring the old Ascendency were directed against the intellectual tyranny which threatens to stifle with its rank growth the tender shoots of nascent nationality,' wrote Sir Horace Plunket. If Joyce cared little for shoots, tough or tender, he saw less sense in shooting but might have doubted A.E. when he declared, 'The theory of physical force has been gradually ebbing away from politics in Ireland.' Indeed, Joyce seemed to fit in nowhere. Anxious for disciples, he was unable to follow any leader less than Ibsen, and with the unreasonableness of genius thought that the society in which he lived should accept him at his own evaluation, although he showed nothing but contempt for its gods. But Dublin has always had plenty of good talkers with brilliant futures and only time would tell if this young man was going to come to anything. Yeats is said to have remarked that he had seldom met a young man with so much pretension and so little to show for it.

SANDYCOVE

At length Joyce obtained some teaching at Clifton School, Dalkey, and discovered that the tower beyond the little bay at Sandycove, just above the Forty Foot bathing-place, could be had very cheaply. According to an account of Oliver St John Gogarty,[1] Joyce undertook to pay the rent and he provided the furniture. At first all went well. They were probably installed by the late autumn of 1903, for William Magee recollected a Christmas spent there, the cold kept out by plenty of whisky. Among the young men who joined them at week-ends was Arthur Griffith, who was to play so important a part in Irish affairs later. During the warm weather they slept out in the open on the gunrest. For a while Joyce must have felt better; he was away from his family, had some work, a group of friends. Then a third resident was introduced and trouble began. Gogarty brought a young Anglo-Irishman to the tower, a Gaelic enthusiast, who later committed suicide for love of an Irish lady. He bored and irritated Joyce, and when he dreamt of black panthers and used his revolver, the young man could bear it no longer.

For many years the Martello Tower had been kept locked, and Joyce's mind had quietly returned there to bring into words the atmosphere of that morning in June 1904 which is described in *Ulysses*. The parallel with the departure of Telemachus in search of his father was by no means forced. It was inherent in that material of his own life which Joyce quarried, cut and shaped for his art, and the tower stands as a symbol of the end of his childhood and youth in Dublin. Stephen, having given Buck Mulligan the key, reflects, 'I will not sleep here tonight. Home also I cannot go.'

Fortunately the trams had not yet disappeared when we went out to Dunlaoghaire one afternoon. Our long, angular chariot sang past Merrion, Booterstown and a fairground which might have been that of 'Araby', on then to Blackrock and Monkstown. Each of these trams had a personality to express, gathered perhaps from the route, the people it served, and was known intimately to the driver, for, as Bloom considered, 'Everything

---

[1] *Mourning Became Mrs Spendlove*, and other portraits, Oliver St John Gogarty, N.Y., 1948. As Richard Ellmann has established, Joyce did not leave the school in June but finished the term there. Stephen wears mourning in *Ulysses* but it is doubtful if Joyce himself would have done so a year after his mother's death.

speaks in its own way.' The day had been showery and Howth seemed nearer than usual, and yachts racing in the Bay looked like cabbage whites scattered on green leaves of sea. At Sandycove the curves of a modern house repeat the theme of the Martello Tower, one of a number built against French invasion early in the nineteenth century, the only monuments of their period to Wolfe Tone, Lord Edward FitzGerald and Robert Emmet. Iron steps, like those of a fire escape, lead to the first floor entrance, painted a naval grey. As the narrow, heavy door of studded metal swung slowly across the threshold stone, I called 'Joyce, Joyce!' and then with a laugh, 'Jimmy, Jim; are you there?' But when we entered through the narrow passage my mood became serious, as though this had been an invocation; it was so many years since the name had sounded here. Strange that with the intensity of imagination, Joyce had brought so many readers to this bare-floored, egg-shaped room, which gave no sense of a vitiated past, the worn-away atmosphere of places visited too often.

Two shafts running upwards aslant the thick, white-washed walls provide a certain light, and these are mentioned in *Ulysses* as being clouded by the smoke of the fire. This may have been the small rusty range with an oven and open grate. Except for one high shelf running round the room, the place was empty. A very narrow, rail-less flight of stone stairs turns upwards to the roof, so that Buck Mulligan must have carried his shaving bowl carefully, his yellow dressing-gown brushing against the walls. The raised gunrest circles the outer wall like a step. To the chin are the huge blocks of grey-white granite, clean and flinty, with little bits of quartz shining in them, as if brought straight from Glencullen on the hills. A bunch of grass waves here and there in the cracks, and all around is the view of the mountains and the sea, with the two spires of Dunlaoghaire like needles waiting to be threaded.

We went down again and tugged at the heavy door to close the padlock, for the huge key is not in use, and turned towards the ordinary-dayness of Dublin again. So many impressions seemed to overlie one another—Joyce working on *Ulysses* at Trieste and Zürich, in those hot rooms in Paris, and that odd coming together of circumstances and creative ability whereby a moment's experience can be given a life so much longer than our own.

When Joyce began *Ulysses* at Trieste in 1914, although he had thought of the theme for a long time, he did not know just where the book would take him. The Homeric parallel had already been found in his own wanderings, his struggle with people and circumstances, to be worked out in terms of a series of events on a certain day in Dublin during the summer of 1904. In *James Joyce and the making of Ulysses*, Frank Budgen mentions that he saw in the writer's flat in Zürich a photograph of a Greek statue of Penelope with her finger uplifted as though listening —the gesture of the little boy figure which Marion Bloom found so fascinating. Joyce too was listening, waiting all through the writing of *Ulysses* for the sound which would bring him round again to the beginning.

On June 10th, according to Gorman's biography, Joyce met Nora Barnacle for the first time, and it is now clear that the rupture with those living at the Martello Tower took place a few days later, probably in the early morning of June 16th, when Joyce called at the Library and mentioned the incident to William Magee. J. F. Byrne was not living at 7 Eccles Street until 1909, so the address probably meant nothing to Joyce at the time and evidently he stayed the night elsewhere. All we can be sure of is that this date, now called 'Bloom's Day', marks the end of one part of Joyce's life and the beginning of another.

No direct reference to Nora's uncle, Michael Healy, has yet been traced in Joyce's writings, but some interesting letters to him have survived. This kindly Galwayman may have been in Dublin at the time and provided part at least of the 'adopted father' theme of *Ulysses*. Born in 1862, he was a member of an old Galway family, brother of Mrs Barnacle of the Bowling Green, Galway. He entered Customs and Excise in 1883 and served in Galway until transferred to Dublin in 1916. A bachelor, he lived with his mother in Ormonde, a large house in Clontarf Road. In 1922 he retired and may have taken another job in Dublin, but later returned to St Mary's Terrace, Galway. He died while attending mass in the Abbey Church. Said to have been an extremely religious man, a member of the Sodality of the Jesuit Church, his loyalties lay with the old régime and he had little use for the Free State. He appears to have helped Joyce financially, owned copies of all his work, and, perhaps, visited the family in Trieste.

'St Stephen's my green.' 'Why should Joyce have chosen that?' someone asked me as we looked at a photograph of the little park taken early in the century. 'He usually had a good reason. . . .' This brought to mind the remark of a friend who had known Nora Joyce much later. 'I remember her saying she noticed Joyce in a park—could it have been the Phoenix or St Stephen's Green—and that he was so goodlooking, dressed in a white suit. She thought he was a foreigner, a Swedish sailor maybe.' Confused as this seems, it suggests that Joyce was wearing his white cap, which must have been unusual in Dublin, and that they came across each other for the first time in that square of trees and little lakes which Joyce had crossed so often on his way to college. In *Ulysses*, p. 573, Stephen murmurs a poem, Yeats' 'Who goes with Fergus?', and Bloom reflects 'In the shady wood. The day's white-breast . . . A girl. Some girl. Best thing could happen to him.'

> Who will go drive with Fergus now,
> And pierce the deep wood's woven shade,
> And dance upon the level shore?
> Young man, lift up your russet brow,
> And lift your tender eyelids, maid,
> And brood on hopes and fear no more.

It is probable that Nora Barnacle was then working at Finn's Hotel, Nos. 1 and 2 Leinster Street, part of a house running over Groggins ('Milliners and Ladies' outfitter', according to *Thom's Directory*) which at the back overlooked the grounds of Trinity College.

Those who knew Mrs Joyce stress her attractiveness. She always had something lively and humorous to say, and never came to see friends without a little gift or helpful gesture. She had that responsiveness which would welcome both husband and wife with a kiss, that overflow of warmth which comes from good health. In a small house in Galway, where a picture of Trieste under the Austro-Hungarian Empire hung near the door, to meet one of Nora Joyce's sisters was to catch something of the vitality which they both shared. Their background was simple. Their father had been a confectioner or baker, but they had not only inherited good looks but something of that social sense and acuteness which is not the prerogative of any stratum of society. I have been told that as the family grew Nora Barnacle was sent to live with her grandmother and was educated by nuns, which made her feel rather pushed aside so that she was ready to understand Joyce's own sense of exile. And although she was untheoretical and could shrug off a great many things, as it becomes clear when Joyce's last year in Vichy is described, there remained in her that strong subterranean current of psychic presentiment of death and fatality which underlies so much of Irish life.

HOWTH

In *Ulysses* that obsessional quality which is so much a part of any writer's make-up is shown by the way in which Bloom thinks of Blazes Boylan's appointment with Marion throughout the day, and the time itself—four o'clock—probably had a significance for Joyce in a very different set of circumstances. While Nora was working at Finn's—what use Joyce was to make of that name!—this was probably the hour at which she could most easily slip away to meet her Swedish sailor, perhaps again in St Stephen's Green. The choice of country may have been an after-confusion, as it were, for Joyce probably talked of his communication with Ibsen and his having learnt Danish to read the plays. Nora was always vague about his work, and indeed read very little of it.

On the other hand, they may have taken the tram to Howth, along the curve of the Bay through what was then green, houseless countryside bordering great sandy stretches at low tide. Perhaps they continued to the summit, their vehicle hissing and groaning up the hills as if Ariel, and Caliban too, were shut up inside; then suddenly bucketing, tin-sounding into the dips of the way, jerking itself back into high-pitched song again. On Sundays and holidays all the different accents of Dublin were heard on that tram, voices which echo in and out of *Finnegans Wake*, from the Coombe and Gardiner Streets, the quays or Ballybough.

The headland is varied enough to be a country in itself and has quite a different character from the wide flat lands of County Meath beyond and behind it. Yeats spent part of his childhood at Howth, James Stephens found there the themes for some of his best poetry. On the east it is a place of cliffs and little bays, bracken and bare slopes; to the north, sheltered from most winds, there are the rhododendron woods of Howth demesne, smelling of peat and leaf-mould. Feminine, exotic, they are one of those surprises of the Irish climate. The Ponticums and larger trees seem to grow out of one another, covering rock surfaces and narrow ravines. Based by ferns, like tropical paintings by Rousseau, they are entered by narrow, stone-ledged paths, red-setter colour and dry from the pine-needles which protect the smaller, lightly branched rhododendron species, whose flowers seem lit from the inside by their colour.

Here and there in this forest, openings show 'Howth Castle and environs', toy size, with turreted walls and towers of a beech-trunk grey, cut into the green of lawns, gardens, paddock; and over a strip of water is the old Celtic-Romanesque church on Ireland's eye. Westward, Joyce and Nora would have turned towards the sands of the Bull, the caterpillar legs of the wooden bridge to his bathing place as a schoolboy, and, synthesized by distance, pencil-blue, the shape of Dublin spread out along the harbours and variations of the Bay.

In *A Portrait* there is that sense of a predestined union, cast as it were by the stars, which is also to be found in such novels as *Wuthering Heights*. In a less overt way it is implied in *Ulysses*. At the same time, the story *The Dead*, in *Dubliners*, and parts of Molly Bloom's monologue suggest a return by the people concerned to a first, never-to-be-renewed emotion, which Joyce and Nora had themselves experienced before meeting one another. Contradictory as these two elements seem at first, they are very much part of human experience.

Some commentators have shown that Stephen's encounter with Bloom is a father-son relationship on the spiritual level, the return of both Ulysses and Telemachus to their rightful place. Joyce's work has as many layers as an onion; peel off one and you will find another. It is therefore possible that it was also the image of the other, dead parent which Joyce recognized in the woman who accepted and perhaps sheltered him. 'Amor matris, subjective and objective genitive, may be the only true thing in life.'

As Joyce did not know exactly where his odyssey was to take him, he searched for that final word which lay somewhere in all the material—

personal, racial or Dublin-shared—the rubbish heap from which, like the hen of *Finnegans Wake*, he had been able to scratch out a letter. He did not find the word or phrase until long after that summer day (part of which was surely spent with Nora Barnacle), not until their relationship had changed, suffered jealousy, antagonism even, been affected by the pull of hard-to-define, deep-lying reasonings of the body and psyche which neither could control. Because experience was for him a circular movement, Joyce sought for some sort of return, and *Ulysses* is as much a book of double ends joined as *Finnegans Wake*. Not until in 1921, on a warm, June-like afternoon sitting in a garden outside Paris after *déjeuner*—relaxed, half-asleep as though from the effort of creation—Joyce heard, in another medium, another voice, the word which carried him back in one way to that moment on the Hill of Howth and forward in another to the assurance he had so much needed: '*and yes I said yes I will Yes*'.[1]

NORTH STRAND ROAD

James Joyce never really left Dublin. After his departure with Nora Barnacle in 1904 one or two people provided a lifeline between Ireland and those many addresses in Switzerland, Italy and France where, for some part of each day, he imagined himself walking Dublin streets again. His brother Stanislaus and Eva, a sister, when they joined him abroad, contributed to that nostalgia. It seems Joyce did what he could to help those of his family who remained in Ireland, paying for English and music lessons, and 'when one of us was in difficulty we had only to wire Jim for the money and he sent it' said another sister; presumably on those occasions when he had it himself.

In Clare Street, above a desk, there is a portrait of Alfred Bergan, a solicitor's clerk, small and robin-like he seems, who figures in *Ulysses* and supplied Joyce with much material. Certainly someone obtained for Joyce (if he had not taken it with him) a copy of *Thom's Directory* for 1905, which was exhibited in London in 1950. Another important source

---

[1] 'The whole climax of *Ulysses* is a single moment of intimacy' (Stuart Gilbert). 'Autour de cette parole et de trois autres également femelle l'épisode tourne lourdement sur son axe.' Joyce to Valery Larbaud, 5.6.21.

of information was Joyce's aunt, Mrs Josephine Murray. Some of the letters written to her between 1904 and 1922 reached the National Library in Kildare Street from a London saleroom. These enabled my husband and me to find the address in a district of modest houses, off the North Strand Road, to which Joyce had posted so many communications. Children took us to Mrs Byrne, a nurse who had been a neighbour to the Murrays at that time. Her kind Scottish voice not only told us where some of the family now lived, but as she put a broad hand on my arm she said, 'Mrs Murray was the *nicest* lady you could meet.' Reading my account, Stanislaus Joyce contrasted the recollections and gossip of the professional talkers with 'the sincere and therefore more interesting' memories of Joyce's cousin, Kathleen Murray,[1] who talked of what she really knew. 'Her mother—the "Aunt Josephine" of so many of my brother's intimate letters, gay, hopeful, desperate, and again full of resurgent hope—had been my mother's most trusted friend. Dying at an early age, my mother had recommended her young and helpless family to this aunt's care. She gave that care generously. Her house was always open to us and we lived almost as much there as in our own. There was just no limit to her patience. She had known my brother from his infancy and followed his progress from childhood to youth with almost maternal interest. My brother found in her tolerance and good humour, understanding and wise advice in his difficulties. She tried to counteract the wildness of his student days, and, as his last letter to her shows, it became habitual with him to turn to her in all the crises of his life.'

'She was very religious,' said her daughter as we talked of those days, 'but took Jim less seriously than his mother, hoping that some day he would find a way out of his doubts. I remember him saying that he envied her faith. "Do you believe in a Supreme Being?" she once asked. "Yes," he answered, and she left it at that.'

The family had been very concerned with the Feis Cheoil singing competition, which Joyce might have won but for his inability, or refusal, to sight read. A tradition had grown up that Joyce had competed with John McCormack, but this was inaccurate, as a study of the programmes has shown.

[1] In *Ulysses* Molly Bloom mentions 'these romps of Murray girls' who were friendly with her daughter, p. 726.

In 1950 J. H. Cousins wrote in his biography, *We Two Together*, published in Madras:

> I recall the stir made by an awkward country boy from Connaught who seemed to be able to climb beyond the tenor clef with ease. . . . At a later Feis I heard a young man with light pompadour hair and hardish grey eyes, the son of a singing mother, render 'A Long Farewell' seraphically. But he moved from music to letters, and in 1925, in Paris I heard a lady warmly recommend to another her purchase of a book on the ground that the author was 'frightfully famous'. My curious eyes sought the name of the author: it was that of the former singer, James Joyce.

Although I find rather exaggerated the statement made by one of Joyce's sisters (recorded by W. R. Rodgers for the BBC) that Joyce never recovered from this disappointment, years and years later—in France when Hitler was in occupation—Joyce told of his near success as if it had happened yesterday.

'I remember how annoyed Jim was!' said Kathleen Murray. 'On the way back to our place he threw the bronze medal, given him as runner up, down into the area. My mother went and rescued it. "You can keep it," he said, flinging it across the table: later he took it back to keep as a souvenir.'

A little girl then, Kathleen Murray was there on the occasion when Joyce told his aunt about Nora Barnacle, and naturally Mrs Murray remonstrated with him. 'It would never work out, besides, he was only twenty-two, without a proper position. . . .' The child, who was used to getting what she wanted from Jim, asked for a red badge or flower in his buttonhole, and for once was refused, for Nora had given it to him.[1] Eventually Joyce brought the girl to see Mrs Murray, who recognized her qualities. Later, in 1906, when the Joyces and their son Giorgio stayed nearby and had their meals with the Murray family, Nora, all agreed, was 'a lovely person'. 'She knew just how to deal with Jim, he wasn't always easy: she remained calm and unperturbed.'

[1] An incident recollected by Miss Murray on seeing the photograph of Joyce taken by C. P. Curran. This shows him in pinstripe jacket and waistcoat, with lighter trousers. When asked what he was thinking about at the time, Joyce replied, 'I was wondering if he would lend me five shillings.'

Few of Joyce's female relatives have read *Ulysses*: the revelations and dramatizations of *A Portrait* had been very unpleasant for members of the family who had continued to live in Dublin. Joyce sent copies of his books to Aunt Josephine, and with the same hopeful persistence with which the student tried to interest his mother in Ibsen, moving from chair to chair in the small kitchen at Royal Terrace, he begged her to read Lamb's *Adventures of Ulysses* before tackling his own volume. She only sent a brief acknowledgement, and Joyce, who did so want to be appreciated by his own people, waited for some time and then wrote pointing out the value of the book and its recent success.

'There is a difference between a present of a pound of chops and a present of a book like *Ulysses*. You can acknowledge receipt of the present of a pound of chops by simply nodding gratefully, supposing, that is, that you have your mouth full of as much of the chops as it will conveniently hold, but you cannot do so with a large book on account of the difficulty of fitting it into the mouth.'

But Mrs Murray was not to be joked into acquiescence: she locked the book away carefully, in case it should fall into the hands of the younger generation.

Many of the recollections of Joyce's relatives who remain in Dublin are therefore unselfconscious and sometimes provide an interesting comment on Joyce's work. 'I remember the time Jim wrote that poem "Bid Adieu" in my mother's kitchen, on a white Becker's tea-bag.[1] I can see it as clearly as anything,' said a cousin. In *A Portrait* Stephen uses a cigarette packet in the same way. 'Funnily enough, Jim was very scared of thunder. One day, he was quite a young man, there was a very bad storm. My mother began to say her beads without any fuss while Jim sat there in a basket chair, quite pale. "But you can't be afraid," she twitted him. "You don't believe in God, do you?" ' Many commentators have mentioned this trait and *Finnegans Wake* is punctuated by a rumbling thunderclap.

---

[1] Wyndham Lewis mentions in *Rude Assignment*, 'Odds and ends of phrases were always floating about in his pockets, he would put his hand in his pocket and take out a packet of cigarettes and bring out with them a scribbled scrap of conversation scratched on an envelope, or notes of the names of objects.'

SANDYMOUNT

Although I do not think they saw each other again, Joyce wrote to his aunt from abroad over many years, asking her for details regarding relatives and friends they had known, some of them the originals of his characters, enquiring about places, and anxious for information of any kind, from newspapers to novelettes, tram tickets and penny handbooks, which would help him with *Ulysses*. Sometimes he sent her a list to complete. It must have occurred to Mrs Murray that her nephew's taste was sometimes rather odd, but believing in his genius, it seems she did all she could to help him. One of her sons told how he used to be sent out to verify whether a certain fanlight was in coloured glass or plain! When he worked at Conan's, the tailoring establishment in Kildare Street, he arranged that Joyce's famous white cap should be made there. He told me that Joyce chose the material, a white blazer flannel, and was particular about details, such as seeing the seams were gimped properly and lay flat, so that it became rather a family joke. Joyce may well have had other clothes there, for there is a reference in *Finnegans Wake*. At one time Joyce was anxious to find out details concerning the Star-of-the-Sea church at Sandymount which is mentioned in the Nausicaa episode of *Ulysses*—if the surrounding trees would be visible from the shore and if there were steps leading down at the side of it from Leahy's Terrace. It would seem that Aunt Josephine put on bonnet or hat and went down to Sandymount. In *Ulysses* mention is made of these steps, which have since disappeared. 'And among the five young trees a hoisted linstock lit the lamp at Leahy's Terrace.'

These trees are still there but the Star-of-the-Sea no longer has ivy on it. The interior remains much the same, 'tastefully arranged', one might say. The weed-grown rocks along the shore have gone and the tide is hardly within sounding distance of the church now. New houses stand on the land created by the building of a sea wall and roadway, taking the view of the Bay from those residents who once heard the waves wash against their gardens.

The ships passing up to the docks behind the long strip of land to the Pigeon House are like stage properties drawn by hidden strings, moving among the houses it seems. The electric power station has chimneys like the fingers of a giant's hand, but beyond them Joyce would recognize again the wide brown sands at low tide, shellcocoa coloured, 'his boots crush crackling wrack and shells', and ask, 'Am I walking to eternity along Sandymount Strand?'

ECCLES STREET

In *Stephen Hero* the young man was passing down Eccles Street one misty evening and overheard a conversation between a young lady 'standing on the steps of one of those brick-brown houses which are the very incarnation of Irish paralysis', while a youth leant on the rusty railings of the area. The scrap of conversation overheard not only sent Stephen composing some ardent verse entitled 'A Villanelle of the Temptress', but suggested the idea 'of collecting many such moments together in a book of epiphanies, by which he meant a sudden spiritual manifestation'.

This street, which Thackeray had noted as giving access to the open country, is one of the most important landmarks in *Ulysses*. Bloom starts from there in the morning, passes the end of it on his way to the cemetery, and brings Stephen back in the early hours. Joyce, who used fact as a basis for fiction, made several enquiries about number 7, which was empty between 1903–4.

On the day that we went to see for ourselves this house which is visited in imagination by so many readers, we chanced upon another link with the writer of *The Irish Sketchbook*. Thackeray had been surprised to find his window at the Shelbourne Hotel supported by a broomstick:

> You don't see such windows commonly in respectable English inns, windows leaning gracefully up on hearth brooms for support. Look out of the window without the hearth broom and it would cut your head off; how the beggars would start that are always sitting on the steps next door! Is it prejudice that makes one prefer the English window, that relies on its own ropes or ballast (lead if you like) and does not need to be propped by any foreign aid? or is this only a solitary instance of the kind, and are there no other specimens in Ireland of the careless dangerous extravagant hearth-broom system!

It certainly seemed as if something of the same method were still in use. The ground-floor window of No. 7 Eccles Street was propped up by a milk-can and an old man reluctantly swept the doorstep in the warm, time-unimportantness of a Dublin afternoon.

GLASNEVIN

Like Dignam's funeral and many people of Joyce's world, we travelled on to Glasnevin. The approach to the main gate is between two long high walls, built against body-snatchers perhaps, at a time when O'Connell had to fight for a Catholic burial ground. These are overlooked by a round-tower monument to the Liberator, tall, clean and new-seeming, a fortification maybe against the Danes of unbelief. Everything is well-kept and tidy—paths, gateway, mortuary chapel—for death is a prosperous trade. Near the entrance is the wealth and fame of the country; not so much grief is recorded there as pride. Close together, the stone monuments stand like people, suggest character. Some are high thin crosses, others portly, supported by the saddened angels Joyce noticed or provided with urns of the towel and hot-water-jug kind—for freshening up at final awakening.

There are bright flowerbeds for Michael Collins; such a small space for the 'big fellow'. Further on the graves become plainer and grass covers the older ones. Whether by design or a kind of symbolic accident, the Chief's grave is alone among trees, and very unusual. When Joyce knew Glasnevin a cross stood there and those who visited it still held controversy alive in their minds. Now a wide circle of grass surrounds a great stone of Wicklow granite with PARNELL cut upon it in ruler-like simplicity.

Returning through the long walks, with the smell of hay in seed, shrubs and baytrees, one thought of Bloom's reflection, 'How many! All these here once walked Dublin. Faithful departed. As you are now so once were we.'

IV

TRIESTE — ROME — DUBLIN

1904–1912

When James Joyce and Nora Barnacle left Dublin in the autumn of 1904, neither of them can have realized that they would spend most of their lives abroad. Later the decision became part of Stephen Dedalus' 'silence, exile and cunning', although that silence was broken from time to time by protests against those attitudes which made guile inevitable and later was to force many another man of talent to leave Ireland. Joyce had made enquiries as to the possibility of going to Sweden as a teacher but eventually he heard of a post vacant at the Berlitz School in Zürich and made up his mind to go there. J. F. Byrne mentions that they spent a long evening together in Phibsborough Road, when Joyce discussed whether it would be fair to ask Nora to come away with him. Byrne wanted to know if he was very fond of her, and when pressed, Joyce replied, 'Honestly, Byrne, there's not another girl in the world I could ever love as I do Nora.'

A note to George Roberts which has survived shows that Joyce had to borrow money for their fares. It also seems that a sister, Gertrude Joyce, now a nun in New Zealand, did much to help them. I was told of a letter from a former student at U.C.D. which described Joyce's last night in Dublin, with the provoking remark, 'Well, perhaps I'd better not show it to you . . . sometime later maybe.' It seems likely that Joyce had a last tramp round the streets delivering a few copies of *The Holy Office*, a poem against most people in Dublin, for Dr Best and others remember finding it the following morning. J. H. Cousins and his wife wrote in *We Two Together*,

> When he scraped the clabber of Dublin off his boots (he would have shaken the dust if there had been any but humidity was no respector of similes) he made a ceremonial exit towards Trieste by having a printed

74

copy of what he called 'A Catharsis' distributed to his acquaintances. The copy that was dropt into our letterbox on that farewell night showed that he had not forgotten our hospitality to him, and our mental and musical exchanges that had presumably cancelled occult and diathetic eccentricities. But the point is that Joyce's back of the hand to Dublin did not include me in its vituperation.

Sometime during the day of October 8th, Joyce wrote another rather desperate note to George Roberts, asking him to send a further ten shillings or to meet him at the North Wall boat by nine o'clock. Nora was escorted there by another friend, a fact which was to have a curious sequel some years later. As suggested by Cousins, and a passage in *Finnegans Wake*, it was a wet autumn evening when Joyce and that courageous young woman set out for Europe together.

When they reached Zürich, Joyce found that no work was available there and after some weeks he obtained a post at the Berlitz School in Pola. It seems that Nora Barnacle's family in Galway sent a friend to bring her home again. This was probably a Mr Greaney, who on his return reported well of Joyce. It seems all he could remember was that when some officials asked Joyce his occupation, he replied 'Landowner'!

TRIESTE—ROME

The years spent in Austria were known most intimately to Stanislaus Joyce, who joined his brother in Trieste in 1905. Among Mrs Murray's papers in the National Library of Ireland there is a postcard by the young man describing the hot, dusty springtime, when the hoot of a steamer in the port reminded him with nostalgia of the fog-horn sounding from the Pigeon House.

When I met him in 1954, he had returned to London for a few weeks with a group of students from the University of Trieste where he had been a lecturer in English for many years. He had not been in England 'for half a century'. Strongly built, with well-shaped head and deep-set blue eyes ('inherited like my brother's', he said, 'from our mother'), he seemed much more of an extrovert than James. At one time an oarsman, he remained interested in the sport. 'I was the bachelor—Jim, even before he met Nora, was the married man.' The anti-clericalism of Maurice in

Stephen Hero had not been replaced by Joyce's latterday detachment, and he was convinced of continued hostility to the writer in Ireland. When we discussed his projected visit there he asked, 'But what shall I do about the language?' Direct, clear-minded and pungently assertive, he undoubtedly provided from his diaries, anecdotes and a good memory, much material for Joyce's first three books and perhaps figures as part of Shaun the Post in *Finnegans Wake*.

In July 1906, Joyce, with his wife and son, moved from Trieste to Rome, where he took a post as correspondence clerk in a bank. Difficulties arose with Grant Richards over the stories of *Dubliners*; Joyce worked on poems for *Chamber Music* and planned *The Dead*. He told Stanislaus of the beginnings of *Ulysses* but was too harassed to write much. Early in February 1907 they returned to Trieste and Joyce managed to obtain a teaching job there. In May of that year, due to the help of Arthur Symons, the book of poems, *Chamber Music*, was published by Elkin Mathews in London. On July 26th, St Anne's Day, his daughter Lucia Anna was born.

In Ireland the personal legend, like nicknames, is very much part of everyday life. Certain characters, out of uneasiness or vanity, tend to begin a snowball process by which anecdotes, criticisms and quotations gather round their name. Mention the person in a pub or sitting-room and someone else will have a new item to contribute. Although Joyce provided a certain amount of material for a time, Dublin had almost forgotten him for a few years. *St Stephen's* contains a passing reference, but a new group of students and their friends had formed there. Many of those he had known were married and settled down, yet when Joyce reappeared with his son Giorgio in the summer of 1909, some of his exploits, real or imagined, were pulled out of the talk cupboard again.

If he had regularized the position by going through a church ceremony in Ireland, perhaps the staider people who had once been his friends might have forgiven him, but it was not his intention to do so. 'I remember how my husband insisted we should cut him,' said one lady. 'People were much stricter in those days. We met in Rutland Square I think it was. Joyce gave me a straight, hard look. I passed on. I was sorry then . . . and much later, oh, in the twenties, sent a message to him.'

Joyce must have experienced that odd sense of return which a few years away from a familiar background can give at the age of twenty-five. Although the cities where he had lived on the Continent were perhaps not very large, what he had known as a child and youth must have shrunk, become just as much removed from him. Gorman records the remarks of relatives and friends. Mrs Murray found Joyce had lost his boyishness, A.E. thought he looked like a businessman, and all noticed his thinness, and air of care, melancholy. During Horse Show week Bernard Shaw's play, *The Showing up of Blanco Posnet*, banned in England, was produced by the Abbey Theatre and Joyce reviewed it for the *Piccolo della Sera*. He suggested to *The Irish Times* that he should interview Caruso, who was singing in Dublin, but was refused: he made enquiries about a professorship in Italian at the National University. There is no doubt that he would have preferred to live, for a time at least, in Ireland. Richard Ellmann points out that during this visit Joyce was in touch with various journalists and in and out of newspaper offices, storing material to be combined with earlier and subsequent impressions as part of the Aeolus episode of *Ulysses*. George Roberts, with whom he had been friendly in his student days, was manager of Maunsel and Roberts and it was arranged that the firm should publish *Dubliners*. Joyce's sister Eva agreed to return with him to Trieste, where she would be company for Nora, and they left Dublin in mid-September. The visit, therefore, seems to have been a success; Joyce was the author of a volume of poetry, his stories would soon follow. He did not remain long enough for the Dublin atmosphere, with its friendliness and envy, to close over him again.

MARY STREET

Although there is no evidence to show that Joyce went to the cinema while in Rome, he was probably aware of the beginnings of quite a considerable industry in Italy. In 1904, Arturo Ambrosio, an enthusiastic photographer in Turin, with a camera brought back from France, had recorded the Swiss-Italian car races and taken the manœuvres of the Italian Cavalry in the Alps. Joyce might well have seen *The Sack of Rome* made by Alberini in 1905, and known that the firm of *Cines* was drawing on Italian talent for theatrical improvisation. Thus by 1909 its productions were widely shown abroad.

During his visit there in the summer Joyce may have discussed the possibility of bringing these to Ireland. On his return to Trieste, through Dr Nicolo Vidacovitch, he found backing for the project. 'Jim was only interested in the money to be made,' Stanislaus Joyce remarked. Yet his meetings with Sergei Eisenstein in the thirties and the use of images from the 'reel world' (see *Further Notes*) show that Joyce was always aware of the cinema's potentialities. Meanwhile, in 1909, the situation was summed up by the song from an operetta which ran:

> *Orami colle pellicula*
> *Si fanno gran danari*
> *Diventan millionari*
> *I Cinematograph. . . .*[1]

Films had usually been shown as part of variety shows but now most of the larger towns had houses devoted to them. Joyce was soon in touch with four businessmen who controlled cinemas in Trieste and Bucharest. Antonio Machnich was an upholsterer who had invented a new type of sofa-bed, Giovanni Rebez, a leather merchant, and Giuseppe Caris, a draper, while Francesco Novak of Pirano owned a bicycle shop. It says something for Joyce's persuasiveness that they appear to have had little hesitation in putting up the capital to finance cinemas in Ireland.

Unfortunately the outcome of this venture, the *Volta* cinema in Mary Street, had already closed its gates by the time I had realized that this, the first picture house in Ireland, had been opened by James Joyce and his associates in Christmas week, 1909. All I could do was to peer over the top of the barrier at the empty little ticket office and the grimy, once cream-coloured doors with small glass panes which gave on to further darkness.

'A pity you hadn't been here before,' a woman said when I asked her what was to become of the building. 'The man who looked after it for years, from the beginning I believe, only died quite recently. He could have told you anything you wanted to know.'

I looked up at the pleasant little façade, with its stucco garland or two, and thought it was doubtful whether Joyce had known more than a plain

---

[1] Today with films
One can make money
Become a millionaire
With the cinema.

housefront with large notice boards before it. One of Joyce's younger sisters could remember him working in Mary Street, using one of the rooms on the first floor as an office, but if any reminder of that time had survived it lay under the dust and debris there.

On October 21st, 1909, Joyce was again in Ireland under contract to the Societá formed in Trieste, with the object of opening cinemas in Dublin, Belfast and Cork. For a time, as Gorman puts it, 'Joyce the businessman superseded Joyce the artist.' Kathleen Murray remembered him 'with his hat at the Kildare angle', and we find the expression in *Finnegans Wake*, for Joyce used everything, '. . . his hat which he wore all to one side like the hangle of his pan' (p. 50), and again, '. . . with his old Roberick Random pullon hat at a Lanty Leary cant on him . . .' (p. 381).

There was a great deal to do and Joyce found little time for the pubs and literary discussions of his student days. He was kept busy examining possible premises, interviewing the theatre inspector about a licence, enquiring as to regulations. After a serious fire in London earlier in the year, the Cinematograph Act, to ensure greater safety, was to come into force on the 1st of January, 1910. Eventually it was decided to lease a house in Mary Street, near the main thoroughfare of Sackville Street, and to make certain structural alterations. There was bother with the landlord, the builders, the technicians; there was staff to engage, posters to design, advertising to be arranged.

In November three of the partners arrived, without a word of English. John Stanislaus Joyce looked on with amusement. He described one of the party, who evidently knew something about projection, as 'that hairy mechanic in a lion-tamer's coat', so apt a description that it remained a family joke.

When he passed through London Joyce probably called at the office of *Cines* in Charing Cross Road, 'the hub of the bioscope world', to arrange for copies of films to be sent to Belfast. He evidently sent details of the project to the editor of *The Bioscope*, for on December 9th there appeared the note:

ITALIAN BIOSCOPE COMPANY INVADES DUBLIN

A notable development of the bioscope is promised in Dublin. The International Cinematograph Society Volta is about to open a branch in Dublin.

The Society, which has no less than 23 film producing factories, situated in different countries, to rely on for its programs [*sic*], has carried out the bioscope idea on a large scale. Branches exist in a large number of continental cities, though the Society has no counterpart in England, and has come to Ireland direct from the continent. It is the intention of the Society to introduce to Dublin the quick continental system at low prices, presenting only the newest films, with a constant change of subject. Among the novelties they hope to present, besides the films of highly dramatic character for which Italian and French houses are famous, is the 'opera film'. By this 'opera film' the entire story of an opera is vividly presented on a specially prepared disc, while an orchestra accompanies the unravelling of the plot by the rapid, but artistic, playing of a selection from the composer's music for the opera.

The new enterprise has come a long distance to try its luck in Dublin, and is sure to meet with keen appreciation here. The bioscope has certainly a great future before it, and the continental system of performances will prove very attractive to Irish audiences.

Later there follows a description of the hall, capable of holding a large audience, and richly decorated in a colour scheme of crimson and light blue, furnished with every convenience for the comfort and safety of its patrons. Thus in spite of many difficulties, the *Volta*—named in honour of Alessandro Volta—was to open on the Monday of Christmas week. Half an hour before the first public performance the electrician was found to have disappeared and Joyce had to search the town for a substitute. By that time there was such a large crowd competing to enter that police were called to control the situation.

The hall in which the display takes place [noted the *Freeman's Journal*], is most admirably equipped for the purpose. . . . Perhaps its special feature is that it is of Italian origin, and is in that respect somewhat out of the ordinary. . . . As an initial experiment it was remarkably good, remembering how difficult it is to produce with absolute completeness a series of pictures at the first stage of their location in new surroundings. . . . The chief pictures shown were *The First Paris Orphanage*, *La Pouponnière* and *The Tragic Story of Beatrice Cenci*. The latter, though very excellent, was hardly as exhilarating a subject as one could desire on the eve of the festive season but it was very much appreciated and applauded. An excellent little string orchestra played charmingly during the afternoon. Mr James Joyce, who is in charge of the exhibition, has worked apparently indefatigably in its production and deserves to be congratulated. . . .

Hitherto films had been part of a variety show or lecture. Now they were available every hour from 5 p.m., with a change of programme twice weekly, in 'the most elegant hall in Dublin' for 6d., 4d. and 2d., children half price. One of Joyce's sisters remembers seeing a film on Francesca da Rimini which seems to have impressed her, and from advertisements in the *Evening Mail* in January and February 1910 it seems that a number of other Italian films were shown at the *Volta—Nero*, a Sensational Dramatic Story of Ancient Rome, *Manœuvres of the Italian Navy in the Mediterranean, Alboino*, king of ancient Lombardy, together with such attractions as *Fatal Forgetfulness* and *The Abduction of Miss Berrilli*.[1]

BELFAST

We know from the biography that Joyce and his partners also went to Belfast in search of further premises but failed to find them. *The Bioscope* shows that other interests were developing the cinema there, for a note appeared on December 16th, 1909, that '*London has its eye on Belfast*'. St George's Hall and the Alhambra were booking films and a London syndicate was planning a new Picture Palace. In those days, copies of films were often sold outright, for they usually ended in a deplorable condition. Such firms as Erskine Mayne's and Lizars' hired out projectors and complete programmes to the church and missionary halls now using this new means of attracting souls to be saved.

When in Belfast many years afterwards, hoping to find some of Joyce's letters for Stuart Gilbert's collection and perhaps a memory of Joyce's visit there, I went to see J. M. Moore. He apologized for his overalls, having just come from his private workshop, a link with the time he made a film projector of his own, and his continued concern with engineering. A relative by marriage of W. B. Yeats, and with many interests, he talked of early days in the cinema and show business, when he travelled with his father during the fairground phase. On one occasion

---

[1] Summaries of certain films in *The Bioscope*, such as *The Girl Detective*, suggest themes in *Finnegans Wake*. The naval manœuvres are mentioned on p. 480.

when with Albert Smith's company at Hove, he fell into a pond. No; he had no recollection of Joyce—ah! but yes! (Was I at last to find something?) He *did* remember a film about horsemen crossing the Alps—very fine it had been. *Nero* . . .? No, it meant nothing to him.

When I mentioned the *Volta*, he told me that Irish Theatres Ltd had taken over the house early on, perhaps from the Societá. The offices had then been used as a distribution centre for films required in the cinemas which the company controlled in different parts of the country. He remembered it well, for one spring morning at 8 a.m. he rang up the person who was in charge—dispatch had to be made early—and settled some point of business. Later he learnt that at eleven that day the man was shot on the roof of the G.P.O.—it was Easter week 1916.

All very interesting but not just what I wanted, a glimpse of Joyce as he was then at twenty-seven, with money behind him for once, and hopes of returning to Ireland with Europe and the modern world at his back.

It was Joyce's interest in music which eventually brought me to a neat house off the Cave Hill Road in Belfast. Gorman mentions that when looking for a site for a cinema—a building suitable for conversion more likely—Joyce was in touch with W. B. Reynolds, music critic of the *Belfast Telegraph*, who had set several of his poems to music. His widow, left with several small children to bring up, told me that she had moved house several times. 'And your husband's papers—his music?' 'Ah . . .' she drew it out, 'I asked an adviser of ours what I was to do with them; my husband collected a great deal of traditional music, you know. This man told me that no one could make it out now and that it was better to get rid of it all. The BBC were enquiring about it not long ago.'

'A pity,' I said. 'There might have been letters from Joyce there too.'

'Mr Joyce? Of course I remember him.' Her good, quiet face smiled. 'My husband used to go to the Feis in Dublin, it must have been there that they met. The last time that we saw him—it must have been in . . .' she searched, 'well, before the first war, anyway. I remember he came up one Sunday morning on a sidecar, quite unexpectedly. We only had lemonade to give him. Very nice he was.'

I asked if she remembered talk of the cinema. 'No . . . but he was doing something here; had come on business. He was talking to my husband, you know. He wore a Russian kind of cap and spoke of going back to Austria or somewhere abroad.' She smiled, seeing them both again. 'He'd such a manner, Mr Joyce, you'd know there was something special about him.'

Down in Dublin again I went to talk to Dr Best, friend of George Moore and Synge, a considerable scholar, with an amusing visual mind and an ability to convey impressions and ideas as if they were films on a screen before us; a personality so badly served in *Ulysses*.

> I remember Joyce coming up to me in Bewley's café, in 1912, just as we waited to pay at the desk. I did not recognize him—with a beard, neat, prosperous-looking. 'Hello, Best,' he said . . . He came round later to the Library —I was on duty from five to ten—and sat there talking until I left [with a laugh], studying me perhaps. We walked as far as my place in Percy Street. No; he would not come in. . . . I found him very pleasant indeed. There was a great deal about himself and his plans for literary work. He talked about Gabriele D'Annunzio too, how he'd like to do something as important. I didn't know—how could one?—what Joyce could do. I remember he took out a wad of notes, like this—casually, so that I could see. Oh, I thought, he must be going well. Later I heard about the cinema project, the *Volta*, you know, in Mary Street. . . . Then afterwards he used to send me cuttings of his articles from Italian newspapers. I put them in a drawer, like this; I couldn't read Italian, and one day turned them out. How could one know . . .?

Yet it was not until this book was in proof that over the London telephone a pleasant voice, with just a touch of the North in it, gave me the portrait I needed—Joyce in the cinema itself. Charles Duff was in his teens, already learning German and Italian, when he met in the Phœnix Park 'a sturdily-built, clean-shaven native of Trieste, a young man with longish fair hair'[1] who sold chocolates. They became friendly and he was introduced to a friend or relative, one of Joyce's partners at the *Volta*. On the strength of linguistic sympathies he was allowed to see the films free in 'a plain comfortless hall, with wooden benches and hard kitchen chairs for the élite'. An upright piano was played by a gentleman who drank Guinness from a frequently replenished cup, with saucer, 'and his music to horses galloping made us all move with the horses' until the hall rattled. Joyce himself was tall, thin, in a long overcoat with collar usually

---

[1] Details quoted from *Ireland and the Irish*, 1952.

83

turned up, and sometimes he would sit down beside the boy and when the show was over treat him 'from a very light purse' to a bun and cup of tea, often with the chocolate-seller. 'Whoever cannot speak and understand a language when spoken, does not know it,' Joyce emphasized. Many years later in Paris, Charles Duff told Joyce over a good dinner how much the chance association had encouraged him to perfect his Italian.

In 1929 there appeared *James Joyce and the Plain Reader* with an introduction by Herbert Read, in which he maintained that each of Joyce's works was more genial than its predecessors; as to *A Portrait* . . . 'It was a fearful brooding and sadly disturbed man who wrote it.' This, Mr Duff agrees, goes back to his impression of the author in 1909.

In a letter published by Gorman, Joyce describes a day trip when 'For five rainy dreary hours we were mooning about Cork' where, as shown by *The Bioscope*, two cinemas were about to open. As suggested earlier, something of that mood of frustration was worked into Joyce's autobiographical novel later. J. F. Byrne mentions an incident which may have taken place at that time, when Joyce came one afternoon to 7 Eccles Street in a very disturbed state indeed. When they had talked for a while Joyce gradually recovered, spent the night there and went away feeling better the next day. Stanislaus Joyce explains that his brother had been upset by the implication of the original of Lynch in *A Portrait* that Nora had 'done a line with him' before their elopement. This Stanislaus was able to disprove, for Nora had told him of these unwelcome attentions at the time. The matter may have been on Joyce's mind on that visit to Cork and later influenced him to hurry back to Trieste, where in any case his family were in danger of being evicted from their flat by a landlord impatient for his rent.

During the New Year the *Volta* appeared to be doing well and it was a pity Joyce could not have nursed it through its first season. For some months Novak the cycle dealer carried on, but he disliked the climate and all was too difficult for him. Joyce fought hard against the partners' decision to sell to an English company, but in June his participation in the Societá came to an end. One more attempt to keep in touch with Irish life had failed.

Yet, as Joyce knew, events are part of a spiral, not a straight line.

Therefore any point of impact upon the past is of value as a centre from which to work outwards. To study in greater detail the implications of this small, almost forgotten episode of the *Volta* might be to stumble on something larger, to see a local event as part of Europe's social history. For instance, it would be interesting to try and trace the subsequent careers of Messrs Machnich, Rebez, Caris and Francesco Novak. Did they return to their previous professions or become large cinema proprietors as the film business continued to expand? Perhaps a septuagenarian, having seen so many changes in Trieste, may still remember something of the months passed in that strange, damp country of Ireland, where promises are so easily made—and forgotten.

NORTH WALL

When Joyce returned to Trieste from Dublin in 1910 he faced one of the worst periods of a difficult life—lack of money, frustrations, family quarrels. Then came the prolonged negotiations with Maunsel & Co., the publishers, and their insistence that parts of *Dubliners* should be changed or deleted. In 1912 Joyce and his family had a brief holiday in Galway with his wife's relatives, then he returned to the battle of the book in Dublin.

One day, having tea at the Kildare Street Club with Joseph Hone, the biographer of W. B. Yeats and George Moore, I asked him about Maunsel's. Together with Professor Bodkin and Edward MacLysaght, he was a director of the firm which in 1909 had undertaken to publish Joyce's stories. He told me half-jokingly that they used to have directors' meetings sitting in the surf at Killiney Strand. Then I mentioned Joyce.

'No, no, I don't want to talk about it—too painful,' he said.

'Oh, well . . .'

'I heard afterwards that Joyce was having a difficult time. . . . I kept his manuscript too long. . . . I was sorry about the whole business.'

Later Mr Hone wrote an account in *Envoy*, April 1951, of how he had given the stories to read to Joseph Sheridan Le Fanu, nephew of the novelist, who had recognized their remarkable quality. Joyce wrote to Mr Hone from Trieste and in replying he probably asked Joyce if he would assent to the exclusion of 'Ivy Day' from the collection. His name was thus mentioned by Joyce when he wrote to George V about the affair later. Although Stanislaus Joyce suggests that sinster powers were behind the refusal, another explanation may have been that Maunsel & Co. were busy printing tracts for the anti-tuberculosis campaign of Lady Aberdeen, the Lord-Lieutenant's wife.

George Roberts, who as manager of the firm figures prominently in Gorman's account of the refusal and ultimate destruction of the first printing of *Dubliners*, left Ireland later and lived in London until his death in 1953 at a considerable age. James Henry Cousins in his autobiography claimed to have 'lured' Roberts down to Dublin from the bookshop where he was working in Belfast. Joseph Hone pointed out that 'Roberts was a very good judge of a book, besides being a fine printer'. He was also interested in the Irish literary theatre movement and published a number of poets and playwrights associated with the revival. Originally from County Down, he was short, blue-eyed and handsome even as an elderly man; Joyce called him a 'red-headed Scotchman'. He never lost his Northern accent, and when W. R. Rodgers made a sound-portrait of Joyce for the BBC, at last George Roberts had an opportunity of showing that he was not responsible for the destruction of Joyce's stories. On the few occasions when we met, I found him a lively, shrewd *bon viveur*, with no rancour against Joyce personally. One evening in Hampstead he showed me part of a book, coverless and unbound. He told me that this was the only copy, incomplete, of that first printing of *Dubliners* by Maunsel's in 1910. The rest of the edition, it seems, had been used to wrap up other books, so perhaps there is still a page or two in Dublin, lining an old cupboard or chest of drawers!

I was anxious that Mr Roberts' copy should be shown at the James Joyce Exhibition at the Institute of Contemporary Arts which I helped to organize in 1950. A collector in the United States had sent over page proofs of *Dubliners* which had been owned by Joyce himself, indeed they may well have been part of the copy held by George Roberts. These had travelled so far and so strangely in Europe, that it seemed poetic justice that for a matter of weeks they should lie under the same glass case together. When we approached George Roberts, he agreed to this at first. Later he hesitated. Would it be safe? We offered insurance to the sum of five hundred pounds. He would see. Meanwhile I included the item in our catalogue and mentioned it as part of our publicity for the Exhibition. A few days before the final date, the book had not come in. I rang up someone near to Roberts and was told he was in 'a terrible state, as he is over any decision', but was assured it seemed likely he would bring us the book in the end. From several such *entretiens* I could just imagine his ups and downs over *Dubliners*.

The day before the Exhibition was to be opened by T. S. Eliot, leaving all other work aside, I asked W. R. Rodgers to help. He telephoned Roberts, who had a great regard for 'the parson' as he called him, and Rodgers taxied up to Hampstead to fetch him. I waited outside the house, annoyed with myself and yet not prepared to give up this wildgoose chase, although those working at Dover Street needed me to settle a number of details. Eventually Rodgers came out followed by Roberts, holding the book. Fortunately a friend had lent me a camera and I photographed him before we left for Piccadilly. There, in the ornate halls of Barclays Bank, after much sealing and signing of forms, the book was made safe until the following day, when it was on show at the Exhibition. At my suggestion Roberts wrote a note to accompany it:

> *44a Denning Road,*
> *Hampstead, N.W.3.*

Dear Mrs Greacen,

The proof copy of *Dubliners* is now in your hands (incomplete) for the purpose of including it in the James Joyce Exhibition.

You ask me to give you reasons as to why it was not published and I am afraid I have little to add to my recent broadcast on the subject.

There is one error that has persisted in all the controversy, that is *Dubliners* was *not* burnt, but was beheaded by the printers' guillotine. I was told that shortly after portions of the mutilated body were discovered by a Dublin bookseller used as wrapping paper for some printed goods by the same printer.

The printer was forced to this decision owing to Joyce's persistent refusal to make the alterations he demanded, notwithstanding the opinion of my legal adviser, and even Joyce's legal adviser.

So far from being censorious, I may say that some years before, when I had published *The Playboy of the Western World*, by John M. Synge, I was proud to be the victim of an unofficial boycott in consequence. I remember several instances, when I was exhibiting it at the Oireachtas, of people walking up to the stall where copies of the *Playboy* were displayed and saying 'Come away, we won't buy anything from the publisher who traduces Ireland.' I was asked to remove the volume by an official of the exhibition, and I said, 'Certainly, I will not only remove that book, but will remove all my stall.' As there were several books in Gaelic the official grinned and declined my offer. So the *Playboy* remained and was a best seller, particularly to the Gaelic speakers of the Western World.

Yours sincerely,

(Signed) GEORGE ROBERTS

One of Joyce's cousins has provided a glimpse of Joyce at the time when he was trying to get *Dubliners* published. 'I was older then and can remember how Jim used to return exhausted and angry in the evenings, for they were staying with my mother at the time. What was it . . .? The publishers refused to print something about Queen Victoria and King Edward, and Jim would not withdraw it. On the day he had the final rumpus with Roberts, he'd been walking about the streets for hours and came home very fed up. I remember my mother had prepared some supper rather specially, but he just went upstairs and began playing the piano; some love song he sang. Nora, feeling that my mother had been put to trouble and her husband was behaving badly, stayed below.

"Ah, do go up to him!" said Mrs Murray, realizing the situation. "Can't you see, all that is for *you*!" '

The North Wall is a treeless area of warehouses and goods sheds through which cattle are driven between the drays and lorries as unwilling emigrants. When Joyce left there one evening in mid-September, 1912, it was to be the last of Ireland for him. During the long journey third class, by boat, then train and boat again to Europe, his bitterness at the narrow foolishness of Dublin life as he knew it had to be expressed on paper. In a dim station waiting-room at Flushing, he wrote a poem about the rejection of his work, giving a 'dig', as they say in Ireland, to friend and foe alike. At first it rushed out, without a title maybe, a series of associations given a blue, forked flame by his anger. As he looked up towards the light, with eyes already injured by anxiety and bad health, he saw there the image of his own emotion, bright against the darkness, and called it *Gas from a Burner*:[1]

> But I owe a duty to Ireland:
> I hold her honour in my hand,
> This lovely land that always sent
> Her writers and artists to banishment . . .

[1] Gogarty suggests that the title contains a reference to an evening when a group of young men went to the Hermetic Society rooms, found there a bag of underclothing and distributed it among their lady friends . . . Stanislaus repudiated this and also the story of the title of *Chamber Music* originating from a joke about a night jar.

V

ZÜRICH—TRIESTE—ZÜRICH
1904–1919

Joyce may have been one of those travellers who send their minds, like luggage in advance, to imagine a place long before the body gets there. In the autumn of 1904 Zürich had become more than a name on a map and Joyce already saw himself teaching at the Berlitz School. As mentioned earlier, that year the city had only proved a stopping-place between Ireland and the Austro–Hungarian Empire, though later Zürich became a refuge during the First World War and was Joyce's last destination in the winter of 1940.

On that first occasion, after arrival the young couple probably left their luggage at the station and set off down the Bahnhofstrasse, past the statue of Pestalozzi and the many shops, warmly lit by gas in those days, the restaurants heated by huge tiled stoves. At the Berlitz School Joyce found there was no post vacant but he seems to have met with sympathy and a promise that enquiries would be made about similar work elsewhere. Perhaps the name of a pension was suggested, and they took the tram from the Paradeplatz to the suburb of Enge.

Few tourists must reach the nondescript quietness of the district, with its streets of grey rough-cast houses and here and there larger residences with fair-sized grounds. Joyce, as he said long afterwards, was amused to find that number 18 Reiterstrasse was called *Gasthof Hoffnung*, which means *hope* in German—and indeed they had very little else. Yet for all the anxiety, now they were on their own in a city which Joyce soon came to like, they spent a few comparatively happy weeks there, until news came of a job in the Berlitz school in Pola.

The Joyces evidently retained pleasant memories of Enge, but in June 1915 when they arrived after a difficult journey from Trieste, with two young children and rather more luggage, they found the place had changed its name to *Gasthaus Doeblin*, after the proprietor. As Joyce remarked later, the name of his native city, or its sound, followed him everywhere, and many of these echoes are found throughout *Finnegans Wake*. Although much of the Reiterstrasse remains the same, with the view of a little neo-Gothic *schloss* in the distance, No. 18 has been rebuilt. In the quiet of late autumn, as I went along Schulhausstrasse there was the sound of children playing, dogs barked, and on a corner where the road mounts steeply was a great rough-trunked aspen, its branches curving down over the pavement. As trees age so much more slowly than people, I imagined its leaves turning about in continual movement as Joyce passed there on a walk up the hill, past Enge church and the pines before a college and down again to the broad roads above the wooded gardens of the Mythenquai. Once the effects of their exodus from Trieste had worn off, his return to Zürich became one of those phases of re-vision of the past which can be so valuable to a writer. Joyce looked back perhaps to their elopement from Dublin, and if much later he was to say to a friend that perhaps they had made a mistake in leaving so suddenly, it was as an older man who realized how little they had known of the difficulties before them. It was now eleven years since he had first spoken, half jokingly, of 'Frau Joyce'. Their life together had been subjected to considerable pressure; besides Joyce's precarious livelihood from teaching and his disappointments over *Dubliners* and *A Portrait*, Nora had to learn Italian and bring up children in a country not her own. Born and reared a Catholic, she was too wise to try and change Joyce or his views. Yet for all its closeness, other strains on their relationship ran much deeper, those frustrations which lie hidden in the texture of *Ulysses*.

In Trieste Joyce had been in touch with Ezra Pound and Miss Harriet Weaver, both connected with *The Egoist*, in which the first chapters of *A Portrait* were published in February 1914. He had felt optimistic then, but his mood the following year in Zürich was that of the poem 'Bahnhofstrasse' in *Pomes Penyeach:*

> High hearted youth
>   comes not again
> Nor old heart's wisdom
>   yet to know
> The signs that mock
>   me as I go.

An article in the *Journal de Genève* describes Zürich in 1915, with its many refugees, young Germans avoiding conscription, and persons suspected of being agents of the countries at war. 'On a l'impression de se trouver dans on ne sait quel inquiètant Babel.' Nurses complained there were no sick, musical-box makers were turning out gramophones, wool and leather were costly but there were plenty of pleated skirts and boots laced up to 'hauteurs invraisemblables'. Never had such extravagant toilets been seen. . . . 'Et l'on se demande quels sentiments s'amassent dans le cœur de ceux qui, à l'entrée de ce terrible hiver, souffrent de la plus noire misère et ont sous les yeux le spectacle d'une si mauvaise luxe.'

Joyce advertised for pupils and set about finding cheaper quarters. Thus it was not long before they moved to the other side of the lake and fortunately, perhaps with the help of Triestine friends, he found a few pupils. It was from Reinhardstrasse 7, off the Seefeldstrasse, that Joyce wrote to W. B. Yeats, mentioning his struggle to live independently (for Michael Healy was still helping them) and saying that he hoped to get *Exiles* typed in exchange for a number of lessons. In July 1915 the poet wrote to Edmund Gosse that as Joyce was probably in great penury, perhaps a grant could be made by the Royal Literary Fund, and George Moore supported the suggestion. Yeats believed him to be a man of genius, perhaps a great novelist of a new kind. When the sum of £75 was made available, Joyce thanked Yeats and Moore for their kindness.

The house itself has been changed with the widening of the road but the owners kindly provided a photograph taken before the alterations, showing a balcony under which there had once been a forge. The Pphenninger family had opened one of the earliest garages in Zürich and it seems that the Joyces probably stayed with the Lutzes, a childless couple. Another tenant at the time was called Blum, though it is doubtful if the hero of *Ulysses* found his surname there!

'We lived at the side,' Giorgio Joyce told me when we passed that way, 'and were no sooner installed when an inspector arrived, with Swiss efficiency, to see that my sister and I went to school.'

'But you spoke English and Italian?'

'Well, we then had to learn Zürichdeutsch. No, it wasn't easy.'

We went on past Kreuzerstrasse 19 [1] nearby, a tall, unremarkable house where the Joyces also stayed at a time when money was very short. Previously it had been impossible to locate Seefeldstrasse 54 *parterre recht*. 'Indeed, that's not surprising,' Giorgio Joyce told me as he led me between the houses to a one-storied building, ungraced by any creeper, with grey walls and dim paintwork, shadowed by larger neighbours. 'It's years since I've been here but it hasn't changed much. That window there was the room where my mother and father slept, there we children—that was the kitchen. I remember my mother didn't like the mice.' He paused and repeated, 'Ah no . . . things weren't easy.' There came to mind Joyce's remark to W. B. Yeats, 'I hope that now at last matters may go more smoothly for me, for to tell the truth it is very tiresome to wait and hope for so many years.' [2]

During April 1916, while they were living in this little house, there appeared in the *Neue Zürcher Zeitung* a series of articles which must have been read by Joyce, who had lectured on *Hamlet* at Trieste in 1913, 'Shakespeare und die Stadtbibliothek in Zürich' deals with an unauthenticated copy of the folios bought in London, probably on a sightseeing visit, by Hans Rudolf Hess in the early seventeenth century. There followed a review of Ivan Turgenev's book concerning Hamlet and Don Quixote, the introverted and extroverted mind. On Shakespeare's birthday *King Lear* is discussed, and there appeared another article 'Shakespeare and the War', all of which might profitably be studied in relation to Joyce's interest in the playwright.

On a Thursday morning, just after Easter 1916, perhaps while Joyce was still on holiday and sitting in a café with the morning paper, he was astonished to see 'Der Aufstandsversuch in Irland', a news item which had come from Italy via New York, briefly mentioning the events of the previous Easter Sunday in Dublin. During the next few days, when Joyce must have looked through each available edition, there followed an

---

[1] Gorman gives this as number 10 and mentions another untraced address in Gartenstrasse.

[2] *The Letters of W. B. Yeats*, 1954, show how he helped Joyce at different periods. Gosse evidently enquired as to Joyce's political outlook and Yeats wrote '. . . I have never known Joyce to agree with his neighbours . . . he always seemed to me to have only literary and philosophic sympathies. To such men the Irish atmosphere brings isolation, not anti-British feeling'. Gosse was not wholly convinced, as shown by his remarks much later (p. 151).

account of the landing of Sir Roger Casement, the fighting at the G.P.O., round St Stephen's Green and the Four Courts. Gorman mentions that Joyce was asked to write on the situation by the *Journal de Genève*— afterwards to publish one of the stories of *Dubliners*. A glance at its files shows that of course Joyce could not have done so. He was decidedly against both politics and violence, yet he was not a loyalist; hourly his emotions must have carried him back to those scenes in Ireland in which many of his relatives and friends were so bewilderingly involved.

The following year the Joyces were sharing a flat at Seefeldstrasse 73, first with Philip Jarnach, attached to the Stadtheater, and later with Charlotte Sauermann, a leading soprano in the Zürich opera. In the late summer of 1917 Joyce had to go into hospital for eye trouble, and was then recommended by his doctor to seek a milder climate and avoid the Zürich winter. He decided to go to Locarno, with family and cat, so I am told, and as he continued to work on *Ulysses*, he sent Claud Sykes various sections to be typed. Unfortunately Nora was ill and indeed had a nervous collapse at this time. Joyce became rather bored with the place and financially embarrassed, so early in 1918 they returned to Zürich. Herbert Gorman mentions that it was Charlotte Sauermann who introduced Joyce to Mrs Harold McCormick, the daughter and heiress of John D. Rockefeller, who was interested in the development of psychology and also helped a number of artists. Joyce was allowed a thousand Swiss francs a month and could now spend more time writing *Ulysses*, which The Egoist Press hoped to publish in London. Yet his allowance did not go very far to support four people, and later Miss Weaver added another 500 francs a month, a gift at first made anonymously through a bank. Gorman relates how Felix Beran, editor of *Das Blatt*, for which Joyce did translations, was present when the letter arrived, at a time when his eyes were again giving trouble. Frank Budgen has already described in his most valuable book [1] a trip to Ascona with Joyce, when they went across the lake to Circe's isle and were given a suitcase of love letters, which Joyce used for *Ulysses* later. They stayed, he told me, at the Pension Reimat kept by Mrs Knoblauch, behind the post office, and one day, returning from a morning's painting, Mr Budgen found a note from Joyce saying he feared a thunderstorm was coming and had gone back to Zürich. He

[1] *James Joyce and the Making of Ulysses*, 1934.

was somewhat nettled until the real reason was made clear. Joyce loved a mystery: Nora had written to tell him of Miss Weaver's decision to make over a capital sum so that he could draw interest from it regularly. 'So your wife opens your letters!' said a rather catty acquaintance, a remark Joyce did not forgive her.

They had now taken a flat in Universitätstrasse 38. To reach it the tram from Bellevue snakes uphill past the heavy college buildings and their gardens, and indeed the family had literally 'come up in the world', for traffic rolls continually downhill over the cobblestones, which must have been noisy with the horse and carriage traffic of those days. Here the ancient, flaking ropes of that wistaria seen everywhere in Zürich seem to hold the houses together as it divides over balconies and doorways, and in the late autumn the foliage is the yellow-green of light, over-ripe grapes. The house, built in the *Neuklassizismus* style, has medallions along the road frontage and the inscription 'Fortuna' in large letters, an ironical comment on Joyce's situation. If all the complexities of that period cannot now be clearly seen, Frank Budgen—that rare combination of an artist who can also write—has recorded many details concerning the progress of *Ulysses* during the following eighteen months or so. Not tall, but strongly built, Budgen moves with the careful balance of those who have been at sea; his hair, fair to red at one time, is white now, his voice and blue quickly moving eyes show that perception and humour which amused Joyce. In *Ulysses* the sailor at the coffee stall with his yarns grew out of their friendly teasing of each other. His book portrays Joyce as slenderly built, in a brown tweed coat buttoned high, with narrow cut trousers, a walk at times suggesting a wading heron—a man who listened rather than looked at those who spoke to him. His beard, orangy brown and shaped to a point, was much lighter than his hair.

> Behind the powerful lenses of his spectacles his eyes are a clear, strong blue but uncertain in shape and masked in expression . . . in moments of suspicion or apprehension they become a skyblue glare . . . the colour of his face is a bricky red, evenly distributed . . . lips thin, set in a straight line . . . And something in his pose suggests a tall marshfowl, watchful, preoccupied.

Although Frank Budgen did not make notes or keep a diary at the time, he gives a very clear description of Joyce. Later, he was again in touch with Joyce, who doubtless recalled various incidents or suggested interpretations of the different episodes of his book, which the artist discusses in some detail. (*Ulysses*, it must be remembered, was not available in England until 1936, except for smuggled copies, one of which turned up for the James Joyce Exhibition in 1950 in a disguised jacket.) When the Joyces moved across the road to Universitätstrasse 29, 'a modernish house of no particular character', Budgen saw Joyce at work on the Wandering Rocks like an engineer or a surveyor, with a map of Dublin on which the routes of the Viceroy and Father Conmee were carefully planned and their positions plotted to the minute. It was here too one evening that Joyce read out the Proteus episode—oh, that this had been recorded!—with its theme of change, the changes of the sea, sky, man and the words themselves. Here again we find the writer moving, not yet consciously, towards the dream transformations of *Finnegans Wake*.

Fortunately Frank Budgen, like Cranly—or Joyce—had a habit of remembering remarks in relation to places. As they strolled between the avenue of trees on the Utoquai from Bellevue towards Zürich Horn, the discussion centred round *Ulysses* as the most complete personality presented by any writer, and the way Joyce was using the Odyssey as the basis for his work. Going down the Universitätstrasse, Joyce said that he wanted to give so comprehensive a picture of Dublin 'that if the city one day suddenly disappeared from the earth it could be reconstructed out of my book'. Then as they looked down over Zürich from the terrace of the University, he continued, 'And what a city Dublin is! I wonder if there is another like it. Everybody has time to hail a friend or start a conversation about a third party. . . .'

The talk turned continually towards Joyce's youth and Budgen noticed that Joyce was much more a Dubliner than an Irishman, his patriotism being more like that of a citizen of a free town in the Middle Ages. At that time many Englishmen felt uneasy about the policy of their country towards Ireland, which had been so near Home Rule and was now rapidly moving towards open war, but Joyce was inclined to sit on the fence; for him there seemed no immediate solution and violence settled nothing.[1] One day along the Bahnhofstrasse, after he had read the Cyclops episode of *Ulysses*, where 'the Fenian giant, representative of the

[1] In the thirties a friend heard him say, 'Poets should keep off politics.'

most one-eyed nationalism, denounces the bloody and brutal Sassenach', Joyce suddenly said, 'I wonder what my own countrymen will think of my work?'

Frank Budgen was sure they would not like it. '. . . your countrymen are men of violent beliefs, and your book is the book of a sceptic.' 'I know it is,' said Joyce. 'It is the work of a sceptic but I don't want to appear a cynic. I don't want to hurt or offend those of my countrymen who are devoting their lives to a cause they feel to be necessary and just.'

Many years later, when I had first arrived in Zürich, I asked a news-paper seller, a fine mountainy-looking man, for '*Peter*strasse', pointing to the word on the map. 'Ah! *Paeder*strasse!' he said, as if half-talking Irish. In a hotel there, smelling of pine floors and Swiss cleanliness, just below the tower of St Peter's with its huge gold-handed clock, the sound of the great bells went through my sleep. To wake early in the morning was like being in Dublin again as other bells, of the Fraumünster or Grossmünster, were followed by the lesser persistence of a convent or some institution far across the city. I remembered how in Hampstead Frank Budgen talked of Joyce's interest in the way people reveal character through everyday gestures, and the use of little bits of Zürich in the pattern of *Ulysses*, for instance the blind boy, whom they often noticed in the streets there or at the Pfauen Restaurant. He told me of those evenings when they used to meet in the Augustinerhof Restaurant nearby. The company was of many nationalities, and as others discussed the war, their distant homes, art or writing, Joyce would take a small pad from his pocket and note down a word or phrase which floated towards him on that river of language, French, English, Greek or German. When the Augustinerhof closed, Budgen would sometimes suggest that they should call at his office and have another glass of Fendant before starting off down the Bahnhofstrasse towards Bellevue. There the limes grow along the quays and lights still swing across the lake like laburnum trails, and near the greater darkness of the bridge the swans sleep upon the water bent round upon themselves into the shape of white stones.

In one of those garden cities to the north of London, with mown grass borders and avenues of trees which run into the shopping centres, I found pictures of Joyce and memories of his Zürich days in a small house built for people who are not tall themselves but gain stature by their personality, the mental space they take up in the world. Perhaps Claud Sykes will forgive me if I suggest that Joyce might well have used him as a model for the 'Gracehopper' of *Finnegans Wake*—slight-figured, with a long-boned, elf-like face, lively eyes and quick movements, humour in his voice. Yet the suggestion would not be wholly accurate, for both he and his wife belong to that comparatively small number of actors and writers who manage to combine their work with the provision later of a neat and pleasant background.

Nowadays Mr Sykes is best known as a writer, having been an actor until his retirement in the twenties. At one time he was with Leigh Lovel's company, which mainly gave Ibsen's plays in England, Europe and the United States. For a period he was with Tree at His Majesty's, and then for health reasons was obliged to go to Switzerland in 1915, choosing Zürich as likely to be a lively place. He first noticed Joyce reading the newspapers in the Museumgesellschaft, and later they met through a film project called *Wine, Women and Song*, suggested by one of the curious characters in Zürich anxious to make money out of the well-to-do and pretentious. They soon agreed that it was a waste of time. Mrs Sykes, with pale hair now a lovely white, and a thick, high fringe, had trained as a pianist at Manchester College of Music and as Daisy Race had also played with Leigh Lovel's company, taking many leading parts. She laughed over her first meeting with Nora Joyce, for when they went to the Joyces' house she was not invited to take off a heavy winter coat. 'But from Mrs Joyce's manner, which had puzzled me by a sort of tentativeness,' she explained, 'I suddenly realized she was shy! Afterwards when we became friendly, Nora Joyce told me she rather dreaded meeting women but had invited me because my husband said I had not been well.' Later they saw a good deal of each other, and after the Locarno visit, when Nora had been ill, unhappy perhaps, the first person she wanted to see was Mrs Sykes, one of her few real friends in Zürich. Joyce, of course, was anxious to know what people thought of his work and he explained in some detail that *Ulysses* was based on Homer. When Sykes read some of the manuscript he remarked that many of the incidents seemed to be the other way round, and then Joyce carefully explained his methods to him.

'He wanted to hear what *I* thought of it,' said Mrs Sykes. 'We got on well together, you know. I told him that it had seemed rather strange to me, for instance I'd never before read a description of someone going to the lavatory.' 'Well, on the whole did you like it?' Joyce asked. 'I'd say *like* isn't the word. I thought it was *life*—as life.' She laughed. 'I don't know if that pleased him or not!'

Claud Sykes had been in Dublin in 1906 and he remembers how the whole of one afternoon Joyce worried him as to whether Mrs Bandmann Palmer could have played *Leah the Forsaken* in that city in 1904, as he had acted in her company later. Now and then Joyce had an amusing story to tell about his teaching. An inspector at the Berlitz School asked one of the teachers, 'What is a verb?' 'And indeed,' said Joyce, 'he picked on the right man.' With some of his pupils they came across a text-book phrase *'Don't dip your bread into the gravy.'* One of them looked up and remarked, 'Oh, but it is zo very *nice!'*

'Then you organized The English Players and produced *The Importance of Being Earnest*, Shaw's *Dark Lady of the Sonnets* and *Riders to the Sea*, in which Nora Joyce played a part?' I asked.

'Yes, and several more—*The Twelve Pound Look* by J. M. Barrie, *Mrs Warren's Profession* by Shaw, and Stanley Houghton's *Hindle Wakes.*' Mr Sykes continued: 'Some writers have stated wrongly that Joyce ran the English Players and produced for them. As a matter of fact he was the business manager, and the production was entirely in my hands. Neither interfered with the other's job. Joyce knew absolutely nothing about production. After the first night of Chesterton's *Magic,* of which he had seen no rehearsals, he came round to the back and was intrigued about the business in Act II, when a picture wriggles on the wall, a chair falls over and a red light in the background changes to blue. He thought such feats wonderful. I pointed out how they were done, the first two being effected by devices that any competent stage-manager could have thought out even if he had never been a producer, while the third was a routine job for the electrician. He did not seem to realize that a producer has a lot more to do than just see that the actors spoke their lines correctly, that he has to shape the conception of their parts, blend them, dictate the tempo of the play and see that every part gets its right value and fits into the general picture. Of course he was very busy with his work and only looked in at rehearsals occasionally—generally when he had something to discuss with me. But he could not help picking up some stage terms, which come into *Finnegans Wake*.'

Frank Budgen had mentioned a performance in Lausanne of *The Importance of Being Earnest*, when he played Chasuble and all the 'decrowned heads of Europe were there'. On that occasion Joyce was in the prompt box, a theme which occurs here and there in his last book. Unfortunately trouble arose between Joyce and one of the actors, a member of the staff of the British Consulate, over some tickets and the price of a pair of trousers, rather like the Gilbert-Sullivan fuss over a carpet. The incident gave rise to legal action and caused Joyce a good deal of worry and irritation. When this was over he was once again able to devote his energies to *Ulysses*. Claud Sykes tells me that in the autumn of 1919 Joyce was uncertain about his future movements. He had often told him that he would not like to settle permanently in Trieste because he thought it would change for the worse after the war, although he wanted to pay a visit there to see his relations and settle his affairs. One day, so Joyce told his friend, he called at the bank as usual to draw the allowance made by Mrs McCormick, whereupon the clerk at the counter simply said: 'Das Kredit ist erschöpft.' Among Joyce's papers at the Lockwood Memorial Library are two letters from Mrs McCormick, written in a clear, ornate hand, with a suggestion of autocracy in its firmness and the involved signature, as if the habit of composure overlay a sense of uncertainty. Joyce evidently wrote to her immediately asking if he might see her. On October 10th she wrote from the Hôtel Bauer au Lac saying that she was glad an English publisher was appearing. As she was not free on Sunday she would say goodbye by letter. 'I know you will reach Trieste safely, and that you will continue your work there with enthusiasm and with inward conviction.' According to Mr Sykes, Joyce then sent her a part of his manuscript with a request for one more month's allowance in order that he might pay his commitments in Zürich, but she refused. On October 13th—how he mistrusted that number!—she wrote again, this time thanking him for the fine manuscript which she would keep until such time as he needed it, and then went on to say that, as the bank had already informed him, she was unable to help financially but now that the difficult war years were past 'you will find publishers and will come forward yourself, I know'. It is probable that shortly afterwards she made matters worse for Joyce, who found the situation humiliating enough as it was, by returning his manuscript.

Joyce was very upset. What could have happened? Did she fear blackmail or had a Triestine friend been a troublemaker? Perhaps Mrs McCormick had been offended by his brusque refusal to be psycho-analysed . . . None of his friends could find a satisfactory answer. 'All I know,' said Claud Sykes, 'was that Joyce left for Trieste in a great hurry because he could not afford to stay on in Zürich and his brother's flat was the only place where he could under the circumstances be sure of a roof over his head.' It was not until twenty-six years later that Dr C. G. Jung, when the episode was related to him, was able to make clear the reasons for Mrs McCormick's abrupt and disconcerting decision.[1]

[1] Herbert Gorman gives a slightly different version of the incident in which, the day before Joyce's departure, the manuscript was returned to him. When he told the lady it was a gift she coldly said he might need it later to raise money. The next day, Joyce heard the payments were to be discontinued. The above is perhaps a little nearer to the actual sequence of events. Joyce, as he was to mention on Mrs McCormick's death later, remained grateful for the help she had given him during a difficult period.

VI

LONDON
(The Literary Background)
1914–1919

It was at Stone Cottage, Coleman's Hatch, Sussex, that in 1913 W. B. Yeats had again intervened in Joyce's life, as he was to do every now and then until the end. He had already told Ezra Pound of the destruction of *Dubliners* and when the latter asked was there anything in Ireland fit to go into a *Des Imagistes* anthology, Yeats suggested that Joyce's work should be included. Therefore, in a very different atmosphere, among Italian, Slovene and Irish voices, Joyce found a letter in his post one day asking him for permission to use the poem from *Chamber Music* which begins, 'I hear an army charging upon the land'. It was like the cord which is thrown aboard a vessel to haul the stronger ropes in. Joyce seized it at once and from that time Ezra Pound undertook to pilot this unusual shipload into port. The introduction was to mean the acceptance of Joyce's work in England, the beginning of his varied relations with writers and publishers there; eventually it led to the completion of *Ulysses*.

In 1931, when Joyce came to rent a flat in Kensington, with his interest in the loops and knots of coincidence, he must have peered through his thick glasses at those streets and houses to which he had sent manuscripts from Trieste and Zürich. It was Mrs W. B. Yeats in Dublin, as we sorted over some letters written by Joyce to her husband, who told me how to find the place where Pound had lived before the First World War. 'You go up past the church and turn left'—she shut her eyes and gestured—'and cross over a bit and it's there round the corner on your right—I can see it quite plainly.' Back in London we followed her directions. Although Church Walk was bombed during the war, part of its original character has survived. We found the little oblong of paving-stones across which the small, two-storied houses face each other, with that determined, unobtrusive air more often found in English villages, their bricks, fired before Trafalgar, now a dark chrysanthemum colour. Round the corner, as Mrs Yeats had visualized, was the door of No. 10 Church Walk, facing the high wall of the graveyard, now a playground, over which Ito, the Japanese dancer who worked with Yeats on *The Hawk's Well*, had once climbed to rescue a kitten which had strayed there.

Ezra Pound had spent some time on the Continent before he reached London in 1908. Extrovert, healthy and enthusiastic, he soon brought together a number of young writers interested in poetry, all very critical of their elders and, as they thought—no betters. Among them was F. S. Flint, poet and translator, T. E. Hulme the philosophical essayist, and Desmond FitzGerald, whom I was to know as a Thomist in Dublin much later. Harold Monro described 'the light-hearted penury of Ezra Pound', who wrote for *The New Age*, and if his letters [1] mention money troubles they were never his own. Alida Monro described how she first saw Ezra Pound when travelling by Underground to Golders Green one day. In the same compartment was a remarkable young man with a great deal of bright, alive-looking hair and beard, in a grey velvet coat. 'You couldn't help noticing him.' Outside the station he entered the Lady Bachelor Chambers—for the respectable but independent female—and later she realized that he was probably visiting H. D. (Hilda Doolittle) and other compatriots there.

The Imagist 'movemong' was born in a teashop in the Royal Borough of Kensington, according to Richard Aldington in *Life for Life's Sake* (1940), at a period when so many sons and daughters of the still well-to-do families had both incomes and leisure, or could live on little for culture's sake. Sometimes the poets and artists of the neighbourhood met at 'Rotting Hill' (Notting Hill Gate), not far from the offices of *The English Review*, edited by Ford Madox Ford, or in a little restaurant off Church Street, and talked of the Vorticism of Wyndham Lewis or Pound's efforts to clean and re-seed the field of English poetry.

The events which brought *The Egoist* into being came from a different direction. Although *A Portrait* did not appear in the magazine until

[1] *The Letters of Ezra Pound*, 1950.

1914, trace elements of the situation had been in the mixture of events since the time Joyce had been friendly with the Belfast poet, James Henry Cousins, in Dublin. Soon after Joyce left Ireland for Austria in 1904, Margaret Cousins, according to *We Two Together*, became interested in the Suffragette movement and was later in touch with the Women's Social and Political Union which had been founded by Mrs Pankhurst in 1903. Tom Kettle and his wife, the Sheehy-Skeffingtons and others were part of a group in Dublin which welcomed Miss Mary Gawthorpe to speak there. When Joyce returned to Ireland in 1912 to make his last attempt to get *Dubliners* published by Maunsel and Company, he saw James Cousins again and very probably Mrs Cousins gave some account of her activities. At one time she was in prison for several months and had helped to break ministerial windows in London with a volley of potatoes, which can have left no doubt as to the origin of the protest.

Miss Dora Marsden, a graduate of Manchester University who had been a teacher for a time, was working for the Women's Social and Political Union. In 1911 she began *The Freewoman*, which put forward the views of this group, at times so forcibly that her editorials were quoted in the United States at Congressional hearings as evidence against suffrage there. Eventually Dora Marsden found herself among those who regretted the political emphasis given to emancipation by Mrs Pankhurst and her followers, as tending to discredit a movement which she believed could only be successful through an effort towards the development and education of the individual.

The Freewoman was printed by Stephen Swift & Co., who also brought out *The New Witness* and *The New Age*. When the firm went bankrupt Miss Marsden then set about to collect around her a number of former subscribers and friends of *The Freewoman*, and in June 1913 launched a successor, *The New Freewoman*. This appeared fortnightly from the London office of a sympathizer who ran *The Path*, a theosophist journal closely connected with the Blavatsky Institute and to which A.E. and W. B. Yeats occasionally contributed. Dora Marsden herself spent much of her time with her old and very devoted mother in a workman's cottage on the slopes of Helvellyn, and gave most of her energy and limited means to her studies and publications. Interested mainly in philosophy of an erudite kind which makes slow reading today, she published in 1928 and 1930 two volumes under *The Egoist* imprint, *The Definition of the Godhead* and *The Mysteries of Christianity*. A pamphlet, *The Philosophy of Time*, was privately printed in 1955. In August 1913 Pound was writing to a friend that he was in charge of the literary department of our 'left wing *The New Freewoman*, I pay a dead low rate'. Later he mentioned his half-magazinette 'for Miss Marsden must have a corner to let loose in. She has her own clientele who look for her.' She took an interest but did not intervene a great deal in the direction of the literary side of the periodical which, between 1914 and 1919, was to publish many writers who later became well known. As Miss Weaver writes in the notes kindly supplied for this study, 'with the new masculine element which allied itself to the paper, very soon objections to the title were raised'. In December 1913 there appeared a letter to the Editor:

> We, the undersigned men of letters, who are grateful to you for estab-lishing an organ in which men and women of intelligence can express them-selves without regard to the public, venture to suggest to you that the present title to the paper causes it to be confounded with organs devoted solely to the advocacy of an unimportant reform in an obsolete political institution.
>
> We therefore ask you with great respect that you should consider the advisability of adopting another title which will mark the character of your paper as an organ of individualists of both sexes, and of the individualist principle in every department of life. Signed. Allen Upward, Ezra Pound, Huntley Carter, Reginald W. Kauffman and Richard Aldington.

Thus on January 1st, 1914, *The New Freewoman* became *The Egoist*, a title probably suggested by Miss Marsden. Finances were always rather uncertain and at one time during the war there was a question of suspend-ing publication. Few contributors were paid and the working staff received £1 each weekly. Early in 1914 Amy Lowell discussed taking it over, but as Pound shows, soon afterwards '£250 was chucked at its head'. Yet, Pound continues, if Amy Lowell thought of running a quarterly there was a staff ready to hand, 'Hueffer [Ford Madox Ford], Joyce, Lawrence, F. S. Flint and myself'. It was probably Miss Harriet Weaver who came to the rescue when the magazine showed signs of failing for lack of funds. Of a Quaker family living in Hampstead, she had been reprimanded as a girl for reading such writers as George Eliot, then considered an immoral woman. Later she became interested in literature and the movement for woman's freedom. She had been a reader of *The Freewoman* and when circulars had been sent out concerning the change in policy, she had written to Miss Marsden and later met her. When the printing was transferred from the provinces to a London firm, Dora Marsden asked Miss Weaver if she would undertake the practical work of editing and see to the business side. Only those most closely concerned with the affairs of the magazine appear to have realized her unobtrusive support.

It was not long before Miss Weaver was acknowledging the receipt of Joyce's manuscript and stating that Miss Marsden and her advisers would publish it during the new year. This began a correspondence and soon a friendship which was to continue until Joyce's death and is still extended to his family.

For six important years *The Egoist* was to give an opportunity to the innovators of its generation, T. S. Eliot, Ezra Pound, D. H. Lawrence. Wyndham Lewis's *Tarr* was serialized in 1916, Harold Monro, Sacheverell Sitwell, Herbert Read, Charlotte Mew and A. E. Coppard published poems there, while other writers included Edward Mowrer, John Rodker and Leigh Henry. From abroad Pound obtained some of the work of André Spire, William Carlos Williams, Marianne Moore, Remy de Gourmont, and Le Comte de Lautréamont. Madame Ciolkowska wrote about affairs in Paris, André de Segonzac was represented by line drawings, Gaudier-Brzeska published those criticisms of his own and other sculpture which after his death Pound brought out in book form. As Pound wrote, 'Yeats used to say that I was trying to provide a portable substitute for the B.M.'

Looking back, Pound wrote in 1934: '. . . *Egoist* was Harriet Shaw Weaver . . . Titular Edtr: Dora Marsden who wrote the front pages on "philosophy" and left the rest free to letters. As nearly as I can remember I got them to appoint Aldington as sub. edtr. and later got Eliot the job, though I remained unofficially an adviser without stipend. I think the files will indicate what I was responsible for, at any rate I served as katalytic. H.W. deserves well of the nation and NEVER turned away anything good. Also the few articles she wrote were full of good sense. She amply deserves Eliot's dedication of whichever book it was'—*Selected Essays, 1917–32*, '*To Harriet Shaw Weaver in gratitude, and in recognition of her services to English letters*'.

BLOOMSBURY

It was from Oakley House, 14, 15 and 18 Bloomsbury Street, London, W.C.1, that the first instalment of *A Portrait of the Artist as a Young Man* was published in *The Egoist* for February 2nd, 1914. The date itself was a good omen—Joyce's thirty-second birthday.

The name Bloom or Blum has occurred in so many different ways during this exploration—Bloomfield Park as seen from the Dunlaoghaire bus or tram, finding that a family called Blum lived in No. 7 Reinhardstrasse in Zürich, and now Bloomsbury Street once called Blemundsland, after the Lord of the Manor in Henry III's reign. Plumtree and Caroline Streets—suggesting, like Goosegreen Avenue in Drumcondra, a very different period—once ran across the site upon which Oakley House was built as a block of offices before the First World War. Now huge advertising hoardings, brightly selling soap or tinned beans across the wreckage of former prosperity, just allow the outline of a doorway to be seen. At the back among the remains of white tiling, old doors, girders and bits of functionless piping left by the bombing, there emerges the remains of stone stairs which must once have smelt of cleaners' soap and gas to those who passed up and down them on varied business. It is unlikely that Joyce was aware that the firm of Maunsel & Co., which had refused *Dubliners* a few years previously, also had an office in the building.[1] They may have been in the neighbourhood previously, for Joseph Hone recollects meeting Joyce and his son in that area about 1912, and talking of the destruction of *Dubliners*.

We now see *A Portrait* in relation to Joyce's work as a whole and its many 'sons and daughters of'. An important contribution to the movement freeing art, and thus daily life, from certain restraints and out-worn conventions, the novel no longer has the power to surprise. A friend of an older generation said to me recently, 'You can't imagine what it was like —I was only a boy then—to get *The Egoist* down there in Charing Cross Road, and to read something so different as Joyce's work. It was unlike anything we had been used to: I can't describe the effect.'

When *The Egoist* arrived in Trieste sometime in March 1914 surely Joyce had not lost the writer's impulse to glance over his own words, to

[1] P.O. Directory for 1915.

see how they look in that odd detachment of print when they no longer belong so closely to their author? Indeed he probably read the magazine from cover to cover, and it is interesting to see what surrounded the first instalment of *A Portrait*. There was an editorial, several thousand words long, on 'Men, machines and progress' by Dora Marsden, and a review of Christabel Pankhurst's book on venereal disease, *The Hidden Scourge and How to End It*. Richard Aldington discussed novels, and an article by the irrepressible Bastien von Helmholtz (Ezra Pound) goes for a journalist who attacked W. B. Yeats because he in turn attacked the bourgeoisie, in Pound's words, 'the stomach and gross intestines of the body politic and social' as distinct from 'the artist who is the nostrils and invisible antennae.' 'John Synge and the Habits of Criticism', a review by the same writer, must also have interested Joyce, together with the last instalments of *The Horses of Diomedes* by Remy de Gourmont.

There is also an account of a presentation to Wilfrid Scawen Blunt of a work by Gaudier-Brzeska, made by W. B. Yeats, Sturge Moore, F. S. Flint, Richard Aldington, Ezra Pound, John Masefield, Victor Plarr and Frederic Manning, which provides an interesting comment upon two generations of writers. In thanking them, Wilfrid Blunt mentioned that Ezra Pound had a volume of manuscripts in which his insults to the world were so deadly that they presented rather a complicated publishing problem. It was no wonder that Pound had a fellow-feeling for Joyce, away in Trieste, writing that Odyssey of Dublin at the end of Victoria's reign. For ten years, as Joyce was to mention in a letter to W. B. Yeats, he had been cut off from English writing. 'A good job too,' Pound might have said. From Bloomsbury Street *The Egoist* travelled across trenches and bomb-marked Europe to Trieste, a symbol valid for our own time too—that beyond the stupidity of war, of whatever temperature, there are always a few people to keep the mind alive.

The first part of 1914 had been fortunate for Joyce. Ezra Pound had published the statement, 'A Curious History', which drew attention to his difficulties over *Dubliners*. He had received £50 for *A Portrait*, which was appearing serially in the magazine: this was exceptional, for most of the other contributors were not paid. There was talk of publication in book form in England and the United States. A little success, a sense of at last belonging somewhere, will often release material packed in a writer's mind. During the spring of that year Joyce wrote *Exiles* and about the same time began to work on *Ulysses* as we now know it. At last Grant Richards brought out *Dubliners*, and in the issue of July 15th Ezra Pound was reviewing the collection of short stories in *The Egoist* under the title *Dubliners and Mr James Joyce*.

Then in August came the war. Joyce had not only seen his literary projects in danger but found himself a British subject in Austria. In September a note appeared in *The Egoist* informing readers that both Joyce's work and a series of articles by Leigh Henry, who was in Germany, would be suspended as they were unable to send their manuscripts. Efforts were made in London and it was thanks to Madame Ciolkowska, Paris correspondent of *The Egoist*, who arranged for Joyce's work to come through her sister in Switzerland, that publication began in the periodical and continued until the novel was concluded. Joyce was also in touch with the American publisher, B. W. Huebsch, later to bring out his work and become a most sympathetic and helpful friend, who had suggested to H. L. Mencken that he should include stories from *Dubliners* in *Smart Set*.

Thanks to the generosity of Miss Weaver there is now in the British Museum an interesting folio prepared by Joyce, consisting of page and galley proofs of the instalments of *A Portrait* as they appeared in *The Egoist*. Certain deletions made by the printers of the magazine have been inserted. Along the margins are various pencil marks made by readers, evidently querying the suitability of certain passages. Although this collection has been catalogued as corrections made for the first American edition of the novel, I believe that originally these were a set of proofs, etc., put together by Miss Weaver and sent, on the suggestion of H. G. Wells, to Messrs Pinker and Son, the literary agents, as shown by an address label. They went the rounds of various London publishers during 1914-15 but the book was refused by them all and the proofs returned to Oakley House. Later it would seem as if this set was used in relation to a list of corrections made by Joyce himself, to be forwarded to the United States.[1]

As The Egoist Press (a natural development from the periodical) was now contemplating the publication of several books of poems, it was proposed to bring out Joyce's novel under this imprint. This was easier said than done. When estimates were requested from printers they refused

[1] See Appendix A: Changes in *A Portrait* made by Joyce.

to handle the work as it stood and stipulated that certain deletions should be made. 'The printers have gone mad since the Lawrence fuss,' wrote Ezra Pound, referring to the suppression of *The Rainbow*. In an editorial in *The Egoist* Miss Marsden pointed out: 'If Shakespeare had not been wrapped in the funeral sheet of "classic" his work would horrify printers and turn publishers faint, not to mention magistrates, censors and the like', and she asks if *Measure for Measure* would have passed them in this century. Referring to *A Portrait*,[1] she states that it was not because they wished to saddle themselves 'with fresh responsibilities in this difficult time but in order to save a work of exceedingly high merit from oblivion, we propose to publish ourselves'. A very well known and successful writer [H. G. Wells] had drawn attention to the serialized form 'but no commercial publisher would touch it unaltered'.

Ezra Pound, resourceful as ever, suggested to Miss Weaver a way out of the difficulty. 'If all printers refuse (I have written this also to Joyce) I suggest that largish blank spaces be left where passages are cut out. Then the excisions can be manifolded (not carbon copies but another process by typewriter on good paper), and if necessary I will paste them in myself. The public can be invited to buy with or without restorations and the copyright can be secured [on] the book as *printed*. That is to say, the restorations will be privately printed and the book without them "published". And damn the censors.

'Joyce is ill in bed with rheumatism, and very worried, and I hope for his sake, as well as for the few intelligent people who want the book, that it can manage to come out.'

Not only was Pound sending some of Joyce's poems to Harriet Monroe and getting Heinemann to read the manuscript of *Ulysses* but attempts were made to find a publisher for *A Portrait* in America. He told Miss Weaver in March 1916 that he had written to John Marshall in New York, 'a very strong letter re Joyce, advising him to print the Joyce book in preference to my book if his capital is limited. I cannot go further than that.' Elsewhere he notes, 'George Moore has also been reading Joyce with approbation. We'll get the thing started sometime.' It was suggested by

[1] The fair copy of *A Portrait* in Joyce's writing, on large thick sheets, which he sent from Trieste in 1920 as a gift to Miss Weaver, was presented by her to the National Library of Ireland. A typescript had been made from this in Trieste for *The Egoist* instalments.

Joyce that Pound should do a preface to *A Portrait* but Pound thought Edward Marsh could do more for him than he could, also that a series of testimonials about a paragraph long from H. G. Wells, Edward Marsh, George Moore, Martin Secker and others would be a good idea. 'I can hardly add anything to what I said in *Drama*. It was almost the strongest kind of statement one could make. . . . I am not trying to get out of doing a job but I think these things should be tried before the reader of *The Egoist* is required to hear any more of "Me on Joyce".'

In 1917 B. W. Huebsch brought out *A Portrait* in the U.S. The printed sheets were imported into England for the first Egoist Press edition, and in *The Egoist* for February of that year Ezra Pound was delighted to proclaim triumphantly: JAMES JOYCE. *At last the novel appears.*

Dubliners had not done well and in 1917 Joyce mentioned to John Quinn that only 450 copies had been sold. On the other hand, *A Portrait* rapidly sold out and soon a second edition appeared. 'I had no idea how many copies to order at first and asked for seven hundred and fifty,' Miss Weaver told me. 'It was all such a venture.' This was due in great measure to the help of H. G. Wells. It was probably Rebecca West, associated with *The New Freewoman*, who drew his attention to the serialized version. As already mentioned, he had expressed his interest and suggested that Joyce should get in touch with a literary agent. When the first edition appeared, Wells was asked if he would review the book but had appeared either too busy or not inclined to do so. Therefore there was both surprise and delight at *The Egoist* office when an article by H. G. Wells appeared in *The Nation* for February 24th, 1917. (This was also published by *The New Republic* on March 10th, and reprinted in *The New Republic Anthology*, 1936.) Quotations were used as part of a leaflet concerning the book which was brought out by The Egoist Press and this proved invaluable to Joyce. For a number of years we find him including it in his correspondence with numerous people. Letters to H. G. Wells written from Zürich show how much Joyce appreciated his encouragement. Long afterwards they were to meet in Paris and discuss the implications of *Finnegans Wake*.

Although the book came in for a good deal of attention, views were not unanimous. Ezra Pound compiled a summary published in *The Egoist*, June 1917:

JAMES JOYCE AND HIS CRITICS

Some classified comments

CAUTION: It is very difficult to know quite what to say about this new book by Mr Joyce.—*Literary World*

DRAINS: Mr Joyce is a clever novelist, but we feel he would be really at his best in a treatise on drains.—*Everyman*

CLEANMINDEDNESS: This pseudo-autobiography of Stephen Dedalus, a weakling and a dreamer, makes fascinating reading. . . . No cleanminded person could possibly allow it to remain within reach of his wife, his sons or daughters.—*Irish Book Lover*

OPPORTUNITIES OF DUBLIN: If one must accuse Mr Joyce of anything, it is that he too wilfully ignores the opportunities which Dublin offers even to a Stephen Dedalus. . . . He has undoubtedly failed to bring out the undeniable superiority of many features of life in that capital. . . . He is as blind to the charm of its situation as to the stirrings of literary and civic consciousness which give an interest and zest to social and political intercourse.—*New Ireland*

BEAUTY: There is much in the book to offend a good many varieties of readers, and little compensating beauty.—*New York Globe*. The most obvious thing about the book is its beauty.—*New Witness*

STYLE: It is possible that the author intends to write a sequel to the story. If so, he might acquire a firmer, more coherent and more lucid style by a study of Flaubert, Daudet, Thackeray and Thomas Hardy.—*Rochester (New York) Post-Express*

REALISM: Mr Joyce is unsparing in his realism, and his violent contrasts—the brothel, the confessional—jar on one's finer feelings.—*Irish Book Lover*

The description of life in a Jesuit school and later in a Dublin college, strikes one as being absolutely true to life—but what a life!—*Everyman*

WISDOM: Is it even wise, from a worldly point of view—mercenary, if you will—to dissipate one's talents on a book which can only attain a limited circulation?—*Irish Book Lover*

ADVANTAGES OF AN IRISH EDUCATION: One boy from Clongowes School is not a replica of all the other boys. I will reintroduce Mr Wells to half a dozen Irish 'old boys' of whom five—Sir Arthur Conan Doyle is one—were educated at Roman Catholic schools and have nevertheless become most conventional citizens of the Empire.—*Sphere*

COMPARISON WITH OTHER IRISH AUTHORS: This book is not within a hundred miles of being as fine a work of art as *Limehouse Nights*, the work of another young Irishman.—*Sphere*

There are a good many talented young Irish writers today, and it will take a fellow of exceptional literary stature to tower above Lord Dunsany, for example, or James Stephens.—*New York Globe*

IMAGINATION: He shows an astonishingly un-Celtic absence of imagination and humour.—*Bellman* (U.S.A.)

RELIGION: The irreverent treatment of religion in the story must be condemned.—*Rochester* (*New York*) *Post-Express*

TRUTH: It is an accident that Mr Joyce's book should have Dublin as its backrgound.—*Freeman's Journal* (Dublin)

Joyce was also becoming known abroad. For instance, there appeared in *The Egoist* for February 1918 an article on *A Portrait* by Diego Angeli, published in *Il Marzocco*, Florence, on August 12th, 1917. Joyce himself translated this at Miss Weaver's request.[1]

Ezra Pound, to whom much of this varied publicity was due, realized that what he was building up for Joyce and others detracted from his own work. In September 1917 he wrote to Margaret Anderson, 'I must get out of the big stick habit and begin to put my prose stuff into some sort of possibly permanent form, not merely into saying things which everybody will believe in three years' time and take as a matter of course in ten, i.e. articles which can be reduced to "Joyce is a writer, GODDAMN your eyes. Joyce is a writer, I tell you Joyce, etc. etc. Lewis can paint, Gaudier knows a stone from a milk pudding. WIPE your feet!!!!" '

ROBERT STREET, ADELPHI

In 1917 *The Egoist* was moved to No. 2 Adelphi Terrace House, Robert Street, just off the Strand. Here again was a neighbourhood which had known many changes, not only of owners and buildings but the levels of the land itself have been altered. Once the river had been within smelling distance of the main thoroughfare. Now the York watergate, attributed to Inigo Jones, gives upon the lawns and outdoor cafés of the Embankment Gardens and the Thames is five hundred yards away. When the Adam brothers proposed building the houses of the Adelphi, some of

---

[1] *The Personal Library of James Joyce* (a descriptive bibliography by Thomas E. Connolly: University of Buffalo, 1955) lists the copy kept by Joyce.

which are still to be seen there, opposition to the scheme was expressed in verse:

> 'Four Scotsmen by the name of Adams,
> Who keep their coaches and their Madams,'
> Quoth John in sulky mood to Thomas,
> 'Have stole the river from us!'
> Oh Scotland, long has it been said,
> Thy teeth are sharp for English bread,
> Would seize our bread and water too
> And use us worse than jailers do,
>   'Tis hard, 'tis hard, 'tis hard, 'tis true.

Mr Coutts, of the famous Bank in the Strand, insisted that he should be allowed the fine prospect over the Kent and Surrey hills visible from his windows, and Robert Street was made straight down towards the Thames for this purpose. It seems that Adelphi Terrace House was one of the first in that area to be built as offices, which were very much in demand. At the top were residential quarters. The Post Office Directory for 1918 shows that above the activities of engineers, solicitors, insurance firms, Miss Nina Boucicault as secretary for the Actresses Franchise League, the Home Rule for India League, etc., lived, among others, John Galsworthy, Esq., and, at the end of the Terrace, Sir James Matthew Barrie, Bart. So far there is no record of these eminent authors encountering those young men and women of another generation who called occasionally at *The Egoist* office downstairs.

Among these was T. S. Eliot, who had contributed articles and reviews to *The Egoist* for some time. These are particularly interesting in that they show the poet in a transition stage between his American background and a gradual identification with English and European culture. *Prufrock and other Observations* was published by The Egoist Press in 1917—500 copies at 1s. each. The following June T. S. Eliot became assistant editor of the magazine until it ceased publication two years later. In a large notebook which records the readings held at the Poetry Bookshop during the war years, owned by Mrs Harold Monro, I noticed that whereas 335 people were present to hear W. B. Yeats read his own poems in April 1916, only twenty came to encourage the young American poet in January 1918. A friend, Caron Rock, then connected with the Poetry Bookshop, remembered hearing him read about that time—the desk-light on the smooth-skinned, handsome face and birdshaped head. . . . No, he had hardly any American accent, perhaps that vowel or two later to be sandpapered down so as to be indistinguishable. Yet for all the steady sway of his reading, this was a period of difficulties, as profound in their different way as those Joyce was experiencing in Switzerland. At times it seems as if parts of *The Waste Land*, with its many currents and shades of sound, are carried along by the dark flow of the Thames as it broadens out below the Adelphi to curve down towards London Bridge.

One day I arranged to meet Miss Weaver at Charing Cross Metropolitan line station. She was there waiting for me, holding her little bag with a book for the train and an umbrella, and dressed in the light wool, no-particular-fashion coat with a small fur collar which I had seen before —everything inconspicuous, neat, the clothes of a person not very concerned about herself or the impression made. Her head and face moved a little in sympathy to a smile of recognition, and as always she would not let me carry the bag.

'Oh no, I can manage. We go up this way, don't we? It's such a long time since I was here. I know they have altered the Terrace. . . .' Some architectural students were measuring and sketching the Watergate: we went on up those narrow streets, more like lanes, which here and there have tunnels debouching upon them.

'I used to approach it more from the other side, down Adam Street,' she said as we turned the corner.

Opposite us were the ruins of what had been The Little Theatre, bombed during the Second World War. We turned left again and were in Robert Street, skirting a high, large-windowed house. Inside were those impersonal maroon-coloured walls of business premises, dignified by arches and a flight of stone stairs that curved mildly to a series of landings.

'Number twenty-three?' Miss Weaver hesitated before the board. 'It was on the first floor.' As we mounted leisurely she said, 'What shall we say we want?'

'Ghosts!' I said.

She laughed, that amused yet half-regretful sound of a person who long ago left some happiness behind and yet continues to face life courageously.

'This is it.'

Across the back of the two communicating houses which make up the building runs a long passage. Soon we stood before the very ordinary door marked twenty-three.

'What can we say?' She knocked.

'I know—I'll ask for Misha Black.' The name had struck me in the hall as suggesting *Mise Eire*. I knocked: we waited. Anticlimax: number twenty-three was locked!

'It was very small,' explained Miss Weaver. 'One could hardly turn round, for we had a good deal in it. I saw to all the business side, printers, proofs, advertisements . . .'

I wondered again at this woman, who had helped to finance a magazine, enabled a writer she did not then know personally to work at a book which printers would not touch, and much later took on the responsibilities of an intricate trusteeship. Could I find the right word? Modesty was too smudged a term—better perhaps to say that here was someone without a sense of proprietorship, the woman of some possessions who did not go hesitantly away but placed them quietly on the table for other people to use.

As we went downstairs again we talked of the John Rodker edition of *Ulysses* and how it had been distributed.

'There were only a few copies here—the rest I kept in a cupboard in my flat.' She laughed. 'I used to go round to the backdoors of the book-sellers with a paper parcel, for a customer might have ordered one through them.

'I remember I brought Mr Joyce here once, when The Egoist Press, not the magazine, was still functioning.' Now we were in Robert Street again, and Miss Weaver stopped to look up at Adelphi Terrace House, and in whatever moment or past circumstance she found herself again, no one of another generation could follow her.

By 1918 Joyce's work had already a small but intelligent public. A further edition of *A Portrait*, printed in Southport, appeared that year. Elkin Mathews brought out *Chamber Music* again and an unsigned review appeared in *The Egoist*, which Miss Weaver attributes to T. S. Eliot: [1]

This is a second edition; first published in 1907. This verse is good, very

---

[1] 'I have no recollection myself of whether I wrote it or not.' T. S. E. in a letter, 22.9.53.

James Joyce and perhaps Michael Healy,
c. 1912

Michael Healy

George Roberts, with 'Dubliners'

Seefeldstrasse 54, Zürich

Reinhardstrasse 7, Zürich

Universitätstrasse 29, Zürich

Seefeldstrasse 73, Zürich

good; though it never would have excited much attention but for Joyce's prose, still it would in any case have worn well. We infer from it that Mr Joyce is probably something of a musician; it is lyric verse, and good lyric verse is very rare. It will be called 'fragile', but is substantial, with a great deal of thought beneath fine workmanship.

Meanwhile Joyce had prepared a considerable part of *Ulysses*. In his *Guide to Kultur*, published in 1952, Ezra Pound wrote:

In nineteen-twelve or eleven I invoked whatever gods may exist, in the quatrain:

> Sweet Christ from hell spew up some Rabelais,
> To belch and . . . and to define today
> In fitting fashion, and her monument
> Heap up to her in fadeless excrement.

'Ulysses' I take as my answer. . . . The katharsis of *Ulysses*, the joyous satisfaction as the first chapters rolled into Holland Place, was to feel that here was the JOB DONE and finished, the diagnosis and the cure was here. The sticky, molasses-covered filth of current print, all the fuggs, all the foetus, the whole boil of the European mind, had been lanced.

Among Joyce's papers, now at the Lockwood Memorial Library, there is the second page of a letter by Pound written to Joyce at that time, probably kept as a reminder of the pleasure which it must have given him when it arrived in Zürich at the end of 1917. As Ezra Pound used the typewriter to reproduce the intervals of the American language—musical or not—it is interesting to see the page itself. 'Pits' refers to the fact that Wyndham Lewis was commissioned to paint at the front, as described in *Blasting and Bombardiering*, 1937 (see next page).

Soon there appeared an announcement in *The Egoist* that it was hoped to serialize Joyce's new novel *Ulysses*.[1] As Miss Weaver put it: 'In 1918 an abortive attempt was made to publish as a serial the new novel *Ulysses*, which Mr Joyce, handicapped by ill health and very bad eyesight, was working upon in Zürich. The project was to bring the chapters out simultaneously in *The Egoist* and Miss Margaret Anderson's *Little Review* of New York, starting in March 1918. But again there were difficulties in this

---

[1] See Appendix D.

2.

Hope to forward a few base sheckles in a few days time.
Wall , Mr Joice , I recon your a damn fine writer , that's
what I recon' . An' I recon' this here work o' yourn
is some concarn'd litterchure . You can take it from
me , an' I'm a jedge .

I have been doing ten and twelve hours a day on
Arnaut Daniel , which some lunatick clerk in orders wants
to private print in Cleveland Oo. I have for the time
being reduced myself chiefly to a rhyming dictionary
of all the ornrey terminations in the language . Some of
the stuff is at least better that the bloody mess I made
of my first attempt , five years ago.

        Lewis is to paint gun pits for the Canadian records.
It will get him our of the firing line for a few months.
Thank God.

        Let me sink into slumber.

        yours ever

                            Ezra Pound

                        18 · 12 · 1917

country with printers and it was not until 1919 that a few isolated episodes appeared in *The Egoist*.

'*The Little Review* had better luck to begin with, no difficulties with printers. After the appearance of eight instalments, however, the U.S. postal authorities and the Society for the Suppression of Vice gave much trouble, seizing a number of the issues and involving the editors in a law case. Notwithstanding these annoyances they succeeded in publishing the first twelve episodes. But at the end of 1920 a court injunction prohibited the publication of any further instalments of the book.'

Ezra Pound wrote to John Quinn:

> It still seems to me that America will never look *anything*—animal, mineral, vegetable, political, international, religious, philosophical or *anything* else—in the face until she gets used to perfectly bald statements.
>
> That's propaganda if you like but it seems to me something larger than the question of whether Joyce writes with a certain odeur de muskrat.
>
> The present international situation seems to me in no small measure due to the English and American habit of keeping their ostrich heads carefully down their silk-lined sand holes.

Under the title 'Literature and the American Courts' in the March issue of *The Egoist*, T. S. Eliot had already dealt with the prohibition of Wyndham Lewis's *Cantelman's Spring Mate* in *The Little Review*. Here perhaps was the first twist of that odd *sugan* which drew together three such different personalities.

Then in the July number T. S. Eliot commented in *Contemporanea*:

> The Englishman coddles his conception of the Inspired Bard: prose is a humbler vehicle. Mr Joyce ought to disturb this view of prose. This brings in again the critic of *The New Age* who objects to the cleverness of Joyce and Lewis. Mr Joyce can wait his turn until *Ulysses* (immeasurably an advance on the *Portrait*) appears as a book; as *Tarr* (after inevitable delays) is finally ready for the public the case of Mr Lewis is more urgent. . . . Both of these writers, and they are utterly different from each other, have been sensitive to foreign influence. This is disturbing; we may enjoy a borrowed ornament or two but we usually object to any writer who has actually assimilated foreign influence, grown his own lion-skin, become suspect in the fold. *The New Age* is 'mystified, bewildered, repelled'. This is quite intelligible. *Ulysses* is volatile and heady, *Tarr* thick and suety, clogging the weak intestine. Both

are terrifying. This is the test of a new work of art—when a work of art no longer terrifies us we may know that we were mistaken, or that our senses are dulled: we ought still to find Othello or Lear frightful. But this active terror repels the majority of men; they seek the sense of ease which the sensitive man avoids, and only when they find it do they call anything 'beautiful' . . .

As Miss Weaver continues: 'The problem of keeping *The Egoist* going had been a hard one and partly for this reason and partly from the incompatibility of its two sides, the philosophic, represented by Miss Marsden whose editorials were found by many subscribers to have become too abstruse for easy reading, and the literary, the appeal of which was wider, it was decided to suspend publication at the end of 1919 and to concentrate on book publication.'

Thus in December, as English life adjusted itself to peace again, Miss Marsden wrote in her editorial:

> . . . we have had to contend against what has proved a very serious handicap to the serial publication of Mr Joyce's novel *Ulysses*. By that condition of the English law which makes a printer liable alongside the author and the publisher of a work, we have in working practice in England a printer's censorship much more drastic than that of the official literary censorship itself, so that it comes about that an intelligence abnormally acute and observant, an accomplished literary craftsman who sets down no phrase or line without its meaning for the creation as a whole, is faced with a situation in which the very possibility of existence for his work lies at the mercy and limitations of intelligence of—let us say—the printing-works foreman! For our part, the difficulties in connection with *Ulysses* have been very great, and the portions for which we have secured print cannot be regarded as sufficiently substantial rewards. Therefore, as we have at last found a printer willing to make an unmutilated copy of the text, we have decided to abandon its further serial publication and to publish instead the entire work in book form as soon as it is itself completed. The high importance which Mr Joyce's work has already assumed for our generation, both as to literary matter and form, makes the prospect of a new and complete book by him an event which of itself would justify deviation from the convention of a regular issue.[1]

[1] See Appendix D for a comparison between the *Egoist* and later texts.

In the end Miss Marsden's closing statement was to prove too optimistic and *Ulysses* was not available in England until three years later. For Joyce *The Egoist* had meant the publication of some of his work in both serial and book form, while putting him in touch with writers and critics both in Europe and America. Much later some of the associations of that period were to bubble up through the stream of *Finnegans Wake*. Meanwhile there was the problem of completing *Ulysses*. In Zürich, as the varied, war-bound society of refugees, cosmopolitans of different kinds and conditions, began to disperse, Joyce and his family prepared to return for a time to Trieste. From Holland Place Chambers, in the little triangular room full of books and manuscripts above the come and go of Church Street, W.8, Ezra Pound wrote to John Quinn that autumn: 'Our James is a grrreat man. I hope to God there is a foundation of truth in the yarn he wrote me about a windfall. Feel he may have done it just to take himself off my mind.'

VII

PARIS

1920–1922

'Mr Pound wrote to me so urgently from Sermione (lake of Garda), that in spite of my dread of thunderstorms and detestation of travelling, I went there bringing my son with me to act as lightning conductor.' Joyce was writing to Miss Weaver explaining how he reached Paris in July 1920. In the meantime Ezra Pound had described his impressions in a letter to John Quinn some weeks previously:

> Joyce—pleasing; after the first shell of cantankerous Irishman, I got the impression that the real man is the author of *Chamber Music*, the sensitive. The rest is the genius; the registration of realities on the temperament, the delicate temperament of the early poems. A concentration and absorption passing Yeats'—Yeats has never taken on anything requiring the condensation of *Ulysses*.
>
> Also great exhaustion, but more constitution than I had expected, and apparently good recovery from eye operation. He is coming up here later. . . . He is, of course, as stubborn as a mule or an Irishman but I fail to find him at all *unreasonable*. Thank God, he has been stubborn enough to know his job and stick to it. . . . He is dead right in refusing to interrupt his stuff by writing stray articles for cash. Better in the end, even from practical point of view. Also justified in sticking it out in Trieste, at least for the present.

A transport strike was on in Italy and Joyce left Sermione on a tram and eventually arrived back in Trieste, where he had been living since they left Zürich the previous year, in crowded quarters shared with his sister and brother-in-law. If for a time Joyce hesitated to go to Paris, eventually he decided to try and do so. On June 22nd he wrote to B. W. Huebsch in America that they hoped to leave Trieste in ten days' time for a holiday of some months. He also mentions that the last draft of *Ulysses*, the 'Oxen of the Sun' episode, had cost him a thousand hours' work, the whole book having already taken six years, and that he needed a rest. At that time sections were appearing in *The Little Review* and three issues of the magazine had been confiscated by the Post Office.

He told Miss Weaver that he did not believe he could ever manage 'to wheel the caravan of my family' out of Trieste, or that they would succeed in reaching Paris. After a stay in Venice for two days and a stop at Milan, they passed through Switzerland and spent a night at Dijon. Delighted to be in France again, Joyce little knew how important the name of that town was to be to him later. Thus Joyce's return to Paris was tentative; if necessary he could go back to Trieste without loss of face there. As to hopes of a rest and a holiday, he knew well that with *Ulysses* not yet complete these were only a dream.

They arrived on July 9th and stayed at a small hotel in the rue de l'Université in the 6ème which is still there. 'My intention', he wrote to Miss Weaver, 'is to remain here three months in order to write the last adventure Circe in peace (?) and also the first episode of the close. For this purpose I brought with me a recast of my notes and MS., and also an extract of insertions for the first half of the book in case it be set up during my stay here. The book contains (unfortunately) one episode more than you suppose in your last letter. I am very tired of it and so is everybody else.' He mentions the possibility of moving to Passy, the fact that part of *A Portrait* might be serialized in French and that there was a possibility of *Exiles* being produced. 'I hope all this will lead to something practical. It is all due to Mr Pound's energy. . . . The whole book, I hope (if I can return to Trieste provisionally or temporarily in October) will be finished about December, after which I shall sleep for six months.'

Pound, who was in Paris at the time, set about introducing Joyce to people who were later to be of great help to him. He also let it be known that the Joyces wanted somewhere to stay. Madame Bloch, who wrote as Ludmila Savitzky, agreed with her husband that they should offer Joyce the use of a flat in Passy. Quotations from her letter to Ezra Pound, preserved by Joyce, not only show with what tact the suggestion was made but give an idea of the background against which Joyce worked at that period.

9 *juillet 1920.*

CHER M. POUND,

Votre femme m'a demandé si nous connaissions un appartement à louer pour M. Joyce. C'est une chose rare à Paris en ce moment mais nous avons, à deux pas d'ici, 5 rue de l'Assomption, un tout petit appartement que mon mari avait avant notre marriage, et que nous sommes obligés de garder, n'ayant pas assez de place rue de Boulainvilliers pour d'autres meubles. D'ailleurs, nous sommes heureux de garder cet appartement parcequ'il peut rendre service à des amis... Si M. Joyce ne trouve pas ce qu'il cherche, nous serons enchantés de mettre ce logis à sa disposition pour tout l'été s'il veut. Malheureusement c'est très petit; il y a deux pièces sur la rue, une toute petite cuisine; dans la troisième pièce, qui sert de chambre de débarras, couche notre 'Velasquez', car ici nous n'avons pas de chambre de bonne... Mais comme nous devons partir à la campagne et naturellement emmener Velasquez—les Joyce pourraient se servir aussi de cette troisième pièce en notre absence.

Il y a un seul grand lit, et puis celui de la bonne. Les meubles sont très peu confortables, sauf le lit qui est *excellent*... L'appartement est au premier étage, il n'y a pas de vue, mais la rue est *très calme* et elle conduit, en cinq minutes, au Bois de Boulogne... Il ne faut se faire aucune illusion, c'est tout juste habitable pour des gens qui s'accommodent de peu. C'est seulement si M. Joyce ne trouve rien, que nous lui proposerons cela. Naturellement il ne peut être question d'aucune location—cet appartement ne nous sert à rien et nous serons trop contents s'il peut être agréable à quelqu'un de vos amis, et surtout à M. Joyce dont je viens de lire le roman [*A Portrait*] avec une grande admiration...[1]

The Joyces were delighted to accept this generous offer and one is left to guess whether Joyce chose a share of the comfortable bed or found more chance of getting on with his work in the 'chambre de débarras'!

RUE DE L'ASSOMPTION

During a visit to Paris I went to see the rue de l'Assomption, for myself. No. 5 looked large and gloomy, a little courtyard showing the broad doorway with its blue china pattern ornamentation. Further on the

---

[1] Ludmila Savitzky's translation of *A Portrait*, published by Editions de la Sirène, Paris, 1924, has been reprinted a number of times by Editions Gallimard.

road becomes wider, and just about the same time of year that the Joyces were installing themselves, the limes are beginning to give out their sticky summer sweetness, ramblers poke through the grilles and on a Sunday the families who assemble children and dogs for an afternoon outing, the schoolgirls going to some meeting at the convent, remain unaware that some of the most extraordinary chapters in twentieth-century literature have been written there.

In August 1920 Miss Weaver had again made Joyce a gift which enabled him to work at his book, and when Frank Budgen visited him at the little flat Joyce told him how pleased he was to be in Paris. 'There is an atmosphere of spiritual effort here. No other city is quite like it. It is a racecourse tension. I wake early, often at five o'clock, and start writing at once.'

The Circe chapter of *Ulysses*, drawing as it does upon the underlying levels of consciousness, made great demands upon Joyce's energy. At times, he said, it seemed as if it was turning him into a beast.

Among those to whom Joyce had been introduced by Pound was André Spire, who invited the Joyces to his home. Sylvia Beach, in an article in *Mercure de France*, 1950, describes how with her friend Adrienne Monnier she went one Sunday to the Spires' house in Neuilly. Among other guests was Ezra Pound (lounging in a chair, very good-looking, with blue shirt and velvet jacket), his wife Dorothy Shakespear and two comparative strangers to Paris, introduced as Mr and Mrs Joyce. Nora Joyce probably felt rather out of it, for she could speak no French at the time and Joyce himself said nothing during supper. He reddened easily and grimaced every now and then so that tiny lines mounted in waves up to his forehead—a characteristic recorded in a photograph by Madame Giedion.

That evening Sylvia Beach approached Joyce with the words 'Est ce le grand James Joyce?' Perhaps for a moment Joyce hesitated—was this another phony?—but in a moment or two he saw that here was someone genuinely interested in his work.

When he called at her bookshop the next day Joyce wore a dark suit, which did not look new, white canvas shoes and a hat at the back of his head, and carried an ash stick which he said had been given him by a naval officer from Ireland whom he had met in Trieste on board a British warship. He was soon telling Miss Beach of the difficulties encountered over his work and found her friendly and sympathetic.

About this time Joyce was also in touch with Philippe Soupault, and had met Aragon, Eluard and various other men of letters. What was happening to his son of seventeen (boarded out at the time) and the young girl, both of whom had seen so many changes of background and knew something of three languages and were now picking up another? Perhaps during the summer when Joyce worked steadily at *Ulysses*, Giorgio and Lucia explored the Bois nearby and gradually came to know a little of Paris. It was surely during this time that difficulties were gradually shaping themselves which Joyce was to face a dozen years later.

BOULEVARD RASPAIL
1920–1921

That autumn the Joyces returned for a further period to 9 rue de l'Université and began to look round for somewhere to stay the winter. By December they had taken a flat at 5 Boulevard Raspail, that long and rather unfriendly road which runs down from Montparnasse with its confusion of cafés and cinemas to the informality of the Boulevard St Germain. A large door of iron and glass and heavily ornamented balconies of the kind which are never used suggest a certain ugly comfort.

Sherwood Anderson had written to Joyce in the spring of that year, a formal note asking if he and his wife might call. They evidently met subsequently, for in the following autumn, as a further letter now at Buffalo University shows, Sherwood Anderson, writing from Chicago, introduced Ernest Hemingway to Joyce at Boulevard Raspail: 'An American writer instinctively in touch with everything worthwhile going on here.'

It appears, from a note written at the time, that Joyce met Jacques Copeau at Le Vieux Colombier, where they discussed the possibility of producing *Exiles*. Nothing came of it, but ten years later, on a card also preserved by Joyce, Copeau mentioned that he remembered the occasion very clearly.

Robert McAlmon's book, *Being Geniuses Together* (1938), gives a lively if somewhat dramatized account of life in Paris after the First World

War when British and Americans in particular came to France to escape the artistic limitations and social restraints of their home backgrounds. He had been a copy-writer and salesman in the United States, then married an English heiress and later edited a magazine. Miss Weaver, it seems, gave him a note of introduction to James Joyce, whose work McAlmon had read in book form and in *The Little Review*. 'At his place on the Boulevard Raspail I was greeted by Mrs Joyce, and although there was a legend that Joyce's eyes were weak, it was evident that he had used eyesight in choosing his wife. She was very pretty, with a great deal of simple dignity and a reassuring manner.' Joyce finally appeared, having just got up, and soon it was obvious that they liked each other. Neither knew many people in Paris and both enjoyed companionship. 'At that time Joyce was by no means a worldly man,' McAlmon remarks. ' . . . He was still a Dublin-Irish provincial, as well as a Jesuit-Catholic provincial, although in revolt. He refused to understand that questions of theology did not disturb or interest me, and never did.'

Joyce read him parts of *Ulysses* and at other times they discussed Robert Burton's *Anatomy of Melancholy*, or Sir Thomas Browne and contemporary writers such as Ezra Pound, George Moore and Bernard Shaw. Sooner or later Joyce would begin to recite Dante in Italian, 'when that misty and intent look came upon his face and into his eyes I knew that friend Joyce wasn't going home till early morning'.

An incident recorded by McAlmon has a bearing perhaps on the frustrations and tensions lying below the conscious mind of the Irish writer, and which bubble up through the current of *Ulysses*. Joyce talked of the fertility of his forefathers, then he would sigh and pull himself together 'and swear by the grace of God he was still a young man and we would have more children before the end. He didn't detect', McAlmon continues, 'that I, the youngest of ten children of a poor minister, did not fancy his idea. He would not listen when I suggested that if one is to produce children one had better have the money to educate and care for them in childhood years.'[1] For six weeks McAlmon was busy writing some short stories, later printed by Darantière in Dijon, and the title *A Hasty Bunch*

---

[1] Gorman, p. 280, records a curious dream related by Joyce, in which Molly Bloom flung a child's black coffin at her husband. Family limitation and its repercussions below the conscious level is an important theme in *Ulysses*.

was suggested by Joyce, 'because he found my American use of the language racy'.

From the Boulevard Raspail Joyce continued to correspond with an Irish musician, George Molyneux Palmer, with whom he had been in touch from time to time since 1912. When I interviewed Mr Palmer at his home in Sandycove, near the Martello Tower, he told me that his mother had first read *Chamber Music*. She suggested that he should set some of the poems to music. Although they never met, Joyce's letters contain a number of interesting references to music and show the efforts he made to get Mr Palmer's works sung by John McCormack or published in France.

All that winter Joyce worked hard to complete *Ulysses*. The Circe episode—re-written nine times—was now finished. The book, he was able to tell John Quinn, who was helping him in America, would be ready in May 1921, and again he talks of needing six months' rest. After Easter Joyce sent further sections to T. S. Eliot in London, who offered to supply a few names of those likely to be interested in the limited edition which Sylvia Beach proposed to bring out that year. He also put forward suggestions, some of which Joyce incorporated in the final version of *Ulysses*, page 482, John Lane, 1941 edition.

> *9 Clarence Gate Gardens,*
> *London, N.W.6.*
>
> *21 May 1921.*
> MY DEAR JOYCE,
>
> I am returning your three mss by registered post as you require and am exceedingly obliged for a taste of them. I think they are superb—especially the Descent into Hell, which is stupendous. Only, in detail, I object to one or two phrases of Elijah: 'ring up' is English, 'call up' American; 'trunk line', if applied to the telephone service, is English, the American is, if I remember, 'long distance'. I don't quite like the wording of the coon transformation of Elijah, either, but I cannot suggest any detailed alteration. But otherwise, I have nothing but admiration, in fact, I wish, for my own sake, that I had not read it.

When a man gains the attentions of others, as Joyce was to do, intermixed with admiration, there is a tendency to enjoy any story which is also rather disconcerting to its central figure. A number current in Paris during the twenties still survive when Joyce's name is mentioned; for instance, an encounter with Proust at which both writers seemed to have discussed nothing at all. As a matter of fact, McAlmon mentions that they met through Sydney Schiff (Stephen Hudson), and that Diaghilev and Daisy Fellowes were also there.[1] One is usually told of a slight disagreement as to whether the window of a taxi should be up in consideration of Proust's asthma or down because fug affected Joyce's eyes!

In the same way it is surprising the number of people who imagine they were present at a meeting between Wyndham Lewis, T. S. Eliot and the Irish writer which is described with ironical clarity by Wyndham Lewis in *Blasting and Bombardiering*, and which suggests his complicated relationship with Joyce in later years. This is substantiated by a note now in the University of Buffalo from T. S. Eliot to Joyce in which he says that as he is visiting Paris he hopes to meet him at last and deliver a parcel from Ezra Pound. With Wyndham Lewis he stayed at the Hôtel Elysée in the rue de Beaune, and on the evening of their arrival Joyce visited them with his son. 'I found an oddity in patent leather shoes, large powerful spectacles, and a small gingerbread beard,' Wyndham Lewis wrote, 'speaking half in voluble Italian to a schoolboy; playing the Irishman a little overmuch perhaps, but in an amusingly mannered technique. Soon I was to be prepared to be interested in Joyce for his own sake. I took a great fancy to him for his wit, for the agreeable humanity of which he possessed such stores, for his unaffected love of alcohol, and all good things to eat and drink.' With his extraordinary visual memory, Wyndham Lewis describes how they all stood around in the dingy dignity of the hotel room while Joyce lay back in his stiff chair negligently dangling his straw hat, a characteristic pose as shown by photographs. The parcel brought over by T. S. Eliot lay on a centre table and soon Joyce was trying to undo 'the crafty housewifely knots of Ezra Pound'. Eventually he opened the package—word so frequently associated with Pound—and there stood revealed some underclothes and a pair of still quite serviceable brown shoes!

Joyce, who was meeting for the first time two writers connected with *The Egoist* for whom he had a considerable respect, was placed in a humiliating position and the encounter began awkwardly. Lewis knew little of Joyce's work, 'although Joyce on the other hand had, I am persuaded, read

---

[1] In *Furthur Recollections of James Joyce*, 1955, Frank Budgen gives Joyce's description of the incident and notes that they had nothing to say to one another.

everything I had ever written', even if he pretended not to have done so, and thus 'bad jams occurred in the dialogue in both directions'. Frank Budgen in *James Joyce and the Making of Ulysses* mentions that he appreciated *Cantelman's Spring Mate* and Joyce plays on the title in *Finnegans Wake*.

Later, Wyndham Lewis was to read Joyce's work with care, to admire certain aspects and to point out, as if the author were dead a hundred years, its origins in Joyce's personal and social background. On asking someone who had known both writers what seemed to them the basis of this odd attraction and repulsion between the two men, I was told, 'Well, I don't exactly know—but I think Joyce had the idea that Wyndham Lewis thought he was not a gentleman.' This is a reminder of the lines in *A Portrait* where Stephen is being continually exhorted to be one and those passages in his books where Wyndham Lewis suggests his own denial of a superior attitude. For our generation the term means little—for one thing there are no servants to 'Miss' and 'Master' our children—but for Joyce and his period this was all-important.

While Wyndham Lewis and T. S. Eliot were in Paris in the summer of 1921, Joyce insisted, in spite of his difficult position, on playing the host. 'We had to pay his "Irish pride" for the affair of the old shoes,' wrote Wyndham Lewis. 'That was it! He would not let us off. He was entirely unrelenting and we found it impossible to outmanoeuvre him.'

Long afterwards in his eyrie above the traffic of Notting Hill Gate I asked Wyndham Lewis about the episode. During that time, he said, Joyce and he were like schoolboys together, they did not mention serious subjects. As to *Time and Western Man*, Joyce had remarked to someone that he thought 'Lewis was perhaps 10% right' and Lewis admitted to me that he was sorry he wrote in that way.[1] Yet the documents of that time, reflecting both objective and more personal reactions, would have been incomplete without Wyndham Lewis's contribution, or those echoes of Joyce which reach out into the sun-dried, strange world of the *Childermass*. When I mentioned that some of Joyce's friends believed him to have been the original of Pullman, Wyndham Lewis was taken by surprise. 'Well . . . er . . . I hadn't thought of it.' Certainly some of Joyce's pride has a place in *Monstre Gai* and *Malign Fiesta*, but soon an ironical affection for

[1] Frank Budgen also records Joyce saying, 'Allowing that the whole of what Lewis says about my book is true, is it more than 10% of the whole truth about it.'

his hero comes uppermost. Giorgio Joyce mentioned his father's regard for Wyndham Lewis. In some odd way they have been complementary to one another; neither became an enemy.

RUE CARDINAL LEMOINE
1921

Sylvia Beach, in the article already mentioned, shows that Valery Larbaud, the poet and translator, had introduced her to Stephen Gwynn and later she reciprocated by sending him James Joyce. Larbaud had been born in Vichy, where his family owned some of the famous *sources*. He lived much in Italy and Spain, and translated Thomas Gray, Samuel Butler, Walt Whitman and other writers into French. Although his name was not familiar to the wider reading public at that time, he had a considerable position in the literary world. At Vichy, as I shall mention later, his correspondence with Joyce, extending over twenty years, is preserved at the Municipal Library.

Valery Larbaud had read what had been printed of *Ulysses* in *The Little Review* and Joyce lent him part of the book not yet in print. Miss Beach transmitted Larbaud's enthusiastic comment. 'C'est merveilleux! Aussi grand que Rabelais. Mr Bloom est immortel comme Falstaff.' Later it was planned that Larbaud should give a lecture on Joyce's work for *Les Amis des Livres*, to be arranged by Adrienne Monnier.

During the summer of 1921, while the Larbauds were in England, Joyce was lent their first-floor flat at 71 rue Cardinal Lemoine. Once installed, Joyce began to write again at a desk before a window which looked upon trees and a quiet courtyard of old, sand-coloured houses. In June he told Larbaud that some of the typescript of his book had been destroyed by a typist, or her shocked husband, but that proofs of the Ithaca and Penelope episodes were reaching him from the printers and that, although he was nearly killed by 'work and eyes', he was still adding much to the text. It must have been about that time that Joyce sent Larbaud a comic postcard which shows a drunk man in a topper falling into a horse trough, with his umbrella in his hand, entitled, '*Prier pour ceux qui sont en mer*'—pray for those at sea, to which Joyce has added '*Ulysses arrive à Ithaque!*'

To reach the rue Cardinal Lemoine, in the 5ème arrondissement, is to walk over the pavements which Joyce followed so many years ago on his way from the Grand Hôtel Corneille to lectures in medicine in the rue Cuvier. Leaving the students, the cafés and heavy traffic of the Boulevard St Michel, I took the broad rue Soufflot which is surmounted by the huge, blank-walled bulk of the Panthéon. Changed so many times from church to national tomb, now the remains of Voltaire, Rousseau, Victor Hugo, Zola, and the heart of Gambetta are enclosed there. The windows of the Bibliothèque Ste Geneviève seem a dim sea green as the last students emerge; on the Panthéon steps an old woman examines the side of her broken shoe, and an artist sketches in what remains of the evening light.

Having recently purchased *Evocation du Vieux Paris* by Jacques Hilliaret, which deals with each street and its notable buildings in direct, workmanlike manner, my mind was full of the history of the Montagne Ste Geneviève. There was that extraordinary woman and saint who held the people together against Attila, there were the churches and abbeys destroyed over the years only to be rebuilt again, the open-air schools to which students come from all over Europe, and the associations with Héloise and Abelard. In the rue Clovis some of the old ramparts from the twelfth century break out from cement-faced houses, great hunks of building stone-softened by the same pink-red valerian which grows so freely upon Dublin walls.

Although there are links with Ronsard, and the painters Lebrun and Watteau lived in rue Cardinal Lemoine, the Pléiade was founded there, and Pascal died a few doors away, I could find no distinction for No. 71 where Joyce had stayed during the very hot summer of 1921. The number covers a square of houses set back from the street and reached through an archway. Except for an old walnut tree or two, there was nothing to be remarked there, but as I came away I noticed up against the entrance wall the remains of a high iron-barred gate. This is mentioned in a story told by Robert McAlmon in his reminiscences. One evening at the Brasserie Lutetia Joyce ordered, as usual, 'that horrible natural champagne'. He was in a highly nervous condition and when McAlmon jokingly said that he had seen a rat run down the stairs from the floor above, Joyce insisted it was a sign of bad luck and soon afterwards collapsed. McAlmon got him into a taxi and they drove to rue Cardinal Lemoine.

9 rue de l'Université, Paris
now the writing of Ulysses *is at an end*

At Bognor, 1923?

The Strawberry Beds, near Chapelizod

There the high iron gates were closed and McAlmon, with a key 'about a foot long', found it very hard to open them. At last, after ten minutes, wobbling it in and out, they were unlocked and with the help of the driver Joyce was carried through the courtyard and upstairs. Nora Joyce started to scold her husband, but when McAlmon explained she 'turned tender at once, realizing it was fright, not drink which had put him into this condition'.

The next day they all met for coffee at the Café Harcourt. Suddenly Joyce's face showed he was in terrible pain. Nora called a taxi and McAlmon, always kindly it seems, saw them home. This was another eye attack similar to those experienced in Zürich a number of years previously. Joyce, in the correspondence I have seen, never directly mentions the suffering these attacks involved. It is Ernest Hemingway, in a letter written to Joyce some years later, who brings this most clearly before us. 'My little boy, when I picked him up to pot him at night . . . poked his finger in my eye and the nail cut the pupil. For ten days I had a little taste of how things might be with you. It hurt like hell . . .'

RUE DE L'UNIVERSITÉ
1921–1922

It was probably Pound who had decided that Joyce should stay at 9 rue de l'Université when the family arrived from Trieste in 1920. His own hotel was quite near, in the rue de Beaune. Joyce may have regarded the name as a good omen, a reminder of Universitätstrasse in Zürich where he had written some of *Ulysses*. Although Joyce had a hard thing or two to say about the hotel,[1] later he returned there in moments of difficulty.

The street itself was made through the area once occupied by the old University and, beginning in the ancient, more crowded quarter not far from the Place St Germain-des-Prés, moves away from the rue Jacob until it reaches a very different neighbourhood. As Joyce made his way to the space and air of the Esplanade des Invalides, he must have noticed that where the rue de l'Université traverses the Boulevard St Germain, there is a house and small garden which takes up a triangle of ground between

[1] Hôtel Lenox, its present name, was not used on Joyce's correspondence but it occurs in *Finnegans Wake*.

the two roads. On the gate is a large white shield, announcing the Institute of Master Locksmiths of France: in the centre are two crossed keys, a reminder of Bloom's advertisement for the house of Keyes in *Ulysses*.

On October 7th, 1921, Joyce was telling Miss Weaver that he was once more at 9 rue de l'Université, which was to be their base for over a year, and described himself as being with manuscripts, pencils (red, green and blue), cases of books and trunks 'and all the rest of my impedimenta snowed up in proofs and nearly crazed with work. *Ulysses* will be finished in about three weeks, thank God, and (if the printers don't all leap into the Rhône in despair at the mosaics I send them back), ought to be published early in November. . . .

'My eyes seem to be all right for the next three weeks though I know it is madness to work them as I am doing, but I feel around me a good deal of impatience made up partly of expectation and partly of irritation. I am very, very slow, and have just enough energy to write the dry rock pages of *Ithaca*.

'With kind regards and looking forward to the expiration of my seven years' sentence.'

Even with Miss Weaver's generosity, Joyce found it hard to support three people in a city where costs were high and they were obliged to live in a hotel. It is much to Robert McAlmon's credit that nowhere in his book does he suggest that at this period he helped Joyce financially, and Joyce mentions that he did not know what he would have done without such loans. Clothes were again a problem for the family, and Joyce, tired of wearing the same things, on one occasion asked his friend for a nice tie!

With the growing interest in his work which Joyce felt about him, he knew it was essential to press on with the book. There were troubles with the printers, for they were puzzled by all the w's and k's in a language they did not know. Joyce told McAlmon that in a room where three people slept, and without a desk, he was working like a lunatic, trying to revise, improve, correct and create all at the one time.

From Trieste Joyce had already asked his aunt in Dublin, Mrs Josephine Murray, for hymnbooks, songs, the *News of the World*, the *Police Gazette*, and information about the Star-of-the-Sea church at Sandymount. He also wanted gossip about people they had known and enquired what had become of Alf Bergan. Soon he wrote from rue de l'Université to find out some details about 9 Eccles Street. By October 30th, seventeen years and three weeks since he had left Dublin in 1904, Joyce was telling Larbaud that the previous night he had completed the Ithaca episode, 'so that now the writing of *Ulysses* is at an end'.

Some time previously Joyce had made an outline of *Ulysses* and gave Larbaud a proposed programme for the lecture to be held at *La Maison des Amis des Livres*. During November there were rehearsals with Jimmy Light, an American actor who read from the Sirens episode, and Joyce met Larbaud several times for dinner to discuss details. By November 26th announcements of the lecture were published and Joyce wrote to Larbaud that he was glad and honoured to see the eminent names associated with his first 'and possibly last' appearance before a French public.

By Christmas-time Joyce knew that *Ulysses* was all but launched on the choppy sea of French literary criticism, and he was also aware that it would be fatal for the appearance of the book to be delayed much longer. The printers had promised that advance copies would be completed in time for Joyce's birthday on February 2nd, 1922. The firm had taken on extra workers in order to do so, but as Joyce sent them whole paragraphs to change at the last moment it did not seem likely. Sylvia Beach, fearing that the copies might not arrive in time, with her usual determination 'phoned to arrange that the advance copies were to be put on a late passenger train from Dijon. This she met at the Gare de Lyon at seven o'clock on the morning of Joyce's birthday. In ten minutes, down the grey, closed-eyed streets of Paris, a taxi took her to the rue de l'Université. Perhaps the night porter, as deliberate as the one I had known at the Hôtel Corneille, was surprised to see a lady hand in a bulky parcel for Monsieur Joyce and insist that it should be taken up at once. 'Eh bien, ces étrangers,' he must have said to himself, going up the dark stairs to the first floor front, 'ils ne sont pas raisonnables.'

If Joyce thought he was going to rest after this accouchement he was quite mistaken; he was soon saying that he had not had a day's peace since the book came out. Many subscriptions reached the rue de l'Odéon and he was busy helping Miss Beach to make up parcels in a way they were never packed before. A review in *The Observer* had resulted in a hundred and thirty-six orders: both the British Museum and *The Times* had asked for copies.

During the winter Joyce had seen something of Desmond FitzGerald, associated with the Imagist group in London a number of years before. He was then issuing a news sheet or bulletin for the Irish Provisional Government, not yet in being, and acted as Minister of Propaganda. This was before the Treaty was signed, with all its tragic consequences. Joyce ironically remarks that as it was proposed he should be awarded the Nobel Prize, Desmond FitzGerald would either change his mind when he read *Ulysses* or lose his portfolio. Mrs FitzGerald, who had been secretary to Bernard Shaw and later George Moore, told me of their meetings with Joyce, and how he asked about 'gathering places' in Dublin and people he had known there. In May, Joyce also met John Middleton Murry, who had reviewed *Ulysses* in the *Nation and Athenaeum*, and was in Paris at that time with Katherine Mansfield, an incident I will mention later.

That spring Nora Joyce was anxious to take her son and daughter to see her mother in Galway. Joyce was very much against the project as the country was in a disturbed state after the Treaty, and although he managed to hold them up in London for ten days by means of express letters and telegrams, they left for Dublin. There they visited John Stanislaus Joyce and were vastly amused by the curses which he bestowed on his native country and its inhabitants, so Joyce wrote to Mrs Josephine Murray, who was annoyed the family had not been to see her, which they evidently intended to do on the return journey. Robert McAlmon describes how Joyce remained in Paris, at 9 rue de l'Université, feeling himself alone and deserted. 'And do you think they're safe, then, really?' he continually asked. 'You don't understand, McAlmon, how this is affecting me. I am worried all the day and it does my eyes no good.' Then Joyce would sigh, and although McAlmon was sympathetic, 'My humour', he continues, 'told me that friend Joyce has a way of enjoying the martyrdom of his trials and tribulations.'

As a matter of fact, Joyce's fears were not for nothing. In Galway the Republicans captured the warehouse opposite Mrs Joyce's lodgings, Free State troops invaded their bedrooms and planted machine-guns in the windows. This was too much for the Joyce party, who were already nervous and uneasy, so they hurried to the station, only to find that their train was being ambushed all along the line and they were obliged to lie flat on the floor. They hurried through Dublin at night-time, with no thought of the people they were to have seen there, and so back to Paris. It was no wonder that in May Joyce collapsed with an attack of glaucoma and for weeks lay in a darkened room.

LONDON—NICE

In the summer Joyce had recovered sufficiently to go over to England, and in London Miss Weaver met for the first time this writer she had been helping for five or six years. It was almost a decade since Joyce and his small boy had encountered Joseph Hone in Bloomsbury one morning and talked about the destruction of *Dubliners*. Now he returned as a middle-aged celebrity whose work had been banned in the U.S.A. and was being sold in England to the few really concerned with literature and the more numerous hangers-on anxious for something *new*.

The editing of *The Egoist* and Joyce's own work had put Miss Weaver in touch with the literary and artistic world. If she went to occasional dinners organized by Ezra Pound during the war, it was as an observer, and when she met some of the contributors about their work or the business of the magazine for lunch or tea, one imagines Miss Weaver never became part of any particular set. At the same time, those younger men and women, so deeply concerned with working out their ideas of art and life and involved in the inevitable personal entanglements (tensions, disagreements, love and hate affairs of the moment), appear to have had a genuine regard for Miss Weaver. Indeed, Robert McAlmon tried to draw her into what he called their 'less high-minded pastimes', and on one occasion they all went together to a music-hall to hear Nora Bayes sing.

A letter from Miss Weaver to James Joyce which illustrates their businesslike yet friendly relationship has survived in a curious way. The original is preserved in the National Library of Ireland, with one or two other items sent there in 1951 by Count G. O'Kelly of Gallagh from the Legation of Ireland in Lisbon. A covering note points out that he found the documents on inspecting an old copy of Sigerson's *Spring Song of Sedulius*, and that this might have been with books belonging to Thomas

Hughes Kelly purchased after his death. Miss Weaver wrote from the north of England on January 30th, 1923:

DEAR MR JOYCE:

I have been hoping to hear how your operations have gone but have received no word so far. Perhaps you have set off again for the south in dismay at the violent snowstorms and other bad weather of Paris. Or perhaps you have made for Rome in order to superintend the Italian edition of *Ulysses* with which Mr de Bosis, so I hear from him this morning, is occupying himself steadily, confronted by certain difficulties which however he hopes to overcome.

A day or two ago Mr Rodker wrote that the original English edition is now entirely disposed of except for 25 mutilated copies which are being rebound. The new edition of 500 (to replace the lost 400) is ready, paid for and on its way to London.[1] I shall ask Mr Rodker to send you a copy so that you may work upon it when continuing your reading of the book. The original corrections (those contained in the printed eight page slip) are supposed to have been made—but not as yet your additional corrections of the first 290 pages. Mr Rodker sent a further £150 on account and I enclose a draft for this (frs. 10,950). Since the draft was made on Saturday at 73 I see the rate has advanced to 75.

When in London you gave me a sample of your obedience. Now observe mine. You directed or commanded or advised or suggested that I should set aside Rabelais and read the Odyssey, neglected as it has been during all the years of my life. I did not do so. I continued the Rabelais in any odd time I had between September 15th and November 15th—but those volumes have not come away with me. With me has come—not to mention a bulky blue telephone directory [2]—the copy of the Odyssey bought when you were in London and, having had more free time during the last week, I completed a first reading of it last night. I am glad you issued the command though I am not sorry to have delayed obedience until now. The *Book of Kells* [3] will be a constant source of delight I think.

---

[1] According to *A Bibilography of James Joyce* by John J. Slocum and Herbert Cahoon, London, 1953, there is some doubt as to the destruction of these copies by the U.S. post offices, as copies have reached rare book sellers. The second English edition referred to above was seized and confiscated by the Customs at Folkestone in 1923.

[2] *Ulysses*.

[3] A Christmas present from Joyce. Madame Jolas recorded the remark that Joyce wanted his work to be as eloquent as he found its pages.

With best wishes for many happy returns of your birthday and kindest regards,

Yours sincerely,
HARRIET WEAVER

During the visit to which she refers, in the summer of 1922, Joyce's eyes had again been troubling him and they decided to stay in London instead of going to the coast. It was probably on this occasion that he met some of his relatives for the first time after many years. His cousin Miss Kathleen Murray, who was then working in a London hospital, remembers the occasion when she and her sister were invited to dinner by Joyce. He wore a cape, a wide hat, and had double glasses. When they left by taxi for a Soho restaurant, Joyce said that he wanted a fresh pair of socks, perhaps having forgotten to change or buy another pair during the day. It was by that time very inconvenient to return to where they were staying and the driver was consulted as to the possibility of any shops being open. He knew a friend in the East End who would oblige. They had hardly settled down in the restaurant when Joyce was called out and returned in a little while looking very pleased, having changed into new socks, a good instance of the way he could always get people to do things for him.

Joyce soon began to order their food in Italian. It must have been an amusing meal, for they had many old jokes to share—that famous white cap worn by Stephen Dedalus which he had specially made through their brother 'Bertie' at Conan's, the tailors in Kildare Street; Kathleen's recitation, 'The Beggar Baby', for their great aunt's parties on Usshers Quay in Dublin so many years ago. . . .

Yet thinking it over, Joyce realized that for a moment there had been an undercurrent of uneasiness. While the waiters were buzzing about him, as he mentioned in a letter later, he asked his cousins why their mother, Mrs Josephine Murray, had barely acknowledged the copy of *Ulysses* he had sent her. As a matter of fact, she found it both difficult and in places so alarmingly frank that she had locked it away from her daughters.

Kathleen Murray was thus placed in an awkward position. 'Well, Jim,' she had to admit, 'Mother said it was not fit to read.'

'If *Ulysses* isn't fit to read,' Joyce replied, 'life isn't worth living.'

VIII

WORK IN PROGRESS

1922–1928

In the autumn of 1922 the Joyces spent some time in Nice. One day when his wife and daughter had gone to listen to what he called 'ladies' ' music, Joyce stayed behind at the Hôtel Suisse to write letters. Aunt Josephine had evidently forgiven the family for not having visited her in Dublin and suggested that as things had quietened down in Ireland they should all go over there later. Joyce pointed out that the last trip had been very costly and had nearly ruined his eyesight into the bargain; perhaps they might meet in London during the spring. He twits her about *Ulysses* and says he is glad it is locked away as other islanders might not be indifferent to its commercial value. 'You said Charley was reading it and that you would tell me what he said and how he looked after reading it. Is he in the press? If so I hope he gets his meals regularly but how does he manage about shaving? I gather you have not finished it and neither has Berty but I think Nora will beat you all in the competition. She has got as far as page twenty-seven counting the cover.' He sends her an explanatory article, probably in *The Criterion* or *The English Review*, and suggests she buys Lamb's *Adventures of Ulysses* at Gills or Browne and Nolan's in Nassau Street. 'Send me any news you like, programmes, pawntickets, press cuttings, handbills. I like reading them.'

Long before he had finished *Ulysses*, Joyce knew to some extent what he would do next. 'I should like to write a universal history,' he told Miss Weaver when they met in London, but did not give her an idea of how he would set about it. Writing to Mrs Murray when they had returned to Paris, Joyce again asks for her help. 'I have been trying to collect my notes as well as my poor sight will allow and I find several names of people connected with the family who were of the older generation when I was a boy. I wonder if I sent you an exercise book with the names of these persons at the top of this paper would you be kind enough (whenever you have a spare moment and anything occurs to your mind) to scribble down in pencil or pen anything noteworthy, details of dress, defects, hobbies, appearance, manner of death, voice, where they lived, etc., just as you did for the questions I sent you about Major Powell—in my book Major Tweedy, Mrs Bloom's father? They all belong to a vanished world and most of them seem to have been very curious types. I am in no hurry. You could send me back the book in the next month if you like but I would feel greatly obliged if you could fill in any details for me as you are the only one who is likely to know about them.'

This suggests that Joyce thought of *Work in Progress* (a name put forward later by Ford Madox Ford) as a continuation to some extent of the factual, truth-is-more-effective-than-invention method. Yet having conveyed in the last pages of *Ulysses* the on-flow of thoughts just before sleep, Joyce now came gradually to seek for the means of expressing those images which push their way upwards from the many levels of unconsciousness. Having written of a complete day in the life of Dublin in 1904, he set himself to travel through the darkness of a dream-night which would, more completely than *Ulysses* had done, contain the elements of all man's knowledge. He may have planned to begin with those half-remembered figures of a generation before his own. Although Mrs Murray's side of the correspondence does not appear to have survived, it is probable, on account of an estrangement referred to later, that she did not comply with Joyce's request for more details about people in Dublin. Perhaps her silence, the reception of *Ulysses* in Ireland and the fact that its publication had finally separated Joyce from the life he had known there, turned his mind away from individuals and on certain levels drew his imagination outward from himself. For instance, not only did he become interested in the Book of Kells, but the Four Masters, the annalists of Ireland, were to provide him with much material. Thus it happens that many of the personages of *Finnegans Wake* carry historical or legendary associations as well as those of Joyce's own experience, such as the Gaelic hero Finn MacCool, St Patrick and St Kevin, Tristan and Iseult.

Before Christmas 1922 the Joyces moved into a furnished flat at 26 Avenue Charles Floquet, where they remained until the following June. The road runs parallel with the 'Champ de Mors', as Joyce called it, being aware of its previous history as a parade ground, an area now dominated by the huge meccano toy of the Eiffel Tower. It was there, on March 10th, 1923, he began his new work, for he told Miss Weaver in a letter the following day: 'Yesterday I wrote two pages—the first I have written since the final yes of *Ulysses*. Having found a pen, with some difficulty I copied them out in a large handwriting on a double sheet of foolscap so that I could read them.' Fortunately this first draft, marked with a thick red 'A', was preserved by Miss Weaver. It deals with Roderick O'Connor, the last king of Ireland, described as having a wonderful midnight thirst on him and drinking up the dregs after his visitors have left. M. J. C. Hodgart, who has made a detailed study of Joyce's manuscripts, points out that the style is related to that of Molly Bloom as she lies awake in Eccles Street, translated into a rambling and masculine monologue. The subject-matter of the passage, which was not used until Joyce was working on the final text in 1938, suggests the break-up of two distinct phases of Irish history, when King Roderick O'Connor, who abdicated in 1183, was overcome by the Anglo-Normans, and the destruction of the records of the intervening centuries in the Four Courts during 1922.

It was very fortunate that Joyce found in Miss Weaver so careful a guardian of his work. From time to time he posted her sections for typing and later, when this was carried out more conveniently in Paris, he sent drafts and proofs of the various sections of *Work in Progress* to appear in *Transition* and elsewhere. During the past few years Miss Weaver has spent much time sorting the material before presenting it to the British Museum. On the basis of the notes which she provided it has now been rearranged by Mr T. J. Brown of the Manuscript Department, and bound into nineteen volumes. Thus in most instances it is possible to trace a section through the earliest drafts and typescripts and to see how Joyce constantly worked on them, adding words, sentences, and whole paragraphs until the final proofs were reached.

Louis Gillet, who was in touch with Joyce during the thirties, suggested in his *Stèle Pour James Joyce*, published in Paris, 1946, that one day there should be an edition of the book which would show the initial stages of certain sections of *Finnegans Wake* compared with 'le texte remanié, corrigé, compliqué d'entrelacs, de paraphes, d'ornements, de rinceaux et de calligraphes'. Although he quotes Joyce as saying that *Finnegans Wake* had nothing in common with *Ulysses*—'C'est le jour et la nuit'—Louis Gillet goes on to give an excellent description of how both themes are reconciled. 'Au fond, M. Joyce n'a écrit qu'un seul livre, ou, si l'on préfère, differents états du même texte.'

BOGNOR

During the late spring of 1923 Joyce was telling Larbaud that they had given notice, the sweeps were in and everything was upside down. There is perhaps a reflection of this in *Finnegans Wake*, p. 119, 'An Irish plot in the Champs de Mors . . . more blame the soot.' By June he was staying with his wife and daughter at the Belgrave Hotel, 6 Montague Street, W.1. A card from T. S. Eliot, in the Lockwood Memorial Library, suggests that they should have tea together at Frascati's in Oxford Street. Lady Ottoline Morrell would be there and she was anxious to meet Joyce. A few days later Wyndham Lewis made arrangements for Joyce to come to Lee Studio in Adam and Eve Mews, off Kensington High Street. As they went down the cobbled way between the garages, still with a few stables there in those days, Joyce must have thought of the Dublin associations of the name—the church across the Liffey from the Four Courts. Miss Weaver remembers that during their visit the Joyces went to a few London theatres, but did not think much of them. On the other hand they enjoyed the ballet at Sadler's Wells.

Why they should have decided to go to Bognor rather than some other resort is not clear. In a note written at that time Mr Eliot hopes they will not have difficulty in finding a good hotel, and he plans that when on holiday at Fishbourne he will be able to fetch the Joyces and show them 'some of the waste lands round Chichester'. A further letter, written on July 12th mentioning that Mr Eliot has been delayed in London, shows that by that date the Joyces were at Alexandra House, Clarence Road, Bognor. It seemed unlikely, on a visit to this South Coast town, that we should find any trace of the place where the Joyces stayed at the time. A hunded years ago Bognor must have presented a pleasing unity of older Sussex buildings and Regency houses, with their dainty balconies, iron verandas and hooded doorways. Gradually this was broken into by compromises of all sorts and now the pier marks the centre of the front, surrounded by cafés and 'attractions'. Behind are the gardens and tennis courts of Wellington Square, and eastwards, among the residential areas (with the inevitable 'Kilkenny' or 'Avoca' of the Irish emigrant), we soon came upon Clarence Road.

To our surprise Alexandra House was still there, narrow in build, neat, its three tiers of windows like boxes in a theatre, slated with grey to give a certain character. Inside we found cream paintwork and cheerful coverings but were told the atmosphere was very different under the previous ownership. 'The real old-fashioned kind of boarding house,' someone commented later who had known the place in those days. 'Jug and basin in the rooms, all dark paint, and full of things: must have been like it for years and years.'

Of course there were other guests there, with children very likely, some of them early morning bathers maybe. In a note to Miss Weaver written on the back of the draft of 'Kevin and his Tub' sent her for typing, Joyce says, 'I am now on the third floor. Over me, thank goodness, is the roof.'

Joyce certainly worked for part of the day. The next piece of *Work in Progress*, the 'Tristan and Iseult' fantasia, was apparently drafted in July. The tone is that of the Gerty MacDowell (Nausicaa) chapter of *Ulysses*, where Joyce mocks at the romantic love themes of the novelette and woman's magazines of his youth, guyed long ago by Arthur Clery in *St Stephen's*. Two other pieces, a parody of the life of St Kevin and an account, in Joycean terms, of St Patrick's conversion of Ireland, were also written that summer. Thus it would probably be late morning before Joyce, in straw boater, with thick glasses and his walking stick, came down the narrow stairs and into the brightness of the street, pavement-warm in the summer. If he asked his daughter, dark and perhaps a little thin-armed at sixteen or so, the name of the big red house on the corner, and she told him it was a Home of Rest for Women, he probably gave his short laugh and asked her if there wasn't one next door for weary writers.

Long afterwards, in Galway, one of Joyce's relatives in law gave me a photograph of the writer at Bognor, and the original is now in the National Library of Ireland. It was taken perhaps by Lucia experimenting with a box camera, or one of those ambulant photographers of the seaside. Joyce, relaxed, half amused, sits beside a friend. Later, going past the dainty little Victorian bandstand, they may have sat on the beach against the high wooden groynes which grow out at close intervals into the tide. As Stuart Gilbert noticed on other occasions, Joyce did not mind the crowds; he would stretch out under the sun and listen to the sound of the sea. In the cries of the sea-gulls, 'Overhoved, shrillgleescreaming. . . . The winging ones', he heard an ironical commentary on the voyage of Iseult and Tristan as they sailed towards her marriage with the elderly King Mark of Brittany. On a more subjective level, Joyce, with a son reaching manhood, may have felt that he too was now part of an older generation.

Part of this mood was carried on into the 'Mamalujo' episode which Joyce wrote in September, the name suggesting both the four apostles and the four Irish annalists. The waves of the sea seem to carry their talk along with it, four old men 'remembering' [1] the past, confusing names and events, listening half censoriously, half regretfully, to the lovers of a different age. Much later these drafts begun in England become part of the dream of the Dublin publican Earwicker—an old Sussex name—who was to be the central figure of *Finnegans Wake*.

VICTORIA PALACE HOTEL

1923

When they returned to Paris the Joyces again faced the problem of where to live. Joyce had not the means to take a flat and furnish it; the question of what the children were to do would soon have to be considered. I believe there was some talk about Giorgio going in for medicine, and he had an excellent singing voice. 'There is gold in that boy's mouth,' Joyce is supposed to have said. Eventually they went to the Victoria Palace Hotel in the rue Blaise Désgoffe, not far from Montparnasse, where Joyce had visited John Middleton Murry the previous year. Curiously enough, in the last few pages of her journal, Virginia Woolf described how she remembered Miss Weaver, in wool gloves[2] and looking 'very buttoned up', bringing *Ulysses* in typescript to their tea table at Hogarth House. 'Would we devote our lives to printing it? . . . I put it in the

---

[1] Joyce told Miss Weaver that it was a 'study of old age'. *Remembering* shows Joyce's triple-edged use of words, the combination of an Irish pronunciation with the idea of rather boring repetition.

[2] 'And why shouldn't one wear wool gloves?' Miss Weaver said to me long afterwards, with a laugh.

drawer of the inlaid cabinet. One day Katherine Mansfield came, and I had it out. She began to read, ridiculing: then suddenly said, But there's something in this: a scene that should figure I suppose in the history of literature.'

After *Ulysses* had been published in 1922, John Middleton Murry expressed his appreciation in a review in the *Nation and Athenaeum*. Writing to Dorothy Brett that spring, Katherine Mansfield also gave her impressions. At that time she was undergoing treatment for her advanced T.B. while staying at the Victoria Palace Hotel and in the late spring of that year her husband joined her there. Joyce had probably written to thank Middleton Murry for his article, inviting him to lunch, at which it seems they talked about common friends in Dublin, chiefly Gogarty and Sinclair. Shortly afterwards Joyce received the following note, now in the Lockwood Memorial Library:

> *Victoria Palace Hotel,*
> *rue Blaise-Desgoffe,*
> *rue de Rennes. 6ème.*

Sunday.

DEAR MR JOYCE:

I feel that I did not make a sufficient apology for the inadequacy of my article upon *Ulysses*. Long before writing it I had made up my mind that it was quite hopeless for me to try to say anything really worth saying about it within the limits of space imposed upon me, and that I must confine my attention to the business of helping it to get a hearing. My article has no merit whatever. I say this in order that you should not think that I have the indecency to offer it as a *criticism* of *Ulysses*. I hope that one day I shall have the opportunity of giving you the best criticism of which I am capable. But it will have to be done in a book, not an article.

Still, there are many points about *Ulysses* I should like to discuss with you—points on which it was quite impossible to converse at lunch. And my wife (Katherine Mansfield) who knows your book even better than I do has points of her own. We should be very pleased if you would come to tea with us on Wednesday next. If the day is not suitable, please choose your own.

We are here at tea-time every day except Friday, and there is never a soul except ourselves. At four o'clock.

> Yours very sincerely,
> J. MIDDLETON MURRY

Katherine Mansfield, writing at that time, described how they lived 'like two hermits in our caves at the end of a long dark passage'. Mr Middleton Murry, in reply to a query, wrote to me in June 1954, 'The date of the letter would be about April 20th, 1922. The lunch between Joyce and myself (no other guests) took place about then. Katherine Mansfield, being unable to go out, was not present. Joyce came to tea on April 27th, 1922. That date can be checked because he inscribed my copy of *Ulysses* on that occasion with the date. I have written no account of the meeting, neither did Katherine Mansfield. . . .' And in a further note: 'I was much too preoccupied with Katherine Mansfield's illness at the time to do more than register that he was very gentle and sympathetic.'

The Joyces stayed for some time at this hotel but do not seem to have been very happy there. 'How I write in the present circumstances I don't know—influence of *Ad Majorem Dei Gloriam*, perhaps,' Joyce told Larbaud in December 1923, and later he mentions that he feels stunned by the way they are living. Yet in other respects 1924 began well with the fourth edition of *Ulysses* out and the publication of parts of Joyce's new work in view. In a copy (shown at La Hune, 1949) Joyce had written: 'Dear Nora, The edition you have is full of printer's errors. Please read it in this. I cut the pages. There is a list of mistakes at the end. . . .' She had evidently decided to try again but it is doubtful if she read the book in its entirety. The final monologue and some of its implications reached her, for she remarked to McAlmon, half-jokingly, about the nasty things men bother about. Much later, to a young Englishwoman they met near Vichy she said, 'Ah, you wouldn't like it.' But if Joyce's work imposed much uncertainty, indeed hardship at times, upon Nora and her family, and she sometimes threatened to go off home with them to Ireland, they remained very dependent upon one another.

Joyce was now writing many hours a day and the next few months were to see the creation, in draft form, of the main sections of his book. For instance, in a black note-book preserved at the British Museum, Joyce can be seen working from the first straightforward narrative of what came to be known as the 'Hen' piece towards the much more complicated typescript versions made later. He had never shown the slightest doubt as to the value of his earlier work; indeed, one is astonished at how frankly he told those likely to be helpful of publishers and printers who refused it.

Valery Larbaud, who had been collaborating with a group busy translating *Ulysses* into French, was interested in Joyce's experiments but Joyce felt uneasy about Miss Weaver who, it seems, had written in reply to the question of a mutual friend that she thought Joyce was wasting his genius in producing a curiosity of literature. She had not intended this to reach him and it was not in her character to make too drastic a judgment; time would tell, and she did all she could to aid the writer. As the drafts of the new work reached her, isolated parts of a vehicle she could not envisage as getting anywhere, she gradually began to see its form take shape. In recent years she has given a great deal of assistance to students of *Finnegans Wake* and her arrangement of the manuscript indicates that in later years she came to understand and appreciate Joyce's last and perhaps most important work.

Correspondence at the Lockwood Memorial Library shows that Stanislaus Joyce in Trieste had sent his brother his views on *Ulysses* and the way in which it arose from their early background. In a letter probably written in 1924, Stanislaus describes Patrick Tuohy's painting of their father, John Stanislaus Joyce, who was still very much alive in Dublin, as 'a wonderful study of that little old Milesian'. Joyce had asked the Irish painter, whose parents he had known in his youth, to bring him over a likeness of his father. A.E., writing of the portrait later, described the slow elaboration of method employed and the artist's determination to be unhurried whether his sitter was raging or not, for Tuohy, he declared, was 'an obstinate artist'. This is borne out by the story that he took his easel and canvas into the bedroom when the old man retired and continued to work at it there.

Born in 1894, Patrick Tuohy painted a number of the men and women of his generation at a time when they were not well known, among them Sean O'Casey and James Stephens. He only had the use of one hand and was, from what one is told in Dublin, a remarkable personality—intense, highly nervous, humorous and often suspicious. One of the students at the Art School where he taught asked if he was still doing the Joyce portrait. 'Yes, but *don't* tell anyone that!' he emphasized, as if 'there were people ready with palate and brushes to make a dash at him'. 'He was "innocent" in some way,' a friend remarked, 'absolutely honest.' His treatment of the original of Simon Dedalus shows no literary influence; he pursued the

Square Robiac, rue de Grenelle

Portrait by Patrick Tuohy   Patrick Tuohy, Lucia, Mrs Joyce

Giorgio and Helen Joyce, Mrs Joyce, James Joyce, Paul Ruggiero
and Mrs Borach, at the Red Cross Sanatorium, Zürich, 1931

reality of the old man as he found him, and Joyce, when he saw the result, was delighted with it.

An account of their first meeting has been given me by Mrs Stein, then Phyllis Moss, an art student who had been taught by Patrick Tuohy in Dublin and saw a good deal of him whenever he came to Paris:

> Patrick, who was then twenty-eight, had an introduction to Joyce who was living near the Champs de Mars. I waited outside but in a few minutes Patrick came out for me. There was nothing personal about Joyce's surroundings. He and his family were staying temporarily in a flat which belonged to friends of theirs. Flats were scarce in Paris and the Joyces were not practical in the art of making themselves a comfortable home. I gathered they had wandered around rather helplessly and I think they had sometimes lived in hotels. Joyce greeted me and sank back into his chair. His tall, thin form seemed to fold up in it. His long head and slightly protruding chin reminded me of Velasquez's portraits. Joyce almost always looked sad. He appeared to be lost in heavy boredom. I had my first lesson that same day in what not to say. I was only twenty-one, unused to literary silence. I jabbered away. Joyce didn't appear to pay attention, but when I got to a certain point he said 'For example?' Sometime afterwards I heard him say, 'I hate generalities.' I was impressionable and only twenty-one—I learned my lesson. Patrick was inseparably 'Dublin' and at this first meeting and the many future meetings Joyce listened avidly to all he said, everything that concerned Dublin was food and drink to Joyce. He plied Patrick with intimate questions about the streets, the houses, the people. He remembered everything, he was insatiable.
>
> The Joyces ate at the 'Trianon' Restaurant opposite Montparnasse Station, the best eating place on the Rive Gauche . . . when the Joyces asked Patrick to dinner they included me as often as not. Joyce awed me considerably. I confined my conversational efforts to Mrs Joyce. Joyce never sat straight in his chair, always sideways, shoulders stooped, his tired expression wandered around. One day when we ate wild strawberries I remarked, 'I used to cultivate wild strawberries when I was a child and try to make them grow bigger.' Joyce twisted around slightly from his inspection of the remote distance. 'And now you are cultivating wild oats.' This referred to Patrick, who made no pretence to elegance and, however sensitive, however fine of perception, was an uncut diamond. There was something elemental about him which shocked many people. It was curious to watch the gradual interest, sometimes growing into a sort of fascination, which came after this

first shock. But Joyce had understood Patrick immediately, I think. So I learned that Joyce, however little he appeared to be listening, was taking in everything that went on around.

When introducing his new friend to McAlmon in May 1923, Joyce mentions that his talk might be a little difficult to understand at first, for he is 'very Dublin'. Quite apart from his painting, Tuohy was one of those people who brought Joyce material for his work, the turn of a phrase, a quotation half-forgotten, the associations of a family or a place-name.

Among Joyce's letters to Valery Larbaud, now at Vichy, there is the copy of an article by Lucia Joyce and two short letters to Larbaud which suggest one aspect of those disturbances which were later to have such an effect upon Joyce and his family. In February 1924 the seventeen-year-old girl apologized for having taken so long to write 'quelques lignes de rien' as unfortunately she did not take after her father. Later she thanks Larbaud for arranging the publication of her article, 'Je me sens flattée d'être à côté de tants de beaux esprits et d'avoir pour la première fois vue mon nom dans une revue.' The little sketch, entitled *Charlot*, in which she described having seen Charlie Chaplin in the Champs Elysées and watching a Petit Guignol, is slight but carefully turned. It would seem to have been her only appearance in print.

As usually happened in the spring, the Joyces became restless. Joyce had already told McAlmon that he avoided those people who admired him immensely but who did nothing to help them find a flat! As various acquaintances have pointed out, when the Joyces were invited anywhere (and Joyce ignored all social invitations which did not include his wife), the subject of where to live inevitably cropped up in conversation.

Again during this period McAlmon helped Joyce out of difficulties. By the end of May, when Joyce found it impossible to work in the heat and noise of the hotel, he had all his books packed. On June 11th he was to undergo yet another operation for cataract and then they would get away for a change. Writing to Larbaud from St Malo in June 1924, Joyce told him there had not yet been much improvement in his sight. Even there he was not free from letters and telegrams about his work. Some discussions had arisen among his team of translators as to whether or not there should be inverted commas in the French version of *Ulysses*. In the end it was agreed they should be excluded.

Controversy of another kind was to reach him there. In June 1924 Sir Edmund Gosse, reigning critic of the period, wrote from London to Louis Gillet protesting against his discussion of Joyce's work in the *Revue des Deux Mondes*. The letter, reproduced in *Stèle Pour James Joyce* by Louis Gillet (Paris, 1946), declares the character of Joyce's notoriety to be partly political and partly a 'cynical appeal to sheer indecency', written by a 'literary charlatan of the extremest order'. Nor does Sir Edmund forget that at one time he helped Ezra Pound and W. B. Yeats to obtain a grant from the Royal Literary Fund for this 'perfect type of the Irish *fumiste*, a hater of England, more than suspected of partiality for Germany, where he lived before the war (and at Zürich during the war).' In another letter, written the following year and shown at the I.C.A. Exhibition in 1950, he consoles himself by declaring that Joyce 'and his monster will soon be buried and forgotten'. So much for literary prophecy!

Another offensive was less direct. Ernest Boyd, author of a number of books on Irish literature, had on several occasions in New York criticized Valery Larbaud and those who had taken up Joyce for what he considered to be the wrong reasons, as part of a literary fashion and because of his outspokenness about sex. In the *Nouvelle Revue Française* for January 1925, Valery Larbaud in *Réponse à Ernest Boyd* considered that Boyd was really attacking Joyce and his work. Letters now at the Municipal Library at Vichy suggest that if Joyce did not take up weapons himself, he enjoyed preparing the powder and shot for his friends to use.

AVENUE CHARLES FLOQUET

The Joyces, tired of hotel life, now took a furnished flat, again in the Avenue Charles Floquet but at No. 8 this time. Miss Weaver, who visited Paris that year, remembers it to have seemed comfortable but with no remarkable character.

They had hardly settled in there before a disturbing letter arrived from Dublin: Mrs Josephine Murray was seriously ill in St Vincent's Hospital. Joyce, who had looked forward to meeting her either in London or Dublin, had thought about her the previous morning, with the intention of asking her about some point in his childhood she would be sure to know. Now, seeing yet another line of communication with Dublin life slip through his hands, he sat down to write to 'Dear Aunt Josephine' for what he knew to be the last time:

> ... I am very deeply touched that you should have considered me worthy of remembrance at such a grave hour. You attached me to you in youth by so many acts of kindness, by so much help and advice and sympathy, especially after my mother's death, that it seems to me as if your thought of me now is one of reproach. Nothing would give me greater pleasure than to talk with you over many things. I cannot employ the usual language or invoke assistance but if I am estranged in that I am still attached to you by many bonds of gratitude and affection and of respect as well. I hope these hurried words may be acceptable to you. I shall feel glad and honoured always if they are.

What Joyce did not fully realize, and indeed only reached his brother Stanislaus Joyce after my own enquiries had been published in 1950,[1] was the disturbing effect which *Ulysses* had had upon Mrs Murray. Before she went to hospital, so her daughter told me, she began to sort out the letters which she kept in a little black trunk (a relic of her schooldays in Glossop). 'I tried to stop her. It had such a final look. I think there were letters of Jim's among them. . . . Mother would not leave them lying around.'

As Mrs Murray was dying, uneasy still about *Ulysses*, and perhaps at the part she had played in a work in completion feared and misunderstood, she kept saying, 'The book . . . the book. . . .' When Joyce's letter came it gave her great pleasure.

A sample or two of *Ulysses* had been translated for Valery Larbaud's lecture on Joyce in 1922 and some fragments, much worked upon in the meantime, were published in *Commerce I*, 1924, and had caused a good deal of discussion. Valery Larbaud was unable to undertake the entire work but had agreed to help Auguste Morel (who had translated Francis Thompson, Donne and Blake into French) assisted by Léon-Paul Fargue, Adrienne Monnier and Sylvia Beach. The work itself represented great difficulties: now and then the collaborators could not agree as to the exact meaning of a word or a phrase, and Joyce, who annotated their draft translations, was called upon to arbitrate. As Adrienne Monnier has

---

[1] See his comments in *Partisan Review*.

remarked in *Mercure de France*, 1950, at times it did not seem as if it could be done at all, until Stuart Gilbert arrived on the scene. Formerly a judge in Burma, he had retired early. From boyhood an admirer of French literature, in the twenties he married and settled in Paris. Stuart Gilbert's knowledge of classical as well as modern languages combined with a natural sensitivity to words and their *nuances* was invaluable to Joyce both in regard to *Ulysses* and *Finnegans Wake*. Correspondence which has survived shows Joyce skilfully holding the varied shipload together and bringing this literary cargo safely into port. At times mutiny seemed likely and Joyce mentioned to Larbaud that he came through one scene 'by looking more like an idiot than usual'. A note, now at Buffalo University, suggests the more humorous side, as when Sylvia Beach mentions in a letter to Joyce how they tried to render the seedcake which Molly Bloom eats on Howth and could find nothing more suitable than 'brioche', even after Léon-Paul Fargue had paid a visit to a pastry-cook's wife to see if there was anything comparable in France.

Before the first French edition of *Ulysses* went to press, Valery Larbaud wrote to Joyce in his excellent English:

> Well, dear Joyce, I am very glad to have been able to go on with this revision and finish it and I thank you for having managed things in spite of so many difficulties, so as to bring about this result.
>
> *In summa*, thinking about it, the French *Ulysses* can be considered as a collective work (comprising as it does a few renderings due to Miss Beach and Miss Monnier, and even to Renert [?], Méchin and Léon–Paul Fargue) in which Morel had the principal and you the decisive part.
>
> The completion of my work of revision will be celebrated on my birthday [August 29th] by a great 'franzo' in a wayside inn at the top of the Bracco mountain, halfway between here and La Spezia, and instead of milk and mineral water I shall drink white Coronata. I wish you could be with us. At any rate you may be sure I shall drink your health and make *brindisi* to the success of *Ulysse*.

When the volume appeared after five years' work in 1929, published by *Les Amis des Livres*, a dinner was arranged on June 27th at the Hôtel Léopold at Les Vaux de Cerney outside Paris, where the collaborators— then an innocent enough word—were joined by their friends, Edouard Dujardin and Paul Valéry being among them.

SQUARE ROBIAC

Joyce really needed a study of his own, where he could have all his books and papers about him. For a long time they searched for an unfurnished flat. 'Nora got so tired of moving about—yet in a way she was the restless one. She liked change and grew tired of a particular environment,' a friend told me. At last in the spring of 1925 a suitable one was found in a convenient district off the long and varied rue de Grenelle which uncoils itself from the Place des Invalides to the Avenue de la Bourdonnais, a lengthy but interesting walk for anyone exploring the 'Joyce country'. When the Joyces went to live there the block had only recently been built. 'In fact, it was so new that part of the ceiling fell down as soon as we got in!' Giorgio Joyce said in his quietly humorous way. Although it is called a square, the house stands on the corner of a little cul-de-sac, concluded by a high, rough-stone wall which suggests an earlier period. At first it seemed as if the very usual frontage, with palms of victory over the entrance, refused to give me any peg upon which I might hand the patchwork of this narrative. The concierge, standing at her veiled glass door in the hall near the lift, had never heard of the Joyces but told me there was another writer living there, perhaps he might do! Disentangling myself gently from her helpfulness, I went out into the street again, now thinking about a cup of tea after that long walk from the rue de l'Université. At the opposite corner I gave a last look back and then noticed a link with Joyce's habitation there. A plaque in soft, yellowing stone, which looked like part of a previous building, had been placed between the windows of the second floor, to announce that this was *La propriété de la Société d'Assurance*, VENISE–TRIESTE. Strange how the association with their previous life was continued there.

Neither Joyce nor his wife was interested in visual taste, the expression of personality through decoration and pictures. What furniture they chose for their flat was solid and unfanciful, some good bookcases, comfortable leather armchairs, excellent beds. . . . The family portraits by Comerford of Joyce's ancestors from Fermoy and Cork looked down upon a very different society from their own. John Stanislaus Joyce was there, as if starting forward from his chair, together with a reproduction of the *Head of a Girl* by Vermeer, which Joyce admired. There was also a photograph of the Customs House in Dublin and one of the riverine heads by Edward Smith which ornament the façade, for Louis Gillet, visiting the Joyces later, recollects Joyce's remark, 'That's the Liffey and here is Anna Livia.' It was at this flat that many of his friends from Dublin saw Joyce and his family; such as J. F. Byrne on holiday from the United States, and another fellow student, Dr Kerrigan, with a practice in Donegal, who talked of their 'barmedical' days and about Haines, whom everyone ragged, and other acquaintances. Joyce, always on the lookout for material, asked him about the rivers of Northern Ireland and later worked some of their names into 'Anna Livia'. Eugene Sheehy was also there and noticed pictures and sketches of old Dublin on the walls and even the design of a large rug portraying the corkscrew course of the river Liffey, made, so Giorgio Joyce remembered, by Adrienne Monnier. Joyce enquired about J. B. Hall of the *Freeman's Journal*[1] and if he still walked about with his overcoat over a shoulder in all weathers. Judge Sheehy also records him saying, 'And how does Sallynoggin look now?' Then, as they talked, Lucia might come in, as someone else remembers, 'dressed in a fur coat, with her hair curled and looking nice'.

Patrick Tuohy painted his portrait of Joyce at No. 2 Square Robiac. 'He was always there in the middle of the floor with his jam-jars and his brushes around him,' as Arthur Power said. Phyllis Moss tells me: 'They got on one another's nerves during the sittings, and Patrick had a hard time of it for he admired Joyce very much. Joyce wrote to Tuohy on 6th December 1926, pointing out that there was a lawsuit pending against a 'crook' American who was pirating and imitating *Ulysses* and that 'my own new work takes up all my time. Yes, I will try to give you a few more sittings though, as I told you, I am not greatly interested in the visage in question. I don't think you quite understood what I wanted in the case of my mother.'[2] Then Joyce was not satisfied with the

---

[1] Author of *Random Records of a Reporter*, Simpkin Marshall, London. Joyce's copy is now at the University of Buffalo.

[2] The photograph included here was presented to the National Library of Ireland by Miss Kathleen Murray as being her aunt, Mrs May Joyce, but Stanislaus Joyce thought it more likely that of an actress whom she resembled. It was taken by M. Glover of Dublin. On page 681 of *Ulysses* there is a faded photograph at 7 Eccles Street, of 'Maud Branscombe, actress and professional beauty', but the parallel has not been confirmed. Joyce refers to a drawing from a photograph, in the U.S. edition of Gorman's biography.

background and some alterations had to be made. In contrast with John Stanislaus' direct relationship with the viewer, James Joyce seems to be looking at something further away, his mouth held up against questions. Yet of the several artists who portrayed the writer—Emile Blanche, Augustus John, Sean O'Sullivan—only Tuohy, who made no concessions to his reputation, presented him as a Dubliner.

'As you know,' Phyllis Moss continued in her letter, 'Joyce went to infinite trouble over his work. One day Mrs Joyce arrived in my room. . . . "You have Norwegian friends, haven't you? Will you ask them to get this book from Oslo—my husband wants it at any price." Joyce was tracing the influence of the Scandinavian conquest of Ireland in his writing of Dublin. I think I am correct in saying that he took lessons in Scandinavian languages to this end. I remember curious little incidents. One afternoon I called at Square Robiac to go out with Mrs Joyce and Lucia but first of all she had to prepare something for Joyce to eat. They spoke together in Italian, as they always did *en famille*. He wanted soup. When it was ready Mrs Joyce went off to tidy herself and I sat, while Joyce ate in silence. When he had finished he laid his spoon down with a final air, "Now you have seen me eat," he said, and for a moment a small smile twinkled in his face. I laughed. Another time, on St Valentine's Day, I was again in their Square Robiac flat, where they seemed to have found a home at last. Joyce came into the room in the white coat that he always wore when working (he said the reflection of light on the white material helped him to see better). He handed me a carbon copy—it was a limerick he had written about my friend Patrick Tuohy. "I thought you would like to have this," he said, and taking out his pen wrote in minute letters "J. J." at the foot of the verse. This was in 1927. After that date I returned to Ireland and I don't think I ever saw the Joyces again.'

Early in 1925 Joyce was again working on the 'Hen' piece of *Finnegans Wake* (now, much elaborated, pp. 104–25) which he was preparing for *The Criterion*, and it had nearly driven him crazy. It was hard to get a satisfactory typist and sometimes he had to call upon his son Giorgio, Auguste Morel, and other friends to help him. Again threatened by eye trouble, he was anxious to get it completed before things became worse. That winter and spring Joyce was busy on the preliminary version of other sections and he felt he had the book fairly well worked out in his head.

That summer the Joyces were in Belgium and from the Hôtel Astoria in Brussels Joyce sent Miss Weaver the early drafts of what he called 'The Muddest Thick that ever was Made', the children's study period into which so much knowledge is condensed, now *Finnegans Wake*, pp. 260–308. During this visit they went to see the battlefield of Waterloo. A postcard to Valery Larbaud written on September 22nd, 1926, with 'salutations cordiales' shows *La Belle Alliance*, with a quotation from E. Dessaux's account of the battle printed below it. On the barn of the café is an incongruous advertisement for *Auld Reekie* tobacco! As there has never been a Wellington Museum in Dublin, so far as I have heard, Joyce evidently wrote his amusing tour of the 'museyroom' on pages 8–10 of *Finnegans Wake* after seeing the Museum near Brussels and transposed it upon the dream landscape of the Phoenix Park.

Stuart Gilbert has recorded that Joyce was pleased when a critic pointed out that Leopold Bloom had been portrayed 'in the round' like a piece of sculpture. He now maintained that his present work really had no beginning or end. It is certainly possible to start with the final chapter and move across the last sentences to the first,

> The keys to. Given! A way a lone a last a loved a long the . . . riverrun, past Eve and Adam's, from swerve of shore to bend of bay, brings us by a commodius vicus of recirculation back to Howth Castle and Environs.

The book, when seen in this way, is like a lampshade upon which the history of man's ideas has been written, as illuminated by one person's mind. Yet, as we begin, it is impossible to know it all in a flash of understanding, as if the current had been switched on; a start must be made somewhere. Joyce knew that however circular his book might be in form, the reader is finally influenced by the point of departure. His method of writing, as shown by so many of the manuscripts, was to prepare the centre of an episode and later to add an introduction and expand the body of the text. Earwicker and his Agnomen, Part I. ii, might be an important doorway into the house that Joyce built: what about the porch and the entrance way?

Joseph Prescott has published an interesting note [1] concerning Miss

[1] *Concerning the Genesis of Finnegans Wake*, Joseph Prescott, PMLA, N.Y., December 1954.

Weaver's repudiation of certain legends concerning the genesis of *Finnegans Wake* and her account of how Joyce wrote to her in September 1926 saying that it would be amusing if she would 'order' a piece or episode for the book. She was staying at the time near Penrith in Cumberland and came across a pamphlet about what was reputed to be a giant's grave in the churchyard there. A copy of the publication, *A Short Historical Sketch of St Andrew's Parish Church, Penrith*, by the Reverend James Cropper, is reproduced. Joyce set to work at once on Miss Weaver's esteemed order, which forms part of the first chapter, though not the opening page.

It was not long before Joyce was again working on the Anna Livia chapter (first published in *Navire d'Argent*, 1925), which was to become the most frequently quoted part of the book; indeed certain readers do not seem to have gone beyond this fantasy of all the rivers of the world flowing as one. Others have been carried along by the talk of the washerwomen on the banks of the Liffey, the confused babble of waters and voices, the mixture of dream and place associations, to an appreciation of the whole which now moves inevitably towards the sea. Joyce himself was nearly distracted by the writing of it. The editors of *Transition* were anxious that this extended version should appear during the autumn of 1927, but it was not until the end of October that Joyce really finished it. The proofs, now in the British Museum, show a mass of insertions, and later on, in preparing the chapter for book publication, Joyce again made many additions.

Somerset Maugham in his *Writer's Notebook* has given an interesting description of the *mores* of the French literary world as compared to those in England. There it is usual for an author to read part of his work before its publication to a group of friends and critics. That November Joyce planned to do so, and thus we find him asking Robert McAlmon to be at Square Robiac on a certain Wednesday punctually at 3.30 on account of the light. *Being Geniuses Together* contains an account of the occasion which suggests that McAlmon's attention wandered at times from Anna Livia's toilet. Although everyone seemed much impressed, Joyce ironically remarked that the two dozen or so men and women present were a small proportion of the world's population. Over the years, did he but know it, the number of people who really came to appreciate 'Anna Livia'—published separately by Faber & Faber in 1939—has, like herself, grown riverwise. Joyce was left very exhausted by this work and seemed to have suffered from the stomach cramp which was to be so dangerous later. During 1928 he wrote the fable of the *Ondt and the Gracehopper* and finished the Shaun section for publication in *Transition*, which was again worked upon later.

Long ago in Zürich Joyce had written to thank H. G. Wells for the article in *The Nation* which had helped him so much at the time. As Wells was in Paris during the last part of 1928 they had lunch together, so Joyce told Miss Weaver. Wells had expected to meet a tall, aggressive man in a frieze coat carrying a heavy stick. They evidently discussed Joyce's work, for H. G. Wells wrote a letter which Joyce found friendly and honest, the original of which is now at the Lockwood Memorial Library:

> *Lou Pidou,*
> *Saint Mathieu,*
> *Grasse, A.M.*

November 23, 1928.

MY DEAR JOYCE:

I've been studying you and thinking over you a lot. The outcome is that I don't think I can do anything for the propaganda of your work. I've an enormous respect for your genius dating from your earliest books, and I feel now a great personal liking for you, but you and I are set upon absolutely different courses. Your training has been Catholic, Irish, insurrectionary; mine, such as it was, was scientific, constructive, and, I suppose, English. The frame of my mind is a world wherein a big unifying and concentrating process is possible (increase of power and range by economy and concentration of effort), a *progress* not inevitable but interesting and possible. That game attracted and holds me. For it, I want language and statement as simple and clear as possible. You began Catholic, that is to say, you began with a system of values in stark opposition to reality. Your mental existence is obsessed by a monstrous system of contradictions. You really believe in chastity, purity and the personal God, and that is why you are always breaking out into cries of c——, s—— and hell. As I don't believe in these things except as quite provisional values, my mind has never been shocked to outcries by the existence of water closets and menstrual bandages—and undeserved misfortunes. And while you were brought up under the delusion of political suppression, I was brought up under the delusion of political responsibility. It seems a fine thing to you to defy and break up. To me not in the least.

Now with regard to this literary experiment of yours. It's a considerable thing because you are a very considerable man and you have in your crowded composition a mighty genius for expression which has escaped discipline. But I don't think it gets anywhere. You have turned your back on common men, on their elementary needs and their restricted time and intelligence and you have elaborated. What is the result? Vast riddles. Your last two works have been more amusing and exciting to write than they will ever be to read. Take me as a typical common reader. Do I get much pleasure from this work? No. Do I feel I am getting something new and illuminating as I do when I read Anrep's dreadful translation of Pavlov's badly written book on Conditioned Reflexes? No. So I ask; who the hell is this Joyce who demands so many waking hours of the few thousands I have still to live for a proper appreciation of his quirks and fancies and flashes of rendering?

All this from my point of view. Perhaps you are right and I am all wrong. Your work is an extraordinary experiment and I would go out of my way to save it from destruction or restrictive interruption. It has its believers and its following. Let them rejoice in it. To me it is a dead end.

My warmest good wishes to you, Joyce. I can't follow your banner any more than you can follow mine. But this world is wide and there is room for both of us to be wrong.[1]

At the end of that strenuous year, Nora Joyce was seriously ill. A letter headed Maison de Santé, Neuilly, written broadly, in thick, smudged pencil, suggests Joyce's nervous state at the time. He tells Larbaud that his wife had been operated on the previous week and given radium treatment. It had been a terrible strain on them all. In November he began to write again a description of madness and blindness coming down upon Jonathan Swift, yet this externalization of one of Joyce's darkest periods was not used in *Finnegans Wake*.

[1] See *Further Notes*, p. 245.

IX

EN VACANCES

Fortunately by the spring Joyce was able to tell Larbaud that his wife had made a splendid recovery. Soon they were thinking about going away for a change. Although Joyce worked hard and suffered a good deal, there is no self-pity in his writing. He also knew how to enjoy himself. During the years spent in Paris there were dinners with friends, excursions here and there, many evenings at the Opéra to hear the best performances of the time, visits to the theatre and ballet. Very often when the light had gone, in the interval before an evening meal at home, or in a favourite restaurant such as the Trianon at Montparnasse, Joyce would go with Eugene Jolas or Paul Léon to the cinema. At times he saw very little there but enjoyed the music; at others he seems to have gained a certain amount from the enlarged images of the 'reel world' as he called it. In *Finnegans Wake* he strides ahead of his own period into our own, and introduces television into a Dublin pub. (See *Further Notes*.)

'Joyce didn't need to travel, you know,' Stuart Gilbert said. 'He might just as well have stayed in his flat in the Square Robiac, for he had such an extraordinary memory, with so much in reserve there—that interior vision upon which he drew for his work, a compensation maybe for loss of sight. To write *Finnegans Wake* he need never have left Paris.' Yet if Joyce and his wife disliked crossing the sea and never left Europe, like most writers from time to time he needed a change of place and company. It amused him to listen to different languages and to draw into himself part of the atmosphere created by other people. All practical arrangements were made by the writer himself. 'You'd often see him over a timetable, however bad his eyes, working over details,' a friend said. Once the Joyces had arrived and were installed in a comfortable hotel—Joyce had done with boarding houses and liked the best of food and wine—postcards were sent to their friends. A number of these were preserved by Valery Larbaud and they suggest Joyce staying at Ostend, St Malo, Toulon or North Wales, and often contain a reference to some phase of his literary activity. The French writer was also a great distributor of *cartes postales* (as shown by the collection which I went to see at Moulins) and among these was a photograph which he took for Joyce of the monument to Vico in Naples.

Occasionally, Joyce had a definite reason for wanting to visit a place and sometimes he made preparations in advance, as when he learnt Danish before going to Copenhagen. In a letter dated June 30th, 1928, dealing with the translation of *Ulysses*, Valery Larbaud wishes him a good journey to that country and adds, 'I do not think you will find anything rotten in it'; and in July he asks Joyce if he has seen Hamlet's two graves at Elsinore. Possibly Joyce had hoped to go that year but the visit was postponed, for Miss Weaver had no recollection of their doing so. He was certainly in Denmark during 1936, for a letter written in October of that year by Levy-Bruhl, thanking Joyce for a copy of one of his books, suggests that they met at Copenhagen and talked on several occasions to each other there.

The Joyces were at Salzburg in the summer of 1928 where they encountered John Drinkwater and his wife, Daisy Kennedy the violinist, who was performing at the Festival. They became very friendly and Mrs Drinkwater told me that they went on various excursions together in the neighbourhood. From London John Drinkwater later wrote to Joyce, who was back in Paris, thanking him for Number 13 of *Transition* and sending some photographs taken at Salzburg. He said how much they had enjoyed meeting him, and 'my wife, under your influence, exclaimed towards the end of the journey that she was sick of bluggage'.

Later John Drinkwater wrote again to Joyce:

'Anna Livia' interested me very much. I do feel that you set your readers the devil of a problem, and I think it is one that very few of them are likely altogether to solve. When one thinks of the immense labour that the work has been to you who have all the clues, one sees how difficult it must be for people to get your precise meaning without them. And although it is plain that you do not mean the work to be understood in terms of common language, I know that as an artist you do mean its significance to be precise. And so you have set a very pretty poser even for the most sympathetic reader. Nevertheless, in spite of all difficulties, I flatter myself that I have been able to get a good deal of your intention from the book. What effect the work will have upon your followers I suppose nobody can say. It may show to some of them a new way of doing things, but it may make a few light-headed people tipsy. But in any case this seems to be a relatively unimportant aspect of the business. What is important is that you have really something to say and have been evolving an entirely personal way of saying it. You may puzzle us but I do not think anyone can be for a moment in doubt that here is something of real importance, expressing a beauty of its own, however elusive that beauty may be to unprepared minds. I got frequent glimpses of it through the mist of difficulties, and I wish your independent spirit every kind of good fortune.

Stuart Gilbert also remembers being at Salzburg with Joyce, probably another year, when they visited Max Reinhardt's castle and a number of churches, Joyce being particularly interested in baroque. They also went to see Stefan Zweig, who had written to Joyce about *Exiles* long ago in Zürich.

'Although he liked to try and look at things for himself,' Mr Gilbert mentioned in conversation, 'when, for instance, the light was bad in a church Joyce would ask me to examine a detail and describe it as well as possible afterwards. He was a most stimulating companion, everything interested him.'

Joyce came over to England several times in the summer with his wife and sometimes his daughter, and on one occasion he was in London during April 1927 for a short stay accompanied by Auguste Morel, to attend the P.E.N. Club Dinner, at which he was a guest of honour.

In his *James Joyce's Ulysses*, Stuart Gilbert mentions that the atmosphere of Dublin in Joyce's youth had much in common with that of one of the larger residential towns in the south of England where he had spent much of his own boyhood. Therefore, it was probably Mr and Mrs Gilbert who suggested in 1929 that the Joyces should go with them for a holiday to Torquay. Miss Weaver, who joined them for a week, remembers they went to see 'Kent's Cavern', famous for its contribution to the study of prehistoric man. While the others probably preferred to sit in the sheltered gardens, or listen to music on the promenade, the writer and his friend went for walks in the town and neighbourhood. Some evenings, as Mr Gilbert records, they sat in a local pub and ordered cider, and Joyce, who cared only for wine, often got him to finish his glass for him.

He seemed to be able to listen to several conversations at once and used to ask for the explanation of a word or expression used by the workmen and fishermen about them.[1]

At other times Joyce would buy a bundle of children's newspapers and the guests at their expensive hotel would be amazed to see a dignified gentleman, with grey hair and learned appearance, reading those brightly coloured pages with the attention they gave to *The Times*. Joyce, who did not care for modern novels, was always interested in children's games and literature. Besides—he was looking for material for *Finnegans Wake*.[2]

In a letter to Valery Larbaud, written from the Imperial Hotel at the end of July, Joyce mentions that the previous six months in Paris had been very trying and that he had literally worked night and day on the Shem and Shaun part of his book. In spite of the fact that he had been sleeping badly and his sight was worse, Joyce speaks of himself as the 'escaped continentalized Dubliner inflicted with the incurable levity of youth'. He mentions too that he had fallen and hurt his arm. In conversation, Stuart Gilbert said that with one of those curious *sursauts* of energy which came upon him at moments, Joyce had vaulted over a wall and, not being able to see very well, fallen down on the other side. He remembers too, on the beach, how Joyce would finger small stones and pebbles to learn their weight and shape, to measure the sensations of warmth or coolness they gave, to store everything that came his way for future use.

In London Joyce did not know a great many literary people and avoided publicity, for this reason choosing the smaller restaurants where he could get good continental cooking. There were certain friends to see such as Herbert Hughes, the musician. The late John Dulanty, then the Irish High Commissioner, remembered his visits very clearly. The artist Frank Budgen and his wife were living in Hampstead, and there Joyce talked of their life in Zürich and discussed Budgen's book. He also saw Robert Lynd, and Arthur Symons, who had known him as a young man.

[1] Jacob Swartz, also at Torquay that year, mentioned Joyce's pleasure at seeing the Fay brothers act there.

[2] *The Personal Library of James Joyce* lists fifteen titles of periodicals purchased by Joyce during July and August 1929. These include *The Baker and Confectioner, Boy's Cinema, The Furniture Record, Poppy's Paper, The Schoolgirls' Own, Woman, Woman's Friend, Justice of the Peace, The Hairdressers' Weekly*.

Le Pont Neuf
Tell me tale of stem or stone. Besides the rivering waters of

The Liffey and the Bann, by Edward Smyth, 1787, on the Custom
House, Dublin

La rue des Vignes
He lifts the lifewand and the dumb speak

Tiny fragments remain of those later visits to London. Alida Monro, wife of Harold Monro the poet, remembers meeting him in Bloomsbury, perhaps on the way to the Poetry Bookshop, and noticing his bright suède shoes, for Joyce, after all, lived on the Continent and in those days the Englishman's clothes were far more restrained than those worn abroad. One of Joyce's legal advisers remarked to me, 'Joyce dressed in very much the French style and was not untidy but, if anything, rather dapper.' When their business talks were over, Joyce would enquire about his family and very often they got on to the subject of cricket.

The Joyces often stayed at the Euston Hotel, to which he had taken a fancy, so Miss Weaver maintains, perhaps because he heard so many Irish voices there and now and again met an acquaintance from his Dublin days. It is likely too that, without admitting it, he liked to remain at this grimy entry to the world he had once known, listening to the noise of the trains and the last far whistle of the Holyhead Mail.

As a student in Dublin, and later in Trieste, Joyce had shown little regard for the work of George Moore. Indeed, according to Herbert Gorman, he had been inclined to mock at it. In 1924 Edouard Dujardin had tried to bring them together and McAlmon suggests that they all but met at Sylvia Beach's shop on one occasion. Yet it was not until 1929, when Joyce was again in London, that they eventually did so. George Moore left an amusing record:

> ... He was distinguished, courteous, respectful, and I was the same; he seemed anxious to accord me the first place. I demurred, and declared him first in Europe. We agreed that our careers were not altogether dissimilar and he added, 'Paris has played an equal part in our lives.' This morning he sent me a book, and pleaded that I had promised to accept a copy of the French translation of *Ulysses*. I was conquered.[1]

And a few days later:

121 Ebury Street,
London, S.W.1.

11th September, 1929.

DEAR MR JOYCE:

When we look back upon our lives, our lives seem fateful. I never

---

[1] *Letters of George Moore,* Ed. John Eglinton. 1942.

understood why I avoided reading *Ulysses*, for I was curious to read it, and when I was in the Nursing Home somebody whose name I cannot recall at the moment, sent me a present of a reading desk, and I wondered what could have put it into his head to send me such a useless piece of furniture. Now I know! I am reading [the translation of] *Ulysses* and if you were here for a longer time and could dine with me, we would talk about the French, which I think wilfully exaggerated in places.

Thank you for sending the book: I look forward to reading it all the winter. And I have to thank you, too, for the volume of essays explaining your new work in progress. The best of these seems to me to be by Stuart Gilbert.

Padraic Colum has written a very pretty introduction to the still unpublished work and I remember him at the outstart of his career, when everything seemed against him.

Moore then sends Joyce a copy of the *Brook Kerith* 'scribbled all over in search of an improved diction, sometimes attained and sometimes missed' and he writes to Joyce later, 'There is so much to be said about the book [*Ulysses*] that I shall have to wait until I meet you in Paris during the spring. If I begin to tell you my doubts about the inner monologue I shall fill three or four pages.' They do not appear to have met again, but on May 10th, 1930, Moore was again writing to Joyce:

My anxiety will be great until I hear from you that the Swiss oculist promises you the sight of one eye. One eye is quite sufficient; a man is as well off with one as with two. Now about Dujardin. I enclose a copy of a letter I have written to him, and hope he will understand that the human mind is not like a weather cock and cannot be diverted from one subject to another —I may live for a few more years, and if I do I shall naturally devote them to my work. Moreover, I know nothing of the question which apparently agitates France, the discovery of the monologue intérieure. In England we don't believe that any discovery has been made. We think, rightly or wrongly, that the monologue intérieure existed from time immemorial.

In James Stephens and his wife, Joyce found associations with both his Irish background and the Continent they all knew so well. At the Lockwood Memorial Library there are several letters in the poet's beautiful handwriting which suggest both their appreciation of one another and the difference of kind between them. Joyce was anxious James Stephens should read *Little Eyolf* by Ibsen, but he was not to be persuaded into accepting that 'dark man of the north'. In the same letter Stephens declares, 'There are two things about you which are unchangeable: You are the most subtle man, and the most continuously kind male creature I have ever known. . . . I got the Ibsen book you left with my concierge— to think of you with your poor sight, navigating the wildernesses of Paris merely to give me a book, scandalizes me and makes me proud—I send you my love in return, but that is so easy to send by a postman that it is not worth a receipt for at the other end.'

To visit Kingsbury in the north-west of London and talk to Mrs Stephens is to touch for a moment the reality of Joyce's own experience— the little house full of books, original drawings, Chinese ivories and biblios, the garden across the lawn with its patches of lily-of-the-valley under the apple trees. There, one day after tea, she pressed the Joyces to stay to supper and they all sat outside shelling peas. At one moment James Stephens must have pointed out the wild strawberry plants brought from Mespil House, near the Grand Canal in Dublin, for Joyce a reminder of how Stephen Dedalus used to pass there long ago beside his Emma Clery.

All holidays come to an end, and by September the Joyces were once again preparing to return to France, like most holiday makers, half reluctant to take up their usual life again. As Joyce had discovered a pleasant place at Dover called the Lord Warden Hotel, where the Irish manager read *Ulysses*, they often spent a few days there on their way. On one side were the platforms and docks of the port while to the west was the high dramatic slant of Shakespeare Cliff—reached by King Lear in his madness —and below a curve of beautiful, Indian-corn coloured shingle. In the morning Mr and Mrs Joyce used to walk down the long mole leading to the lighthouse. 'What do you think?' Joyce always asked. And Nora, looking at the grey, moving body of the water, would pronounce, more often than not, a decided, 'No; not to-day!' Joyce, of course, could not see.[1]

---

[1] According to Giorgio Joyce his parents often stayed at Calais, on the way over.

X

LONDON—ZÜRICH—PARIS

1931–1938

Back in Square Robiac Joyce and his helpers continued to work at the last section of *Work in Progress* to appear in *Transition*. Some prepared notes from books which interested the writer, although not more than a word or two might be included in the text, others read from newspapers, found songs or children's games for him. I happened to mention to Stuart Gilbert that some of the advertisements echoed in the *Wake* had associations with my own childhood—*Harlene* for instance, the picture of the lady brushing long dark hair. 'Yes, I remember those. I used to read out all sorts of things for Joyce. Often I'd ask him what he was getting at and write it down. I must find my notes sometime. Joyce said to me, I remember, "Trouble is I've no imagination." ' It seems that Joyce did not know a great deal of Latin, and less Greek, although he had a working knowledge of several modern languages. His use was selective, unacademic. In the Lockwood Memorial Library there are several scraps of paper with a scribbled telephone number and a note, such as 'The two sycophants with their amygdaleine' (i.e. almond) 'eyes' which he used in *Finnegans Wake*, p. 94. There is also a letter-card from Samuel Beckett which suggests he supplied Joyce with some Greek which he needed.

'Indeed, if he'd known *you*,' said Stuart Gilbert with a laugh, 'he'd have got you to look up something about Dublin or Cork for him. I never knew anyone with such a gift for getting people to do things for him. I used to call them Joyce's "runabout men". Then of course he'd make some gesture in return, give a signed copy of his work, a book, an invitation to dinner, and offer to help with your own difficulties if he could.'

Thus to some extent Joyce's writing became a co-operative effort and if Richard Aldington and others sensed that at moments there was a

---

certain rivalry between the groups surrounding Joyce, he managed to avoid disruption. At times the revision of some of the previous work took several months, and he often worked day and night to complete an episode. That *élan* which carried him so far along the road in 1923–4 had now disappeared, and parts of the work were written with a kind of agony more than cerebral, as if the whole body and psyche were involved in the struggle. It was clear that this could not go on for much longer.

In the background was Joyce's increasing anxiety about Lucia. A poem in *Chamber Music* suggests that he had been long aware of her instability. She had now been obliged to give up dancing as being too strenuous for her and had become increasingly difficult. There was an engagement, later broken off, perhaps a sense of frustration arising from the strain which Joyce's work imposed upon them all. Their life, with its many changes and financial uncertainties, had left her without a settled background or many friends of her age among more normal households. I am told that she spoke four languages not one of which was quite her own. On asking if Joyce was one of those parents who talked frankly to their children about sex, I was told, 'Oh no, he was old-fashioned about that sort of thing, like myself.' The truth, I imagine, was not that the author of *Ulysses* was prudish, though like most people his character was made up of many contradictions, but that Joyce simply did not think of those matters in relation to his daughter until it was too late.

'I believe at the bottom Lucia wanted to get married,' said a woman who had been sympathetic to the girl, 'but somehow didn't feel very sure of herself.' An older friend of the family, a married man, mentioned how occasionally he used to ask her out on her own for tea or a drink, 'Just to cheer her up.' A woman depends so much on that subtle relationship between herself and the masculine world, and without some attention, however indirect, often feels dried and unattractive. In Lucia's case the younger men among the intellectuals and artists were probably more interested in the writer than his daughter. Sensitive, and without her mother's self-confidence, she may well have been caught between affection for her father and the need to make a life of her own. In this connection Miss Weaver pointed out that 'Lucia was insistent that it was her own idea to be an artist in her own way, carrying this so far that when for a time she attended dancing classes at the Vic Wells, she did not want it to be known that she was James Joyce's daughter!'

At the Victoria Palace Hotel six years previously Joyce had cried out to McAlmon that the task he had set himself was terribly difficult but he believed it could be done. Now, towards the end of the twenties, perhaps earlier, he seems to have become very discouraged. This was largely due to overstrain and unfavourable comments by those who did not understand his technique. His friends cast round to see what could be done.

Among the papers at Buffalo University is a letter from George Borach which suggests that as he had heard Joyce was in ill health, perhaps he would care to consult Dr Alfred Vogt in the Seefeldstrasse, Zürich, who curiously enough also treated Eamon De Valera. Joyce also mentioned to Miss Weaver on March 18th, 1930, that he had heard from two ladies concerning oculists in Wiesbaden and Zürich, both of whom he consulted before deciding to put himself in the hands of Dr Vogt. Thus in May 1930 Joyce underwent his ninth operation, which was so skilfully performed that after a time he was able to see, imperfectly perhaps, but well enough to go about by himself and to write a certain amount.

Joyce was soon anxious to get back to work but of course was not able to do so for a good while. T. S. Eliot wrote reassuringly that he felt things would turn out well in time and that the book would be finished—'a year or two does not matter for a grand thing like this'.

As shown by a letter written on January 31st, 1925, from Claude Road, Drumcondra, and preserved at the University of Buffalo, John Stanislaus Joyce wrote every year for his son's birthday in February. 'By the way,' he asked on this occasion, 'did you receive that portrait of me that Mr Tuohy painted? And I hope you have the other family portraits all safe?' He concludes, 'I am still what is left of me, your fond and loving Father.' The note, with its shaky copperplate writing, is a reminder of someone's remark that they often used to see the old man going up Summerhill in Dublin, 'in a loose overcoat, with his tie out untidily; he was quite a character you know'. Later he was bedridden for a number of years.

On the same date in 1931 Mr Joyce writes again, asking if his son recollects the old days in Brighton Square, 'when you were baby Tuckoo and I used to tell you all about the moo-cow that used to come down from the mountain and take little boys away?' Had Joyce's work refurbished the memory, once provided by the talkative and amusing orginal of Mr Dedalus? And he concludes 'Again my dear boy, may God bless you is the prayer of Your fond and loving Father.'

This was probably one of the last letters to reach Paris, for he died in hospital on December 29th of that same year. When the news reached Joyce it affected him deeply. Much of the past came back into his mind [1] and he regretted that although he had often promised his father to return he had been unable to bring himself to go back to Dublin again, because of the rumours, which some people took pleasure in elaborating, that he 'would be chased out of it there'.

For some time Joyce had not been sleeping well and he complained that the flat in Square Robiac had become very noisy. Again there was talk of where they should live. In the spring of 1931 Joyce had turned out an accumulation of books and papers. He sent Miss Weaver some manuscripts found in 'the house that Joyce leaves'. It was rarely that he spoke of himself in the third person and the phrase also carries the sense

[1] 'Oh father forsaken, | Forgive your son.'—*Ecce puer.*

that once more he must wheel his caravan elsewhere. Giorgio was engaged, Lucia might be better in different surroundings. For testamentary reasons it was now necessary for Joyce to go through a form of British marriage. Therefore they left Paris for London, where they were married in a registrar's office in Kensington. Joyce chose July 4th, his father's birthday. He was most anxious to avoid publicity but the news got out somehow. A witness at the ceremony marched out first when it was over with another lady on his arm, hoping the reporters would make a mistake, but Joyce with his glasses was too well known.

Afterwards Nora Joyce probably returned to their flat to change and Joyce, glad of a little solitude maybe, went to Slater's Restaurant which he had discovered in Kensington High Street. He had no sooner settled down when a friend, knowing he would find him there at that time, hurried in to say there were posters out with his name on them. Joyce, who thoroughly disliked that kind of renown, was rather short to him, but that evening over dinner with friends in Hampstead they were all able to laugh at having successfully dodged the Press who had tried to track them down there.

When the Joyces arrived in England that spring, having stored their furniture in Paris, they thought it a good idea to find a flat in London and to spend part of each year there. As Joyce already knew Kensington and liked the district, through Messrs Marsh and Parsons in Church Street they found an unfurnished flat in 28A Campden Grove, which is just up the hill above St Mary Abbots. The house, facing north, is at the narrow and darker end of the street. Joyce did not care for it there and told Miss Weaver it should be called 'Campden Grave', saying that 'Buckingham Palace was real, and the sooty buildings along the railway lines, but the flat wasn't somehow.'

Yet it would do for a time. Expeditions were made to the big stores, accounting perhaps for the inclusion of their names in *Finnegans Wake*, and the Joyces bought comfortable beds and other things they needed.

Although they generally went to Soho or had a meal at home in the evening, at lunch time Joyce often walked down to Slater's. 'Ah, he could always pick a restaurant,' I was told. The entrance is just beyond the carriage-way to 'Millionaires' Row' or Palace Gardens, now occupied by legations and embassies. One passes over the terrazzo floor of the grocery department of the store to mount wide brown-wood stairs. On the first floor, a long room runs from the back of the building to the front where employees from offices round about and shoppers up for the sales eat their 'fixed price' luncheons. Sometimes part of the room, used in the evenings for meetings and dances, is set with long tables, and large parties of farmers and complete Women's Institutes, or so they seem, have a meal there before going to something at the Royal Horticultural Hall or down at Olympia. There the voices of the people flow into one another, only a word or part of a sentence rises into distinctiveness for a moment and then is carried on by that continuous river of talk.

Sometimes Joyce made his way back under the high plane trees of Palace Gardens. To the right are the green paddocks before what were once royal stables, often grazed by sooty London sheep, and to the left is the house where Thackeray used to live, a line of association running back to the Grand Hôtel Corneille and the epiphanies of Eccles Street. Soon there is a narrow way past the wall of the barracks which comes out into Church Street, just opposite the Doll's House and Pound's doorway in Holland Place. By 1931 the little triangular room had long ago ceased to have manuscripts lying about and the poet was then living in Rapallo. He had shown no enthusiasm for Joyce's experiments and is supposed to have told him, when *Pomes Penyeach* appeared in 1927, 'Put it in the family Bible', a wisecrack Pound himself has no recollection of making. At the same time it seems that when Pound was discussed in his hearing, Joyce always pointed out how much Ezra had done to help him.

It was during this time that Mrs Griffin, a sister of Mrs Joyce, from Galway, stayed with them in London. She remembered excursions to the Tower and how one day they set off for Stonehenge, which Joyce had long wanted to see. Lucia, it seems, was not at all happy in London, feeling rather foreign there. One day she set out to see Mrs Stephens but fled away when she saw there were a number of other people to tea.

By the autumn the Joyces had let the flat for the winter to the cook at the French Embassy and stayed in Paris until the spring at 2 Avenue Saint Philibert, where they evidently had a friendly connection. Joyce was delighted by the birth of his grandson, Stephen James Joyce, that February of 1932, but Lucia was becoming increasingly troublesome.

One morning in April they taxied to the Gare du Nord with their luggage intending to take the train to London, where the flat was ready for them. Lucia had perhaps protested the night before, and now at the station itself she had such a *crise de nerfs* that Joyce, tired, embarrassed, and I should say furious, was obliged to take the trunks off the train. Soon the Kensington flat was given up, although it served to establish English domicile on Joyce's death. Perhaps their failure to return to London during the thirties—Miss Weaver and other friends had pressed them to do so—eventually led to the family becoming involved in the débâcle of 1940.[1]

RUE GALILÉE
1932–4

'Here we are in a hotel again after twelve years in Paris,' Joyce told Larbaud in May 1932. By June they had found a furnished flat for a while at 2 Avenue Saint Philibert in Passy, and the following month were in Zürich as Joyce's eyes needed attention. Their daughter, who had been having treatment, was now in Austria and the Joyces made a short visit there to see her. Then, after Dr Vogt had again seen his patient, they spent a few weeks in Nice before returning to the Hôtel Byron on the Champs Elysées. Altogether it had been a terribly expensive period of disrupted work and great anxiety.

'The flat in the rue Galilée, in the seizième?' a friend remarked. 'Oh, that was a bad time, so much trouble with Lucia. Joyce may have been in favour of taking it because of the English-American chemist on the corner.'

The road runs up from the Avenue d'Iéna to the Avenue Kléber and is divided into three distinct portions by others which run across it. Approaching from the Champs Elysées, at the corner of the centre position, is a confectioner's with windows of ornately coloured glass, deep blue and almost black now, with a fleur-de-lys design in gold on each little pane; further up the road a dairy is surrounded by painted panels with rural scenes of cattle going to drink or a cottage among fields. Apart from

[1] It is very possible that if Joyce had been more closely in touch with English life in the thirties he would have used the radio as a means of putting his work across. David Jones, Dylan Thomas and others have made excellent use of the medium.

these late nineteenth-century touches, the road is severe enough. Almost opposite the house where the Joyces lived is the Hôtel Galilée with a curious terraced entry running parallel with the pavement, as if the architect had been determined to create an impression, however limited the space available. As usual I tried at No. 42 in case there might be some person still there who might remember the Joyces. 'Oh no, the property has changed hands,' I was told. 'The owner used to live down here then, I believe. Sorry I cannot help you. . . .' A young woman was bringing in a pram, and as she crossed the white terrazzo floor with its pattern of green leaves, a little boy followed her. Here, I thought, Stephen must have come to see his grandparents and formulate his first memories of them.

Once settled in a furnished flat in the rue Galilée—after Galileo who would not retract—Joyce worked to complete *Two Tales of Shem and Shaun*,[1] which Faber and Faber were to publish that Christmas. In fact, parts of *Work in Progress* appeared in England before *Ulysses* had been published there. The memory of how copies of the second English edition, published in Paris, had been confiscated by the Customs at Folkestone in 1923, and vehement criticisms of the book, had combined to make publishers reluctant to undertake the risk. The decision to lift the ban in the United States, described in detail by Herbert Gorman, and the appearance of the first authorized American edition in 1934, gave Joyce more hope. Help was to come from an unexpected direction.

During the autumn of 1931 Harold Nicolson had given a series of broadcasts on modern literature. Well aware that hearing D. H. Lawrence and Joyce mentioned among other writers, many of his listeners would 'be profoundly shocked', he maintained them to be two of the most important figures produced by the post-war generation.

Harold Nicolson, in a letter written in January 1956, mentioned that when Lord Reith (then Sir John Reith), the Director-General of the BBC, became aware of the optimistic remark, 'In my next talk I shall discuss the work of James Joyce,' he said that Joyce must not be mentioned. Harold Nicolson threatened to discontinue the series and to explain matters in a letter to *The Times*. In the end a compromise was reached under which no mention was to be made of *Ulysses*. 'I was indignant at the time but I now

---

[1] Publications by Joyce are only mentioned where relevant to the text. For details, see *A Bibliography of James Joyce*.

think that Reith was quite right in saying one cannot mention on the wireless a book, the importation and sale of which was prohibited by the Home Office.'

Hugh Walpole attacked the broadcasts in *John O'London's* and *The Listener* printed letters beneath the heading *Harold Nicolson under Fire* (one correspondent talked of those 'desiccated prigs who in London West Central repeatedly cried "Woolf! Woolf!" '). A letter in the Lockwood Memorial Library shows that on December 16th, T. S. Eliot wrote to Joyce that he thought Harold Nicolson had put up a very good fight in his broadcast on Joyce's work and that he seemed to have precipitated a crisis in the affairs of the BBC. There would probably be a great many wigs on the green before it was finished.

No book-titles were mentioned in the talk. Joyce 'seized the muse of Irish romance by her pallid neck, dragged her away from the mists and wailings of forgotten legend and set her in the sordid streets of Dublin of 1904. In so doing he did well.' Later the speaker pointed out, 'You must abandon yourself to receptivity, you must not expect a lesson or a story, you must expect only to absorb a new atmosphere, almost a new climate.' Joyce had 'added enormously to our capacity of observation: once you have absorbed the Joyce climate, you begin to notice things in your mind which had never occurred to you before. And to have given a new generation a whole new area of self-knowledge is surely an achievement of great importance.'

The controversy was opened by a letter from Mrs Edith Lyttelton to *The Times*, summarizing the general sense of uneasiness at a rumoured change in BBC policy: 'If we are now to be herded into the middle way on every subject, if we are not to hear opposite sides but merely an official view, however carefully framed, the prospect is dangerous.' A few days later the subject came out into the open. Alfred Noyes pointed out that it was merely proposed there should be no more talks on contemporary literature and mentioned the great tolerance of the BBC even when the subjects of the talks 'were, so to speak—known to the police'.[1] Minority

---

[1] Alfred Noyes had written of *Ulysses* in the *Sunday Chronicle* in 1922: 'The foulest book that has ever found its way into print . . . What concerns us all and most earnestly demands consideration is the appalling fact that our Metropolitan criticism should have been treating such works as those of Mr Joyce seriously as works of genius.'

views could find expression in print. 'The British public is quite well enough informed to choose its own literature; or, at least, to find more adequate guides, with more time to spare than any wireless "educator", no matter how rosy and supposedly unsafe his opinions, or how unconventionally unconventional the pattern of his discreetly disguised herdsman's crook.' Individuals protested; the Society of Authors and the Publishers Association opposed the suggestion that novels would no longer be reviewed on the air. A letter, signed by some forty publishers and writers, stated that it was understood that the action of the BBC was due to the fact that critics had refused to accept the condition laid down that certain authors should never be referred to—censorship of books was a dangerous thing. Eventually Michael Sadleir pointed out the general injustice of Alfred Noyes' letter, for there had been talks on a number of other authors and the BBC would continue to give time to literature. The last word was left to a correspondent who thanked Alfred Noyes for speaking against those who defended the subversive. Although Joyce is not mentioned, reference is made to an author 'who has written passages of a nastiness entirely beyond the licence of any civilized age', of whose work it had been written 'it would make a Hottentot sick'.[1]

Harold Nicolson, according to Miss Weaver, had first met Joyce in 1922. Now in February 1934, when staying in Paris, he asked Sylvia Beach for Joyce's address, which was not given to every casual enquirer. At 42 rue Galilée he was shown into a 'dim trim little drawing-room with a parquet floor, a few rugs and many occasional chairs and tables in the style of Louis XV' which had 'the enclosed atmosphere of an unused sitting-room in a neat provincial hotel . . . on each table there were groups of floral tributes . . . evidently the disciples had been celebrating Joyce's birthday on the day before'. When Joyce came quietly into the room he advanced cautiously, feeling the furniture. Very neatly dressed, upon his fingers were several heavy encrusted rings; 'his sockless feet slipped tentatively along the parquet in carpet slippers of blue and white check. . . . From time to time his hand would finger and adjust the loose lenses in his heavy steel spectacles. His half-blindness was so oppressive

---

[1] The original remark was in *The Sporting Times* in 1922: 'The main contents of the book [*Ulysses*] are enough to make a Hottentot sick . . . not alone sordidly pornographic, but intensely dull.'

that one had the impression of speaking to someone who was very ill indeed.'

At that time Harold Nicolson was collecting material for a book on Hamilton Rowan, the eighteenth-century Irishman (published in 1943 as *The Desire to Please*), and he wanted to discuss Joyce's reference to Hamilton Rowan's escape from Clongowes Wood, mentioned in *A Portrait of the Artist*.[1] Although they may have spoken of this in passing, the point was never cleared up for Joyce spoke gently, 'in his lovely Anna Livia voice', of the difficulties encountered over *Ulysses*, which he pronounced in the Triestine manner as 'Oulissays'. Might he send his visitor a copy of the *de luxe* edition so that when confiscated an action might be brought against the administration? Harold Nicolson pointed out that Molly Bloom's monologue would alienate the sympathies of any English court of law. 'The plan was unfolded with such innocence and passion that I became embarrassed', and later 'I left the flat with vague promises to Joyce's trusting sightless eyes'. Yet the question of *Ulysses* was not forgotten, for Harold Nicolson found that the authorities in London were not so unsympathetic as he had expected. It may have been as a result of these enquiries that Joyce was soon able to make arrangements with a London firm and in 1936 *Ulysses* was published in England, fourteen years after its first appearance in the rue de l'Odéon.

When Louis Gillet first met Joyce in 1931, as described in his book, 'With absolute simplicity, quite devoid of pretentiousness, he furnished me with the key to his work. He explained to me the mystery of the titanic figure H. C. E., the unique, many-faceted hero of innumerable incarnations. . . . He told me about the language he had adopted in order to give his vocabulary the elasticity of sleep, to multiply the meaning of words, to permit the play of light and colour, and make of the sentence a rainbow to which each tiny drop is itself a many-hued prism.' [2]

As they came to know each other the Joyces went to dine at the flat in the rue Bonaparte where the Gillets lived for many years. During the occupation they moved to the country, under conditions of considerable

[1] See Appendix F.
[2] Translated by Maria Jolas, *The James Joyce Year Book*, 1949.

hardship, and Louis Gillet, who did much to help Jewish and other friends, died shortly after their return home. When I met Madame Gillet she took me into the salon and talked of their regard for Joyce. Odd the gestures we remember: 'Joyce used to bring his glass of white wine in here after dinner and put it on top of that radiator.' We moved into the salle-à-manger, where the ancient woodwork had once been painted cream and blue. 'There my husband sat; here the principal guest. We used to have Claudel, oh, many others here.' I could imagine the white cloth, the wine and good food presided over by the bearded friendliness of Louis Gillet. 'My husband had known Rodin, Barrès and many artists and writers. He wrote the *Lettres Etrangères* in the *Revue des Deux Mondes* and this put him in touch with English authors too. On a visit to England we met Virginia Woolf among others and stayed with Rudyard Kipling in the country. All I can remember is that he sang in his bath . . .'

As time went on Joyce was increasingly concerned with trying to bring his daughter back to health. Having controlled his own neurotic tendencies by concentration on his art, he now endeavoured to direct Lucia's energies towards another form of self-expression. At his suggestion she designed the cover, an initial letter and tailpiece for a special edition of *The Mime of Mick Nick and the Maggies*, published at The Hague in 1934. The abstract emblems, if they can be called so, are delicately poised, feminine; to my mind counterparts in some way to the dark horsemen of Wyndham Lewis's *Enemy*, though this might only be a period influence. Often it required a good deal of tact on Joyce's part to encourage Lucia to do such work. It seems he even arranged for publishers to allocate her some royalties, probably out of his share. On one occasion he saw that an illustrated Bible was to be found in a certain library, thinking that she would be interested in it. In 1936 the Obelisk Press in Paris published 'An A.B.C., being a Hymn to the holy Virgin, in an English version by CHAUCER, with capital letters designed and illuminated in gold, silver and numerous colours by Lucia Joyce and with a preface by Louis Gillet of the *Académie Française*.'

Yet neither paternal concern nor art could draw Lucia out of her darkness. Louis Gillet often used to meet Joyce in a little café near the Invalides on the corner of the rue Dominique and the rue Fabert, not far from the offices of *Transition*, from whose windows Joyce had once watched the funeral of Marshal Foch through field-glasses. The place was almost empty about five in the evening. 'Through the steam-damp windows, the trees on the Esplanade stood in shivering rows, like plants in an aquarium.' Both being family men, talk soon came round to their children. Joyce would give him news of Lucia and the latest effort to find the right treatment. 'The spectacle of his sick daughter rent his heart, and was almost the only subject of our conversation.' Joyce, who had behind him several generations of alcoholism, felt that he alone was to blame. 'It was his fault, for he was the father. Everything that went wrong with his beloved son and daughter was to be laid at his door because of the abnormal elements of his genius.'

ZÜRICH

Joyce's visits to Zürich gave him the opportunity of meeting old friends there and on one occasion he travelled specially from Paris to hear a concert of music by Ottmar Schoeck, the Swiss composer whom he greatly admired. Among the pinewoods of the outskirts, the house of Professor and Madame Giedion at Doldertal has remained as the Joyces knew it, the warm wood-panelled comfort of rooms with something of that tidy carelessness of people always hard at work. Traditional furniture combines with modern sculpture, against a bookcase leans a recently acquired painting for which there is hardly space on the walls. A great map-like blue fantasy by Max Ernst hangs over a table. Beneath it Madame Giedion helped Joyce to correct proofs. 'In the end he had to stop me asking questions about the meanings,' she laughed. Joyce must have appreciated her sense of words and gift of visual description, and many of her remarks have served to illuminate other incidents in this narrative. Towards the end of the evening we talked of how Nora Joyce liked the rough mountain people of Switzerland, of her kindly impulsiveness, the way she brought gifts on the many occasions when they visited them. For all her cheerfulness, at times she grumbled about life, and when the Giedions talked of moving, Joyce, perhaps reflecting that he had never owned a house, said, 'Don't; you'll be glad of these thick walls.'

As I was leaving, we stood at the gate a moment and there was the sound of a little stream in the darkness. 'Yes, I remember Joyce lying here on the grass one afternoon as we left for a picnic. He was still there when we returned. "Oh," he said, "I begin to feel there is such a thing as peace." ' Now in 1934, as Lucia became worse and Mrs Joyce found it impossible to deal with her at home in Paris or even when she visited them from a sanatorium, Joyce rather reluctantly agreed to consult Dr C. G. Jung. As the psychologist's article, 'Ulysses, a Monologue',[1] was translated into English and appeared in *Nimbus* in 1953, when visiting Zürich I asked him if he would be so good as to see me.

We could only arrange a meeting in the evening. Thus I went out to the village of Küsnacht and made my way down a long, villa-edged road. Going through white gates, at the end of a short avenue of trees I could see a lit doorway in the dark tower-shape of a house. Soon a girl took me to a small ante-room on the first floor. Indian dolls and toys were in glass presses and among books and papers on the table was a recent issue of *Punch*. Downstairs someone whistled and a deep clock struck six across the atmosphere of quiet and good order there.

As I was ushered into a large library, over parquet and Indian carpets, there was only a standard lamp in a corner by the window so that furniture and pictures were indistinguishable. Dr Jung rose and shook hands, a bulky figure with a pleasant voice, and I sat down on a comfortable seat opposite him. By some effect of the light behind his chair, or the angle of his glasses which enlarged the pupils, a curious distortion gave his look the full-powered concentration of a child or an animal. It was so distracting that I shifted my position and it became more usual again.

We talked first of all of my study of Joyce's background, and Dr Jung's brief glimpse of Ireland from a liner stopping at Cobh on the way back from America. I mentioned Joyce's years in Zürich during the First World War and how Mrs Rockefeller McCormick had helped Joyce financially for a time and then abruptly ceased to do so.

'It has been suggested,' I said, 'that you were in some way involved, and that perhaps Joyce had offended the lady by refusing to be analysed?'

'Well, now you tell me the story I may well have been, in an indirect way.' Dr Jung explained that Joyce's name was then unknown to him and he had not met the writer personally until much later, when Joyce, whose daughter was then in a sanatorium, asked for a consultation. Yet

---

[1] *Europäische Revue*, September 1932, pp. 547–68.

he recollected that before 1920 Mrs McCormick mentioned she was supporting both an author and another artist at that time. She was much troubled by the fact that the latter did not work. Dr Jung hesitated to tell her to cease these payments, but when the artist himself became his patient and told him of a recurrent dream in which he was bleeding to death, he advised Mrs McCormick to end an intolerable situation, with most satisfactory results. Although Dr Jung was not informed, she may well have decided to have done with Joyce and the manuscript of *Ulysses* as well.

'In the thirties I was asked to write an introduction to the German edition [1] of *Ulysses*,' he told me, 'but as such it was not a success. Later I published it in one of my books. My interest was not literary but professional. . . . The book was a most valuable document from my point of view; I expressed this, as you know.'

'You said that the experiences related were part of "the cold shadow-side of existence"—I do not think that Joyce cared about that.'

'The peculiar mixture and the nature of the material as presented is the same as in cases of schizophrenia, but dealt with by an artist. The same things that you find in the mad-house, oh yes, definitely, but with a *plan*. I wrote and apologized to the publisher for not being able to provide what he needed for the edition.'

As in the case of *A Strange Necessity* by Rebecca West (see *Further Notes*) it seems as if Dr Jung's comments had really got under Joyce's skin and worked their way through him like a needle. In both cases, it should be observed, the irritations set up by Joyce's work are fully described first and then comes a good deal of praise. With a certain kind of person it is the last taste which remains in the mouth, but other people never get over an initial unpleasantness. Like Wyndham Lewis, with his emphasis on the *petit bourgeois* aspects of *Ulysses*, these criticisms went through the thinnest part of Joyce's armour. Mary Colum in *Life and the Dream* says that Dr Jung wrote to Joyce about Molly Bloom's monologue: 'I think the devil's grandmother knows as much about the pyschology of a woman—I don't. . . . It is a string of psychological peaches'.[2]

[1] Probably the 2nd and 3rd edition, published in 1930 by Rhein-Verlag, Zürich.

[2] Dr Jung cannot remember having written to Joyce, but I have reason to believe that a copy of his letter is extant. Richard Ellmann mentions Mrs Joyce's remark on seeing it: 'He knows nothing at all about women!' She meant her husband.

She later points out that Joyce was much indebted to the work of both Freud and Jung and how she put this to him on one occasion and he would not deny it. Indeed, in *Finnegans Wake* (p. 115) it is half-mockingly acknowledged, 'when they were yung and easily befreudered'.

A remark which has survived may illustrate what appears to have been Joyce's attitude at one time. 'What the Jesuits in Rome have to say about my work makes sense but Jung's comments are just silly.' When Joyce approached the psychologist professionally in 1934, Jung had put the article and his apology for it out of his mind, but Joyce would hardly have done so.

'Certainly he seemed very restrained,' Dr Jung said when I mentioned this. 'Yes, now I remember it, during the hour or so while we talked of his daughter, it was impossible not to feel his resistances. The interview was correspondingly uneventful and futile. His daughter, on the contrary, was far more lively. She was very attractive, charming—a good mind. And her writing, what she did for me, had in it the same elements as her father's. She was the same spirit, oh they cared for each other very much. Yet unfortunately it was too late to help her.'

The neurotic, like the child, is often very absorbent of the atmosphere created by those around him, especially when it in some way involves himself. A remark disparaging the Doctor—'How could *he* know what is going on in my pretty little head'—purported to have been made by Lucia, suggests that no real rapport was possible between them.

'*Finnegans Wake*?' Dr Jung replied to my query. 'I read parts of it in periodicals but it was like getting lost in a wood. Oh no, I could not manage it. *Ulysses* yes, but still I do not understand why so many people read it, so many editions have been published.'

'Well, surely they needed certain things to be said. In the twenties people wanted to read in print what they could not express themselves, about life, sex . . . That generation was freeing itself from so much; we hardly understand its situation now. Then it seems to me that many problems inherent in Joyce's work are also those of the present-day world, in particular the adjustment of personal relations to science, the question of over-population. . . .'

'Yes, yes, that is the *great* problem, all over the world. I have been in India and seen the under-nourished people, the thousands, thousands born there. There is the important question of food, of food production. How are they all to be fed?'

Dr Jung enlarged on this theme in a flow of sentences, one upon another, and with that quick, unsought illustration which characterizes his prose. As he stood up to go I was aware of his fresh, full face, and that there was a particular attractiveness about the man by his very largeness and health of mind.

'I am glad,' he concluded, 'that I do not have to face the difficulties of the future. I shall be eighty in July 1955, you know. They are so very great indeed.'

'Well, I think you have done your share in helping other people— enough for one lifetime. We'll have to try and find a way out anyway.'

'Yes, yes.' As I got my coat from the ante-room I knew that by long habit he was watching, assessing me. With more care than usual, as if to make a good impression, I turned off the light and shut the door.

'Is this an old house?' I asked, to fill the gap before saying good-bye.

'No, but built after an ancient style.' He smiled. 'I am, you know, a conservative.'

Lucia's condition may have improved, for in 1935 she spent a few months in Ireland with an aunt at Bray. Thus Joyce was once again in touch with Irish life. He provided numerous introductions, told her places she should see, and at one moment sent her two volumes of Tolstoy, which suggests that she was already well read. Sometimes he commented, humorously, on items in the Irish newspapers which she had sent to him. All the time Joyce was struggling to draw her back into normal life.

The visit was not altogether a success, and when Lucia had spent a further three to four months in England the situation again deteriorated and Joyce had a good deal of anxiety. Eventually she went as a voluntary patient to the famous hospital at Northampton associated with John Clare. Joyce, to whom it had been suggested more than once, resolutely refused to have her certified, and for this reason she was brought back to a private home at Ivry on the outskirts of Paris. There she remained until the establishment was evacuated to Pornichet near St Nazaire in 1939.[1]

[1] I sent a draft of this account to Dr Jung and the following paragraph summarizes his interpretation of the situation. 'If you know anything of my Anima theory, Joyce and his

7 RUE EDMOND VALENTIN

During 1935 the Joyces moved to a flat at 7 rue Edmond Valentin which was only a short walk from their previous home in the rue de Grenelle. To traverse the Avenue Bosquet and take the street turning between high, shut-away houses is to sense the contrast of those two phases of Joyce's life in Paris. Behind lies the come and go of friends and helpers, the talk of Giorgio's wedding and Lucia's performances as a dancer, Joyce's struggle to convey the charms of Anna Livia, that afternoon eight years ago when Nora prepared one of her excellent teas for those who came to listen to Joyce read his work. The grey-brown buildings with half-closed eyes have heavy doors of iron and glass like those of the Boulevard Raspail, and no one remembered the Joyces there.

Over the past few years Joyce had not been to Montparnasse so often, but met his friends at Fouquets in the Champs Elysées, where the fashionable impinged on the theatrical and literary. Padraic and Mary Colum saw a good deal of him and his wife at this time; Joyce always sat in the same seat at the same table and after they had eaten and while the others talked he drank Muscadet and smoked.[1] As William Magee remarked in a letter written in 1950, 'Curiously, the man himself when I met him in later life was not very interesting. Unlike Moore and Yeats, he seemed carefully to withhold his real opinions about men and things'. Their lives had moved very far apart since the old National Library days but Joyce surprised Mary Colum by remembering numerous details concerning University College, where she had also been a student. Mrs Stephens, who

daughter are a classical example of it. She was definitely his "femme inspiratrice", which explains his obstinate reluctance to have her certified. His own Anima, i.e. unconscious psyche, was so solidly identified with her, that to have her certified would have been as much as an admission that he himself had a latent psychosis. It is therefore understandable that he could not give in. His "psychological" style is definitely schizophrenic, with the difference, however, that the ordinary patient cannot help himself talking and thinking in such a way, while Joyce willed it and moreover developed it by all his creative forces, which incidentally explains why he himself did not go over the border. But his daughter did, because she was no genius like her father, but merely a victim of her disease. In any other time of the past Joyce's work would never have reached the printer, but in our blessed XXth century it is a message, though not yet understood.' (A passage in W. R. Rodgers' broadcasts on Joyce suggests that at times he was under considerable strain.—P. H.)

[1] *Life and the Dream*, 1947.

185

was often at Fouquets with her husband, remarked that Joyce would put in a query or a statement into the general conversation but never held forth. James Stephens could talk the clock round and Joyce would listen to him until the small hours. On one occasion Marlene Dietrich was with Erich Remarque at a nearby table and she was very pleased to have a few words with Joyce, who afterwards remarked to Mary Colum with his whimsical smile, 'I thought the years when I was a lion were over.'

There must have been many evenings when the Joyces stayed at home and Joyce listened to the wireless or friends such as Stuart Gilbert, Eugene or Maria Jolas came in to give some help with his work. Paul Léon, in particular, did a great deal to keep Joyce's practical affairs in order. When they were alone Lucia's illness was no longer a subject for constant discussion, and as a woman remarked, seeing them again, 'Oh you know, there came that kind of silence between people when they are elderly and there is nothing more to say.' Sometimes when she had gone to bed, Nora could hear Joyce, his papers spread over the floor, laughing away to himself over that book of his.

One evening when her husband was out, Nora Joyce began to tidy an old box or a drawer and came across the letters Joyce had written to her when a young man. She hardly re-read them, for the best memories have a thread of pain through them, but she certainly said to someone: 'The other day I tore up Jim's letters to me—what would I want with them?' Although she was often rather brusque with her husband, impatient at the way he overdid things, in a sense he appreciated this, as part of her concern for him. Occasionally this was misinterpreted as disharmony between them. Once Lucia had said to Madame Giedion: 'I know mother's rather crusty but she really doesn't mean it.'

Like Stuart Gilbert, Mary Colum found there was something enigmatic about Joyce. Never had she heard a more mysterious voice than when he used to sit down at the piano in their flat as if he were alone in the room. In spite of his mockery of romantic love, many of his songs were sad love-songs in various languages. One of these was Yeats' poem which carried so many associations—morning on the Martello Tower, playing for his dying mother, the Hill of Howth with Nora. Perhaps he sang it in Mrs Murray's off the North Strand Road, after the struggle over

Dubliners, and on many other occasions. Now, with the tragedy of Lucia's life to face, it held a further meaning:

> And no more turn aside and brood
> Upon love's bitter mystery;
> For Fergus rules the brazen cars,
> And rules the shadows of the wood,
> And the white breast of the dim sea
> And all dishevelled wandering stars.

During the early thirties Joyce had done a great deal to help John O'Sullivan,[1] the tenor, whom he believed to be one of the greatest singers of his time. To some extent this may have been a transfer of his own youthful ambitions and those he had centred round his children; it was also a distraction from his worries to use his influence for a fellow-countryman. At one time Joyce was in touch with George Antheil concerning a libretto he was to write based on Byron's *Cain* in which John O'Sullivan would perform; on another occasion he wrote to Sir Thomas Beecham on his friend's behalf. Joyce put so much enthusiasm into this cause that his literary, and more literal, followers were sometimes embarrassed by it.

As I heard that John O'Sullivan was living in the north of Paris, I went to see him and found that his speaking voice alone would have seduced Joyce from his work, only to return him there later with renewed energy. For me it was like being at home in south-west Ireland again—the high-boned, handsome face of the man, the softening over of the edge of his words, that Kerry intonation which came into the English language from the Irish spoken round about Killarney.

'Yes, my people came from there. You know the Lake Hotel? My grandfather owned it. I was a young boy when my father died and at twelve was sent to an aunt at Forges-les-Eaux in Normandy. After the Lycée Corneille at Rouen, I later took up singing, trained at the Conservatoire you know, and started in 1911 as Romeo and from then—' Mr O'Sullivan went over to a cupboard and brought out a portfolio full of programmes, photographs and letters dealing with his performances all over Europe and in the United States.

'Unfortunately we lost a great many papers during the war, Joyce's

---

[1] He sang on the Continent as Jean Sullivan.

letters among them. You know this?' He held out a copy of *De Honni-soi a mal-y-chance* (*From a banned writer to a banned singer*) which first appeared in the *New Statesman and Nation* on February 27th, 1932.

At the University of Buffalo there remains other evidence of the efforts Joyce had made on his behalf and Stuart Gilbert told me he remembered helping to make out notes for Joyce on John O'Sullivan's career at one time. 'As a matter of fact it was Stanislaus who introduced us. I had known him in Trieste,' John O'Sullivan said. 'Ah, Joyce!' he sighed. 'He did all he could for me.' Then, concluding with a laugh, 'What times we had—I remember he'd be there at the Opera in a box for *Otello* or *Faust* or *Guillaume Tell*.'

By the middle of the decade *Work in Progress* was already well known and some of those who had once read *Ulysses* either for its literary merit or its outspokenness were either disappointed by Joyce's difficult technique or lost interest in an experiment which had not yet appeared in book form. Joyce realized this, for he wrote 'You will have loss of fame from Wimmegame's fake' (*F. W.*, p. 375). Publication had been discussed since 1931, when Joyce was last in England. At Faber and Faber's, in Russell Square, Richard de la Mare, who has been in charge of production since the firm's inception, from a large file of letters provided a few details of the book's evolution. 'We had an awful time of it, I know,' he said good-humouredly. 'When did it start?' He turned to a collection of specimen pages. 'I see the first is dated August 12th, 1931. Joyce had an idea of the length of the book even then—518 pages. It eventually became 618, I think. There were various other specimens; we changed the type. . . . The last . . .' He turned over. 'The last specimen was December 1936; yes, that's when we really started production.'

In March of that year Messrs R. MacLehose of The University Press, Glasgow, who had printed *Haveth Childers Everywhere* in 1931, acknowledged the receipt of some of Joyce's typescript with the remark, 'And now many bitter tears are being shed over it.' Gorman mentions in his biography that Joyce was composing the last part while the earlier pages were being printed, a statement which would need to be checked by the British Museum manuscripts. The printers soon found it was impossible to set from the copy to hand: could it be re-typed? Joyce, who had evidently made many corrections, had himself been doubtful if they could follow it, so the parcel was sent back again to Paris. Perhaps his friends took good care that Joyce did not spend time on changing it again, for eventually production got under way.

With the political situation moving quickly towards war, Joyce was most anxious to have the book published. At last the final set of proofs were posted off to England, but even then there were last-minute telegrams and telephone calls, as Joyce wanted to make slight changes. By November 18th, 1938, the book was finished and Joyce was preparing a little thanksgiving party. It was planned that an advance copy should reach Paris in time for Joyce's birthday in February 1939. On January 30th, Paul Léon, who had conducted most of the correspondence, wrote to Mr de la Mare that this had just arrived and looked very beautiful; he would take it over at once to Mr Joyce who would be very pleased and write tomorrow. Indeed Joyce sent a telegram that afternoon or the following morning, 'MY WARM THANKS TO ALL CONCERNED FOR PATIENCE PROMPTITUDE WHICH I GREATLY APPRECIATE.' What the Glasgow printers said about it all is not on record but, allowing for the fact that at least they understood a few words here and there, their remarks cannot have been very different from those of Maurice Darantière's men in Dijon as they prepared *Ulysses* seventeen years before.

Paul Léon mentioned two further additions which were included when *Finnegans Wake* was published on May 4th, 1939 ;[1] on page 486, *Trothed today, trenned tomorrow* was to be inserted, and on page 614, in a passage in which we find the statement 'It will remember itself from every sides, with all gestures, in each our word. *Today's truth, tomorrow's trend.*' A not unprophetic conclusion.

[1] For a summary of press comments see Appendix C.

XI

PARIS—VICHY—ZÜRICH

1939–1941

The Joyce road round Paris was to take one more loop again out towards Passy—'in my end is my beginning'. On at least two occasions the Joyces had gone back to number 2 Avenue St Philibert, not far from the rue de l'Assomption where Circe had been written. I had always found it worthwhile to go to the district where Joyce had lived, to collect the tiny scraps of association left behind him. Thus, one winter day I took the Metro to La Muette and went down the rue Boulainvilliers and soon found myself in the rue des Vignes, which is a quiet, fairly narrow street with frontages softened here and there by tiny gardens behind *grilles*. On number 32 there was a plaque to Gustave Fauré who had lived there for many years before his death in 1924; and further on at an angle runs the rue Albert Bruneau, once the rue Saint Philibert.

The high block of flats there had nothing to suggest but over-emphasized respectability, so I returned to look for 34 rue des Vignes, which stands back from the pavement beyond a little space overcome by ivy, the strong dark kind, thick-stemmed as a tree. I remembered how the song 'The holly and the ivy now both are well full grown . . .' echoes through the *Wake*.

Pushing the magic button which foreigners find so fascinating in French houses, I went into an empty, well-kept hall with a glass birdcage of a lift. As there was no answer from the concierge, feeling balked, I tried the door; which opened into a tiny room. The place smelt of time, a lifetime of washing and polish; here, surely, no great changes had taken place. It seemed strange that everyone should be out, for French people do not, like the Irish, leave their doors unlocked. Then I heard a woman's voice from a back room, 'Entrez, entrez! je viens. . . .' I went in and she continued, 'C'est ma mauvaise jambe, je suis en train. . . .' As it was im-

190

possible to explain my mission at that distance I went into the tiny kitchen and listened to the old lady as she wound a bandage round her leg. She was sorry, but at the clinic they told her it had to be done twice a day. Oh yes, she remembered the Joyces—she and her husband had been there for forty years—very nice people they were; just before the war they took a flat there. The concierge at 2 Avenue Saint Philibert, indeed—she knew her well, went to the country and wasn't there long before she died. Yes, probably Mrs Joyce asked if she had anything there and passing number 34 rue des Vignes, she'd seen a flat was to let. They had their own things, yes, nice people, didn't talk much, nor entertain, quiet they were, but amiable, asking how she was and so on. . . .

We went into the front room, with its wide bed screened off in the corner, suggesting the odd life of these people, stretching out sleepily during the night to press that button there, to let in some late reveller, knowing each footstep like a piece of a tune. As Miss Weaver was uncertain when the Joyces went to this flat, I asked Madame Amiel—for that was her name—and she produced a book, recording the payment of the water rate which is made in that area by the individual tenant. This showed that Joyce first did so in April 1939. Thus they probably moved in earlier that year. Madame Amiel pointed to the account, 'Ah, you see, there it says "Campagne"—that is when so many people went away on account of the war. No, we did not hear what became of the Joyces. Those were terrible times.' She stopped for a moment. 'On nageait dans les difficultés.'

'The Joyces did not write and let you know concerning the flat?'

'Oh no, it would have been dangerous as they were foreigners, but a gentleman came, a friend of theirs.'

'Monsieur Léon,' I interposed.

'Yes, tall, good-looking he was, and very pleasant. He wanted to take their things but the proprietor, oh no! He could not get on with him; he sent them all to the Salle Drouot because the rent had not been paid. . . .'

'Well, I believe there were a few things, books, papers . . .?' I did not press the matter.

'I don't know but they were sold and the man didn't come to any good either, for the Germans took him away not long afterwards.'

Joyce's death she heard on the wireless and had cut out his picture in the paper. I showed her some photographs taken by Madame Giedion in Zürich.

'Ah . . . le voilà!' she exclaimed. 'Le pauvre—et Madame Joyce aussi. Que la vie est triste. Oui, des gens charmants!'

As I went down the rue des Vignes I remembered Frank Budgen's voice in the recorded portrait of Joyce. Of all Joyce's friends he was the most observant, with a quick sense of atmosphere. Mentioning that Joyce liked Passy, he told how calling to see the writer one afternoon he read to him the last nine pages of *Finnegans Wake*. Once he had listened in Zürich to the sea-changes of the Proteus, now it was 'that wonderful, unforgettable death of ALP, which was like the death of the human body, death of nature if you like, and the death of the single person.' When it was over there was nothing more to say, so as Budgen had another appointment they went out.

I could see them going down the street, a tall, thin figure, helped now and then at the crossings by the broader, more active man who had been a sailor. Where the river moves in a long free curve towards the centre of Paris Budgen got a taxi and as the door shut heard Joyce, for the last time, calling, 'Lots of fun at Finnegans Wake!'

HÔTEL LUTÉTIA

After Munich, Joyce must have wondered if it would be possible to return to England or to live once more in neutral Switzerland. The reception of his book had been depressing and also he was reluctant to change arrangements with regard to Lucia, who was being well looked after by Dr Delmas. Now his daughter-in-law was also ill. It was not until the end of August that the Joyces went on holiday and when war was declared in the autumn of 1939 they were staying in Zürich. Then they passed through Paris on the way to La Baule, not far from Pornichet where the sanatorium had been evacuated. Louis Gillet, who saw them at that time, mentions that every day Joyce spent a while with his daughter and then went down to the sands. There, behind dark glasses, he relaxed, listening to the cries of the children, the gulls, the sound of the water, in his mind perhaps the idea that he might write yet another book, not carried along by the river this time but the endless variations of the sea.

Back in Paris by October, the Joyces found that many people had already left or were arranging for their families to do so, and the blackout was in force. For the time being they decided to stay at the Hôtel Lutétia, which Madame Jolas visited periodically. She was then busy settling the pupils of her *École Bilingue de Neuilly* into temporary quarters at La Chapelle, a summer residence belonging to a parent, in the province of Allier.

By that curious trick in which later impressions impose themselves over those which must also have come to other people, I can always see Maria Jolas—handsome in a clear-skinned, perhaps Scottish way, for her maiden name was MacDonald—at the James Joyce Exhibition in London in 1950. In the confusion of last-minute preparations she calmly found a job for herself and a corner in which to carry it out and, refusing to be distracted, was yet able to answer queries or make useful suggestions. In the same way during that first autumn of the war, as the Joyces discussed their complicated situation, she would wait until they had finished and then, as if her mind had all the time been working upon the problems involved, might put forward a tentative solution. If this was not entirely acceptable she would not force the issue but search round for another plan.

When eventually their daughter-in-law went into hospital, Joyce arranged that his grandson should rejoin the school in the country. Later, as Madame Jolas shows in an article in the *Mercure de France* [1] which covers this period in some detail, the Joyces decided to accept her suggestion that they should all spend Christmas together at St Gérand-du-Puy, some seventeen or eighteen kilometres from Vichy. Thus on December 24th, Joyce and his wife drove through the familiar streets to the Gare de Lyon for what was to be a week or ten days' holiday.

VICHY

As Stuart Gilbert remarked to me, Joyce hardly ever stayed in the country. He used to say half-jokingly that God was less likely to strike him down in a thunderstorm if he was surrounded by a lot of other and more innocent people. Madame Jolas had taken rooms for them over Christmas in the village about a mile from La Chapelle. The visit was only

[1] May 1950.

to be a short one and Joyce may have been comforted by the fact that just behind their windows ran la Route Bleue, along which cars and lorries rushed with that disregard for place or persons characteristic of the French motorist. Conditions were more tolerable than in Paris, and the Joyces eventually remained at St Gérand-du-Puy for several months, occasionally seeing Madame Jolas and their grandson during the week and going up to La Chapelle on Sundays. In her account of that winter, Madame Jolas mentions that Joyce was then reading Eckermann's *Conversations with Goethe*, but does not record his comments.

Now and then Joyce and his wife went into Vichy, to see about money or do some shopping. For the French the town had long been 'une ville purgative' where Madame de Sévigné stayed, and Napoleon III made many improvements. In England it was still associated with an innocuous table-water.

Out of season, as I found myself, the place is like a well-groomed dog sleeping with one eye open. Many of the hotel and restaurant people have transferred to the Côte d'Azur. A few shops and cafés are busy and preparations are in hand for two hundred or more doctors and several thousand patients in the spring and summer. The streets, where trees touch each other and the houses, lead to squares and pleasant gardens; in the pavilions the brown, warm-tasting water bubbles up under glass domes ornamented by interlacing patterns of brass, or more recently, protected by great plastic shapes like dish covers. Now and then a few people enter to fill bottles for use at home, or an old man stoops to drink from one of the many taps near the continuous underground rumble of the springs. At the beautiful fountain of the 'Sources des Célestins' surrounded by the rich smell of damp gardens under leaves, there is something sacramental about the idea of taking the waters, a worship of natural forces. Since the Romans, perhaps before, the sick and the pleasure-loving have brought their will to live, offering it there.

A few years ago the Municipality had acquired many of the books, pictures and manuscripts, besides a number of letters, which Valery Larbaud had brought together over a long and varied lifetime. At that time these had not yet been arranged, but passing the bookcases I saw a set of *The Yellow Book*, the names of Smollett, Samuel Butler, and Gabriel Miro, and a copy of Auden's *Dance of Death*. What interested me most were boxes upon boxes of correspondence—André Gide, T. S. Eliot, Festing Jones (translator of Larbaud's books into English), Edith Sitwell, who had dedicated *Troy Park* to him, and many others. In the library, high up in the *Mairie*, with the aid of Madame Vigneron, the helpful and enthusiastic librarian, I listed for Stuart Gilbert those letters which Joyce had written to Larbaud over a period of nineteen years. These ranged from the first note starting with the formal 'Cher Monsieur' asking him to dine soon after Sylvia Beach had introduced them, through their collaboration over the translation of *Ulysses*, to the last brief letter of 1940.

When staying at Evian-les-Bains in France during 1933, Joyce sent a card to Larbaud saying, 'I should be at Vichy drinking Source Larbaud instead of here drinking Source Crachet.' Yet he does not appear to have been there before 1940, and although the Frenchman had been an invalid for some years he and his wife were delighted to see the Joyces on their home ground. In the summer they are in the country, but they spent the winter in a house in the rue Nicolas Larbaud, called after the writer's father. There, as I talked with Monsieur and Madame Larbaud, I noticed on the table beside his wheel-chair a number of magazines in French and English, for he is still very much in touch with literature. I was told, a little ruefully, how he had given instructions for his special copy of *Ulysses* to be bound 'with the colours of Ireland' as part of the cover, and it had arrived with a Union Jack ensconced there. 'That raises a nice point,' I laughed. 'For the book was written under the British régime, or about that period anyway. And Joyce was not what one would call a nationalist; he stood apart from it all. Indeed, I think it best to leave it there.'

Madame Larbaud mentioned how they had seen the Joyces a number of times during the spring of 1940, when they were staying nearby. 'Ah,' Valery Larbaud nodded, 'he was such a very good friend.

During those extraordinary months from which the subsequent history of the war was to shape itself, the Joyces stayed at a modest hotel in Vichy and Madame Jolas shows that they were glad to have the amenities of town life again. Yet the news reaching them from newspapers and wireless only increased their sense of uncertainty. Early in April Mr Chamberlain had said that 'Hitler had missed the bus': Reynaud declared his confidence in the Maginot Line and stated that there would be 'no phony peace' as had been rumoured against his government. In the middle of that month Norway was invaded: by May the campaign there was over. Then the Low Countries were entered, Dunkirk followed, and by the 29th Leopold had surrendered.

At that period Joyce may have considered if it would still be possible to leave France. But what about Lucia? He had already been with Madame Jolas to Moulin, about half an hour's journey from Vichy, to arrange for her to enter a hospital there. But it was then too late. By June 11th Italy was in the war and the Germans were now leaving the vaunted Maginot Line behind them.

Thirteen years afterwards, when so much else had happened, I found the Hôtel Beaujolais where the Joyces stayed at that time. It was now closed for the winter and I could only look at the frontage of the fairly old, pleasantly built house with its classical flowers and fruit decoration over the doorway, which made me think of the Volta Cinema in Mary Street, now so many years behind. Through the glass door I could see one of those brown wood halls usual in the smaller French hotels, and beyond, the suggestion of a garden. When eventually I found the man who was its proprietor when the Joyces were there, he told me how on Sunday, June 16th, without warning, the place was taken over, together with other establishments, by the French military. 'And then—oh I forget the details, there was some bother over a cheque which Monsieur Joyce had to give me, on a bank in Paris or abroad, everything was in such confusion. Oh yes, eventually after a lot of bother the matter was settled.' Slight as the recollection may seem, it illustrates what the Joyces were to face at the time, taken like everyone else completely by surprise.

Madame Jolas has described how the Joyces arrived that Sunday at La Chapelle, with their hurriedly packed belongings, together with other friends looking for help. She had no room left, but in St Gérand there happened to be a small flat vacant temporarily while the mother of a pupil was in hospital in Vichy, so the Joyces were at least assured of somewhere for the moment. When she called later in the afternoon, tired I am sure from all the responsibility which had suddenly devolved upon her, she found Joyce listening to the radio and Mrs Joyce making tea.

A further impression of those few days was given me in London after the war by Priscilla Dibblee, a musician who had been living in France for

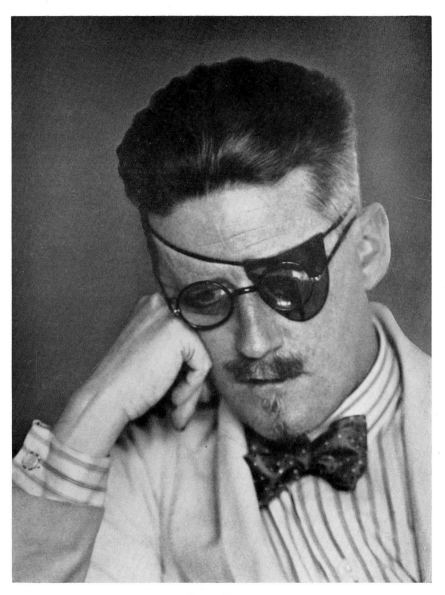

James Joyce
self exiled in upon his ego . . . writing the mystery
of himself in furniture

St Gérand-du-
Puy, Allier

La Chapelle

Hôtel du
Commerce

some years. With her elderly father and mother she had left Paris earlier and because a pianist friend had gone to Allier, her son being with Madame Jolas, they stayed at the end of May in the district. Just before the Germans broke through it seemed as if they could get to one of the ports, but on arrival at the station found that everything was in such confusion they could no longer do so. Therefore with twenty-two trunks, a cycle and, more valuable still, a mattress, they returned to the already overcrowded village of St Gérand to look for accommodation. At last, through the help of a lady who already had people sleeping even in the corridors of her residence, they found a little space in the four-roomed house of an ancient and quarrelsome brother and sister who each grew a patch of potatoes. In the evening the old man would gather up the colorado beetles on his crop and put them on the other, but by the next morning the woman had thrown them all back again with interest!

On the Tuesday of that week it was known that the Germans were approaching and many people must have felt that their desperate exodus from the North had been for nothing. The 'Boche', so much feared during the inter-war years, but until then only a fearsome myth, was soon to become a reality. There was no reliable news: soldiers who had returned and now hid themselves among their own people suggested the complete overthrow of the Allied armies. Rumour of the German advance naturally reached the village first and Joyce sent a note as soon as possible to La Chapelle. Madame Jolas describes receiving it as she crossed the garden with some of the children. Headed *le 18 juin Waterloo 1940*, this was to be destroyed after she had read it. In the event of investigations, would she please say that his son Giorgio was a teacher of Italian, singing, what she liked. . . .

Priscilla Dibblee remembered how for hours the tanks and heavy armament rumbled through and the people shivered in their houses, wondering what would happen. In particular the Jews, and there were a number among the refugees, feared to be discovered; the Joyces could possibly pass themselves off as Swiss or at the worst be sent to an internment centre. Not a soul was to be seen on the *place* or in the little streets as the Germans installed themselves at the school. To everyone's relief no house-to-house search followed. Had they but known it, negotiations were in progress which resulted in the withdrawal of the German forces the following week behind a line some kilometres away, into what then became the occupied zone.

The personal relationships of that moment will never be known in detail, although some Tolstoy-like mind writing another *War and Peace* might reach back from the future and reconstruct them—the fear of those who refused to shelter the Jews, others who risked much by hiding them, people who were soon prepared to accommodate themselves to the invader. Yet throughout the rumours, those dark and brutal possibilities of suffering, there continued that mixture of humour and kindness, hard-headed calculation and impulse which is part of the French mind. Now, as in Ireland after the civil war, there remains much more bitterness against fellow countrymen than against the enemy.

As the Germans withdrew everyone turned towards Vichy. The Embassies which had been moved there made a link with the outside world and through them allowances were made to British and American subjects. Joyce, had he wished it, could have claimed Irish citizenship and it was certainly suggested that he should fly to the United States. I do not think he had ever been in a plane and he dreaded the sea, especially with its war-time dangers. His chief concern at that time was to obtain permission for Lucia to go with them to Switzerland, where she could enter another sanatorium.

Before the armistice in July separated the French into two main groups, those who accepted or opposed Pétain's government, Louis Gillet went to Vichy to bring his influence to bear in helping Jewish friends to escape. Knowing that Joyce was in the region, he went to see him at St Gérand, a very different atmosphere from that of his pleasant salle à manger in the rue Bonaparte, or of those talks at tea-time in the little café overlooking the Esplanade des Invalides.

'Je le trouvai agité ce jour-là d'une angoisse mortelle. Il brûlait de s'envoler ailleurs, il ne pouvait tenir en place. Pendant le repas, il ne put s'asseoir, ne fit que tourner autour de la table et ne s'arrêta qu'a la longue, épuisé de tourment, pour prendre une gorgée de vin. . . .'

It is not easy to understand what the invasion of France meant to the pysche of a people completely unprepared. 'We simply couldn't believe it, not until the Germans were right down as far as Moulin,' I was told. During the First World War Vichy had been a hospital centre and during

1939 many families of Jewish origin came there from the eastern frontiers. After the break-through it had seemed as if Bordeaux would shelter the Government, but accommodation was very limited there and it was decided to move to Vichy. Thus in a few bewildering hours the town had become the centre of that phase of secondary shock after accident from which the body of French life has yet fully to recover.

'Ah . . . so much happened then.' The eyes of the woman in the book-shop near the Place Albert 1er looked out of the window as if she was watching the projection of events filmed over a dozen years ago. 'We had to put away all English and Jewish authors. But people read then—any-thing that was black upon white; there wasn't much else to do.' Priscilla Dibblee, on her cycle trips to the town from St Gérand, found the atmosphere there very unpleasant. Opportunism and a kind of youthful optimism prevailed, 'for of course people didn't know how things were to go'.

Now that Vichy had returned to its winter quietness, I had an oppor-tunity of seeing what remained of the centre round which that curious period had moved, leaving another word, *le vichyisme*, to be added to the French language. One bright morning I crossed the Casino Park where gardeners were sweeping up the brown branches lopped from the trees, and found myself before the outwardly solid bulk of the Hôtel du Parc, built sometime between the wars in that plain style which suggests quiet luxury. The main entrance was boarded up. 'Oh, this would take millions of francs to restore,' our guide said, opening a service door. 'And there aren't many wealthy clients about these days.'

What had been the hall now seemed wrecked and dismal in the light from the shuttered windows. The terrazzo floor, scratched and grubby, was worn to the earth where the Marshal's guards went up and down in nailed boots; a wide stain showed where people had stood before the re-ception desk. There only the key and room board remained, with an advertisement for the resident hairdresser, a reminder of that morning, after the *déjeuners* had been served, when the civil life of the hotel came abruptly to an end.

'We were informed that General Weygand and his staff would take over,' I was told. 'It was a matter of hours: some of the guests had to sit outside on their luggage until arrangements could be made. After a short time the military left and the place became the headquarters of Marshal Pétain.'

A dusty velvet curtain and lampshades with beaded fringes suggested past glories—in a corner were piled a number of gaunt iron bedsteads, used when the building had been a temporary hospital after the war. We passed through to the great room, hung with mirrors and elaborately ornamented, where a *bôite de nuit* had recently been started, and abandoned. It was here that Pétain's press conferences were held and receptions given, or gifts presented to the Marshal by delegations—a wonderful crystal sword, model trains, leatherwork from Algeria, much of which was to disappear at the liberation. Here, after the Germans left, a dais had been erected for a military tribunal.

'Ah . . .' said a woman who had worked there at that time. 'So much happened during those years, so many people were here. Fancy, at the Ministry of Finance an ante-room carpet had to be replaced twice in three years, just worn to holes!'

'Passons chez Laval!' Our guide took us up the stained marble stairs, for Pétain's special lift was not working. At one turn I noticed the marks where a barrier had been installed at the time when the Marshal was more heavily guarded, 'in case anything should happen'. We now reached a long passage, with perhaps two hundred doors, which was terribly cold and damp-smelling. At the end of the red carpet, daylight fell across a purple chair, like a setting for *Electra* or the *Agamemnon*.

Laval's small office overlooked the park and was crowded with odd pieces of bedroom furniture. The grey walls and ornate fireplace told nothing of the man who had worked and disputed there. As we left I remembered hearing of his apathy during the last few months after Normandy when his secretary could get no letters signed.

Upstairs, past the secretaries' office, we were shown the glass-panelled entrance to the Marshal's suite, one side of which was missing. In August 1944 the Germans wished him to leave and he had refused. On the 18th, after an evening of great anxiety, the old man had gone to bed. Early the following morning the door had been broken when the Germans came to fetch him. Thus Pétain left this little group of rooms where he had lived for four extraordinary years.

Now the cream walls were bubbled and flaked into patterns and the

Bureau had as little to relate as that of Laval below it. Much of the office furniture, the splendid Empire desk for instance, was returned to Paris, but Pétain's bedroom had been left in some measure as he knew it. There were tables and a few chairs with the specially woven tapestry of wheat sheaves and double-axe design, besides a large ordinary brass bedstead with a bright pink mattress upon it. The little balcony, where he took the salute each day, overlooks the clipped trees of the park and the long serpent of the covered way. The sunshine there is as bright, as indifferent to political preoccupations, as he would have seen it on any similar morning a dozen years ago.

ST GÉRAND-DU-PUY

The evening bus to St Gérand was large, very warm and crowded. The workers and shoppers who packed themselves in all seemed to know one another. I made room for a handsome, fair-haired Alsacienne beside me. As we moved from the outskirts into the country, tilled fields and mauve-blue woods, chrysanthemum-coloured roofs and squares of meadowland made a continual pattern of tones and shapes, bright with that vigour which shows out just before darkness. Soon we began to talk. Yes, it was my first visit but I knew other parts of France. She lived just beyond St Gérand and would see I got out at the right place. A friend, I mentioned, had been there during the war and I was going to make some enquiries; what times they had passed through! Oh indeed, and they had listened a great deal to the British radio, the only way of getting news, for no one could believe the papers then. . . . 'Yes, it was very dangerous to do so; several people were caught and penalized. We owned lorries, did some haulage business, as well as the farm, and the Germans would requisition these with one of our drivers to fetch supplies. They paid, oh yes, the Germans were very correct, one must say that for them, until the last phase, and then of course—what with the *miliciens* and the partisans, or those who said they were resisters, no one knew where they were.

'Just to show you—one evening in came a chauffeur of ours, tired out he was, and said he must have a meal before going on to Vichy. I asked the officer in German, for I knew it as a girl, and he agreed the man should do so. We were in the kitchen and the meal being prepared. "What will

201

I do?" I asked the others. "It will be awkward to have him sit there watching us eat?" Quite a young man, and he had made the journey too. Well, in the end I asked him would he eat with us. He disappeared into the toilet for a full five minutes and came out all washed and brushed up. We sat down and food was served.

' "What about the T.S.F.?" someone asked. "It's time for the news. He'll hardly understand what *poste* we're on." I was afraid but the others turned it on. No one said anything and we continued with the meal. Suddenly it was announced from London that Rudolf Hess had landed in Scotland. . . . "Hess?" the German said at once. "He's one of our people. In England?" Very reluctantly I was obliged to translate. "He must be mad, *mad!*" was all he said.'

When they had finished the officer clicked his heels together and thanked her for the food. As the lorry disappeared into the darkness, the family were left wondering if there would be serious consequences.

'The next morning, there was the officer again, with a superior. You can imagine what I felt. He saluted as if he'd never seen me before. Ah, the Germans are all right if they haven't someone over them.'

Our bus had become a long cabin of electric brightness, but now it stopped and abruptly I found myself leaving that stuffy friendliness. The large, rough-surfaced *place* of St Gérand-du-Puy stretched as far as the winged figure of a war memorial. On two sides were houses of an elderly, unpretentious pleasantness, with that indrawn look of the time of day when life begins to centre on the kitchen or the salle à manger. For a moment, in the greyish light through which colours still showed softly, I seemed to meet all the frustration of Joyce's last few months there. 'Ah . . .' I thought, 'this is how he must have seen it, coming back from Vichy one day after hours of trying to get visas, permits, money. . . .'

In the Hôtel du Commerce the young proprietress was feeding her baby and a few workmen sat talking at the marble-topped tables. Soon I was being taken up the wooden stairs, past a wheel which worked a little lift and some pictures of Nice painted many years ago. The bare cleanliness of the little bedroom increased my depression: it had been foolish to come, no memory of the Joyces could have remained here. What I needed was some food.

'Yes, I remember Monsieur and Madame Joyce,' the young woman said after providing an excellent dinner—her father had been chef at the Ritz in London. 'They used to shop at the grocer's opposite, where I was working then.' She stopped to visualize. 'He was very nice, Monsieur Joyce.'

All that evening the proprietor and a commercial traveller talked of the war and occupation, of dramatic escapes from the Germans during the débâcle, long treks homewards through the confused and terrified countryside, the hiding, waiting and the gradual reversion to old jobs or finding new ones, descriptions of a period which had been so terrifying and yet so fully lived. Like most people, they had some often-repeated adventure, those bright-coloured selvedges to the material of history.

That night I slept well under the big puff of the eiderdown. Then suddenly I was trying to wake. Outside on the Route Bleue a heavy vehicle had suddenly stopped, with a harsh abrupt hiss; there were sounds of a shot being fired. For a moment I could not place myself nor the period; was it still wartime and the Joyces there? For a moment I seemed cut off from my own past and projected into another. Then across the landing the baby whimpered and, reasoning that it had only been a lorry with a puncture, I went to sleep again. The next day, in the village, people asked one another about an unusual disturbance, so it had not been altogether imaginary.

By daylight St Gérand-du-Puy had that usual air of amiable decay given by old stonework, crumbling mortar and an ancient well. Beyond it were the fields where German petrol-cans lay in the ditches and farms were sheltered by their trees. It was suggested that I should see Madame Pontherier, in whose flat the Joyces stayed while the tenant, also a refugee, was in hospital. A neighbour directed me along the street to a yellow door, waiting to wave me on and perhaps curious about a stranger in a place which now has few visitors at that time of year. The owner of the house, elderly, pleasant in voice and manner, welcomed me at once and we sat in her small front room with its bright red paisley coverings. The flat upstairs, she explained, had really been intended for use in the summer, but with the war a number of people had been there, including the Joyces. He was almost blind and used to feel for the pavement with his white stick. She would certainly show me the place.

We went along a narrow passage to the back. 'There is the little garden.' Although surrounded by three high walls and the open side of an old barn with thick black beams, there were many creepers and flowers growing in the small space, which seemed warm and sheltered. She gestured towards a bright green bench in the corner. 'Madame Jolas liked to sit there, talking to Monsieur or Madame Joyce when she called.' Then it was not literature they discussed—how far away *Transition* and their life in Paris seemed—but the news or lack of it and how to escape from their difficult situation.

The stairway turned round upon itself within the deep walls like that of a tower until we reached the door of the flat on the first floor. While the old lady opened the kitchen shutters I noticed that damp, memory-holding smell of closed rooms. The window gave on to the tiled roofs and a tiny view of the garden. With what sense of having found a shelter did Nora Joyce look out on the afternoon they first went there? 'How long?' Joyce certainly thought, 'for how long?'

'There! This is where they cooked. Not that Madame Joyce did much. They had their meals mostly at the Hôtel, I think. Oh no, I did nothing for them. Everyone fed as best they could at that time.'

The plaid design of the wallpaper was very marked around the stove. 'Someone seems to have been frying, anyway,' I said. 'Ah yes, that was the American lady, she wasn't used to it, poor thing,' she sighed. 'Everything is very shabby, I'm afraid. Oh, in those days there were so many people! Others came in here later!' It was a remark I had heard so often. 'After a time I had to go to Paris and could not get back here.'

The tiny entrance hall had an electric light bracket like a gargoyle from Notre Dame and there was a nice wrought-iron hat-rack and one or two pictures: Rembrandt's 'Man with a Hawk' and a very dim water-colour of Paris.

In the little *salon* the covers and the walls were of the same faded blue linen—little chalets, dancing boys and girls in eighteenth-century costume, graceful with a dim gaiety of repetition. High up ran that brown bookshelf which often accompanies a divan in France, as if the solitary are given to much reading in bed. The old leather volumes, propped against each other, had been ignored by summer visitors—Caesar's Comment-aries, St Augustine, a yellowed Universal Geography and an ancient History of the Church. . . . I wondered if *Ulysses* or *Finnegans Wake* had once stood against them. Certainly Joyce wrote at the round table there, for I had seen the address of the house among his letters.

We stood now in the bedroom, seeing it through the barred light from closed shutters. The two Victorian prints might have been chosen as an ironical commentary on Joyce's situation, if he happened to peer at them. They were *The Return* and *The Departure*, showing ladies with muffs and high-hatted gentlemen of Victorian England enjoying the novelty of railway travel. . . . Above the broad bedstead of polished wood and gilt was a huge picture of the Sacred Heart.

'It was here she was so ill, poor Madame E——, very young she was.'

Early in July the invalid had returned from Vichy and the Joyces went to the Hôtel du Commerce, then occupied by Madame Jolas and the remainder of her pupils and staff. The weather was very hot and, nursed by her mother, the young woman was near the end. On her last day a message was sent to the Hôtel du Commerce but Madame Jolas was in Vichy. Joyce himself volunteered to go, putting aside those deep fears which had followed him since the shock of George's death at Windsor Terrace and the months of his mother's sickness. It seems he never allowed talk of the subject and feared omens, an empty bottle on the table, three nuns seen in the street or a black coat laid across a bed. Faced with its reality again, there is no knowing what he thought during those long warm hours beside another woman who did not die easily.

As the Germans withdrew and tension lessened, people began to sort themselves out. Some moved south in the hope of leaving through one of the ports or across the Spanish frontier. As they were the only other British subjects there, the Dibblees saw a certain amount of the Joyces. Priscilla remembered evenings when they had music together—Joyce said he liked the Strauss she played on the violin—or the walks they shared, often in search of food from the nearby farms. 'We all tended to hoard, of course!' She was only vaguely aware of Joyce's reputation and Nora assured her she would find the books very boring. Joyce was sometimes in a good mood, sometimes bad. No, she did not know about the daughter. He was rather awesome in a way. One day when she complained of the charcoal stove on which she found it difficult to cook, he said his wife had used an open turf fire for years in Ireland, and somehow she felt rather rebuked. Later when she saw him about some business he was very charming and most helpful. It is amusing to find that after all those years and in such odd circumstances, Joyce was once again telling the story of the Feis Cheoil in Dublin and how he might have been a singer, like John McCormack.

At the Hôtel du Commerce the smaller room to the left of the main *salle* was reserved for the use of Madame Jolas and the Joyces. In the evening they dined late and sat listening to the wireless or discussing the next step to be taken. When Paul Léon came to the village, he helped Joyce to make a list of corrections to *Finnegans Wake*, later appended to subsequent editions. For a while it took Joyce's mind off the efforts he was making to reach Switzerland and the difficulties of getting Lucia away from Pornichet, which was near St Nazaire, at that time being heavily bombed by the R.A.F.

When they had finished work the two friends walked down the lanes or along the main road in the direction of Vichy. Madame Jolas describes how they were often to be seen resting for a while on a fallen tree-trunk at the cross-roads. Passing there, I could find no trace of it now and continued on to see La Chapelle. There was a short cut but I missed it and walked up between two lines of trees, along a heavily rutted track, hard and dry on that bright day, a reminder that the property was only intended as a summer residence. Some rather tattered pines were grouped about stables and outhouses, and beyond them was the shape of a house with shuttered windows. The caretaker said that the old gardener, who had known the war-time history of the place, had died recently but there was no objection to looking round. Indeed, it was I who felt like a ghost trying to grope back to those small memories which return on seeing a place again—the trees from a bedroom window, the pattern of woodwork along a gate.

Madame Jolas has described the Christmas she spent with the Joyces there in 1939, when St Gérand-du-Puy only seemed one address between life in Paris and its resumption again. By then the stuffy enclosed smell had been chased out of the house by the come and go of the young people who had spent a term there. The windows would be alight and a warm stove or fire heating the salon. No sooner had the Joyces arrived than he complained of that stomach cramp which the doctors thought was due to nerves, and because this had become increasingly frequent and Joyce disliked a fuss, no one was greatly concerned. Over the meal Joyce seemed depressed, perhaps remembering other Christmases in Paris when all his family had been together. Afterwards the children sang and later he joined Madame Jolas in *Ye Banks and Braes*. Towards the end of the evening a sudden gaiety seized him, he caught Maria Jolas round the waist and danced a valse with her on the little *perron*. 'You know well it's the last Christmas,' he said. It was certainly the last they were to spend together.

As already related, the Joyces did not return to Paris but visited La Chapelle over that fine Easter of 1940 when the weather seemed to mock at war. Sam Beckett joined them, bringing news of the world they had shared. Afterwards came their stay at the Hôtel Beaujolais in Vichy, and on Sunday, June 16th—a very different 'Bloomsday'—when the French armies were breaking up, they drove through that calmly beautiful land-scape to find help and shelter there. In August the last of the school-children had left and Madame Jolas and her daughters arranged to return to the United States. Glad as they were to get away, she was sorry to leave the Joyces there with the chance of reaching Switzerland with Lucia still uncertain.

As the little flat was available again for a time, it seemed better that they should return there, as Joyce hoped. They could leave shortly. Nora Joyce was very reluctant to go where someone had recently died, for she had changed little from the young Galway woman who had run away to the Continent thirty-six years before, and now she experienced a curious presentiment that something terrible was approaching them.

It was probably at this time that Priscilla saw Giorgio Joyce pushing their belongings across the square on a handcart, 'And not looking as if he liked it.' I mentioned this to him when we met in Switzerland and he said it was very probable as that was the only means possible, and they had so many changes there. Later the luggage was wheeled back to the Hôtel du Commerce, which they now shared with other refugees, and he described the humorous side of the situation, for the Joyce family never lost the habit of pooling little incidents which amused them. In the long room up-stairs, once used for marriages and other village celebrations, he slept with a number of other men; one snored, another smoked in the dark and a third had with him the dog of 'son amie', although later it was discovered that she was—less romantically—his wife! Downstairs in the kitchen, various groups did their own cooking, 'looking into the saucepans on the stove to see what other people had managed to find for dinner'. Over the marble tables of the *salle* the ladies sat for hours, discussing the loss of their silver spoons or wondering what had become of valuable furniture. 'I spent most of my time with the village people,' said Giorgio, 'and very friendly they were.'

From them I obtained a further picture of Joyce at that time. 'I remember him well,' said an ironmongeress. 'He came in here to get his stick mended. And one day everyone was saying how he had very nearly been run down by a car near the hairdresser's.' I thought of how Priscilla had tried to describe Joyce's curious way of walking, 'kind of floating, it seemed', not being quite certain of where he was going.

The chemist, a middle-aged man whose intelligent face had seen a good deal of life, told me that his wife had read *Ulysses* and they talked of books with Joyce, but unfortunately she was ill at the time and I was unable to see her. He used to wear a grey overcoat, chilly he was, and indeed he recollected him looking for sheets of coloured paper on which to work. At first I thought this might have been a reflection of the articles which appeared after Joyce's death, but he may well have used such sheets when working through the corrections of *Finnegans Wake*, although Madame Jolas has no recollection of this. All that is known to exist is a notebook, probably written in Paris, with references, phrases and words, gathered together for some work never even begun.

'Ah . . . Monsieur Joyce!' said the chemist, looking out over the bottles and sponges towards the square. As with Miss Weaver, standing outside number 2 Adelphi Terrace House, I heard in the long vowel sound and saw in his eyes some accumulation of knowledge, regret and yet amusement, brought back by that name.

The hairdresser also sells newspapers and the shop is a centre for much lively talk. Madame Ronchon told me that Joyce first called when her husband was in the army and she maintained she could only cut ladies' hair, but he sat down and was so persuasive that she did her best for him. He was so pleased with the result that even when her husband returned after the débâcle he did not want to transfer to him.

'He got me a bottle for my eyes when they were sore one time,' she said. 'Madame Joyce? Oh yes, she was handsome, with that white hair, which she liked elegantly arranged; particular about her appearance, you know.'

'We had great talks,' Monsieur Ronchon said. 'He was so amusing and knew any number of languages. He told us how he learnt Danish—which he found the most difficult of them all—in order to visit the country. It was hard for them here, they hadn't much money at the time, like a lot of the other people.

'I often think of Monsieur Joyce when I go out into the country and see one of those barns we have in these parts. There's a little door inside the larger one and it has a particular kind of step to it. Monsieur Joyce asked me to find out the right word for it, "For everything has a name," he said.'

'And do you remember the way he used to go into the shop next to the Café de Paris and through the back passage so that his wife or Madame Jolas wouldn't see him have a Pernod there! It wasn't supposed to be good for him, some kind of pain he had at times.'

'Eh bien, il était bien rusé,[1] Monsieur Joyce!' Her husband laughed.

'There was the time he lost a gold ring and everyone was looking for it. He took his grandson Stevie with him and they found it on the *grande route*. He was very fond of the boy.'

Some ten years afterwards I showed Giorgio Joyce photographs of St Gérand and mentioned this remark about a ring. 'When I come to think of it,' he said, 'I remember returning from one of those cycle trips to Vichy about business and there was my father and Stevie sitting together after tea. He was telling him one of those stories from Homer which the boy loved to hear. As I was going upstairs, Stevie called out, "Father, do you know what Nonni has promised me? His gold ring!" "Has he indeed; very nice," I said, and didn't think anything more of it. When my father died Stephen reminded me of the fact and I sent the ring to him. I hadn't realized it had been lost; strange that those people there should have remembered it.'

In the autumn of 1940 Joyce at last obtained permission for Lucia to be taken to Switzerland, but arrangements for their entry were not yet

[1] In Ezra Pound's *A B C of Reading*, p. 45, he mentions Amadis Jahym, Secretary to Henry II of France, calling Ulysses 'ce rusé personage'.

complete. Madame Giedion was eventually obliged to mortgage their own property to cover the large guarantees necessary to allow four persons to live in a country already full of refugees. Then, when all seemed settled, Lucia's permit expired. Joyce, or rather his family, could resist no longer. What was to prove a bitter winter, with little food and fuel, was already upon them, and it was increasingly clear that Joyce needed medical care.

When it seemed that they must leave on December 13th, Joyce, in whom an irrational sense of dread was deeply set, tried to change the date, but nothing could be done about it. Giorgio described how with trepidation he went into Vichy to have their passports stamped by the German authorities, for he himself had no visa. 'Put yours on top,' advised the Frenchman in the waiting-room. 'You might get away with it.' Fortunately there was no investigation but there was still the chance of inspection to be faced on that long, war-dark journey across France.[1]

Thus, on December 13th—the feast of Saint Lucia—exactly a month from the date on which he was to die—Joyce lit a candle for his daughter in the salle à manger. 'And the darned thing was burning away all day,' said Giorgio ruefully. 'Then in the late evening we packed ourselves and what was left of our belongings into the only available taxi and drove to take the train at St Germain-des-Fosses some kilometres away.'

In the little room of the Hôtel du Commerce, where so much talk of departure had been heard, the mirror over the chimneypiece continued to reflect for another hour or two the flame of Joyce's offering there.

ZÜRICH

It was the night on which Pierre Laval was arrested and there was a general uneasiness in the air. During the journey across France in the overcrowded train with its darkened windows, Nora Joyce could not help showing her fear that Giorgio might be questioned. They had coffee at Lyons and parted with friends who were going to the United States. The night was uneventful and at last they reached the Swiss frontier. When their papers had again been examined, they now travelled through the late afternoon landscape of a country where trains were scrupulously

[1] A last note to Madame Larbaud concerns 'Un manteau de chèvre', as she told me, stored for Joyce—hence 'overgoat' in *Finnegans Wake*, p. 35.

clean and the voices those of people who, though surrounded by dangers, were still free.

'I met them at the Bahnhof,' Madame Giedion-Welcke said. 'The group looked like the long thin figures of an early Picasso drawing. They were very shabby and tired but so pleased to be back here again. We went somewhere for refreshment, one of those places decorated in heavy Gothic style, and I remember Joyce looked round as if it was pleasing him. "Oh," he said, "if you knew what it is like to have got away from that *trottoir roulant*, the road at St Gérand." '

The Joyces settled into a pension not far from the Seefeldstrasse and the houses where *Exiles* and *Ulysses* had been written nearly twenty-five years before. At Christmas they went up to Doldertal and spent an enjoyable day with the Giedions and their family. Although the Swiss themselves were doubtful, Joyce seemed convinced that the country would not be invaded. He had been wondering how they were to live, as all foreign credits were frozen, and Madame Jolas was organizing a fund in the United States to help them. In the meantime he appears to have made enquiries about teaching. History was indeed repeating itself.

Two accounts suggest Joyce at this period. Professor Straumann of Zürich University, in an article in the Swiss publication *Du*, December 1948, described his impressions of a meeting, obviously based on careful notes made at the time. He heard Joyce's hesitant steps along the corridor of the *pension*, noticed the careful way he shut the door, remarked on the slim, almost youthful figure and air of quiet elegance. 'One only noticed his reddish-grey, close-clipped moustache after his somewhat darker hair, which was already mixed with grey and combed straight back above a very high, slightly furrowed and impressive forehead. The wrinkles running from the base of the nose to the corners of the mouth lent to his face its proper age; they also gave a peculiar mobility to his features, which assumed frequently and easily an expression of friendly irony, but also one of care and weariness.'

They spoke of music, Joyce's admiration for Ottmar Schoeck, and several musicians known to them both. Joyce mentioned that the Jewish intelligence had always had a great interest for him. He talked 'with a certain light objectivity, as one who has a perfectly well defined attitude towards most things but who is quite ready to revise his thinking with regard to their relationship to each other; almost more like a philosopher than an artist.'

On another occasion Joyce's affection for Dublin was mentioned. 'You see I carry this city round with me always,' he said, and told how even the sound of its name came up in so many different ways. Professor Straumann was anxious to know if a knowledge of local conditions would make Joyce's last book easier to understand. Joyce made it clear that this was not so, and that the reader should not pay attention to the place-names or historical events but let the 'linguistic phenomena affect one as such'. A knowledge of Vico's work would certainly be helpful, he thought.

Léon Edel, who worked with Eugene Jolas in Germany just after the war, stayed in Zürich on his way back to the United States. In *James Joyce, The Last Journey*, published by the Gotham Book Mart in 1947, he gathered a number of memories of that time which might otherwise have been lost. He described Nora Joyce, which few people have done. 'She is deep-voiced and soft-spoken . . . white-haired, her face lined and sad: a woman of natural charm and dignity and of great simplicity. I was struck by her large, strong, bony hands. . . . Her son, George Joyce, in bearing and appearance, down to the long coat, the moustache, the glasses and the way his thick hair is combed back, recalls photographs of his father in his Trieste and earlier Zürich days.'

Although the account of the Joyces' last year in France is sometimes inaccurate, the little book describes how Joyce delighted in showing his grandson the bright shops of the Bahnhofstrasse decorated with fir branches and tinsel, their goods magnificently displayed, and other parts of the town, probably reminding him of his life there during the First World War.

On the afternoon of January 9th, after one of these long walks, Joyce returned with the youngster and seemed in good form. Early the next morning he woke in considerable pain. A doctor prescribed palliatives, but as there was no improvement he was taken to hospital, where it was found that peritonitis had developed from a perforated duodenal ulcer.

During the next few days he could still joke a little with the friends who came to visit him. Two young men from Neuchatel gave their blood for a transfusion and Joyce regarded this as a good omen, but the white star was not to form again for him upon a favourite wine. He passed into

Chez le coiffeur

Salon used by
the Joyces

Bedroom, St
Gérand-du-Puy

Dublin Docks

The Pigeon House

delirium—how strange it must have been—and during the late evening of January 12th he was most anxious that Nora should lie down beside him. Against her will she was persuaded to leave. Thus it was by himself that Joyce set out upon the shadowy waters. '*The keys to. Given! A way a lone a last a loved . . .*'

XII

FINNEGANS WAKE

TIM FINNEGAN'S WAKE[1]

Tim Finnegan lived in Walker Street,
A gentleman Irishman—mighty odd—
He'd a beautiful brogue, so rich and sweet,
And to rise in the world, he carried the hod.
But, you see, he'd a sort of a tippling way;
With a love for the liquor poor Tim was born,
And to help him through his work each day,
He'd a drop of the creature every morn.

Chorus

Whack, hurrah! blood and 'ounds! ye sowl ye,
Welt the flure, yer trothers shake.
Isn't it the truth I've told ye?
Lots of fun at Finnegan's wake,

One morning, Tim was rather full;
His head felt heavy, which made him shake;
He fell from the ladder and broke his skull—
So they carried him home, a corpse to wake.
They rolled him up in a nice clean sheet,
And laid him out upon the bed,
With fourteen candles around his feet,
And a couple of dozen around his head.

Chorus.

---

[1] When shown this version, Stanislaus Joyce said at home the third verse was not
considered proper!

His friends assembled at his wake;
Missus Finnegan called out for the lunch.
First, they laid in tea and cake
Then pipes and tobacky, and whiskey-punch.
Miss Biddy O'Brien began to cry:
'Such a pretty corpse did ever you see?
Arrah! Tim avourneen, an' why did ye die?'—
'Och, none of your gab,' sez Judy Magee.
                                        Chorus.

Then Peggy O'Connor took up the job.
'Arrah! Biddy,' says she, 'ye're wrong, I'm shure.'
But Judy then gave her a belt on the gob,
And left her sprawling on the flure,
Each side in war did soon engage,
'Twas woman to woman and man to man;
Shillelagh-law was all the rage—
An' a bloody ruction soon began.
                                        Chorus.

Micky Mulvaney raised his head,
When a gallon of whisky flew at him:
It missed him—and hopping on the bed,
The liquor scattered over Tim!
Bedad, he revives! See how he raises!
An' Timothy, jumping from the bed,
Cries, while he lathered around like blazes:
'Bad luck to yer sowls! d'ye think I'm dead?'

            Chorus
Whack, hurrah! blood and 'ounds! ye sowl ye,
Welt the flure, yer trothers shake.
Isn't it the truth I've told ye?
Lots of fun at Finnegan's wake.

So far there have been comparatively few references to the text of *Finnegans Wake*. When I was writing of Dublin, Joyce's other books and the city itself had provided more than enough material to study and carry out into life again. Some time previously I had experienced the 'dry-mouthed stage' of 'getting through *Ulysses*', which has been well described by Virginia Woolf or Dr Jung. Once I discovered the trick of reading sentences as if they were a series of telephone wires seen from a train, weaving up and down in a continual pattern of talk or reflection, and found I had a definite journey to go, the book became more and more fascinating.

Joyce's recording of part of 'Anna Livia' suggested that *Finnegans Wake* was perhaps not so difficult after all. Yet faced with that hedgehog of a work at first I could find no way of persuading its meaning to uncurl for me;—page on page of words all in extraordinary disorder, with here and there a place-name or a quotation showing through a verbal fancy dress. Yet it was impossible to believe that the man who wrote *A Portrait* or *Exiles* had spent nearly seventeen years producing an elaborate hoax. As Joyce said in the Hen's letter, 'You is feeling like you was lost in the bush, boy? You says; It is a puling sample jungle of woods. You most shouts out: Bethicket me for a stump of a beech if I have the poultriest notions what the farest he all means' (p. 112).

Later I began a determined reading of the text, with *A Skeleton Key to Finnegans Wake* by Campbell and Robinson, several dictionaries and an encyclopaedia within reach. Although the American scholars had done their best to throw light on a difficult subject, the effort was so great, even distasteful, that I marked the date of each attack to shame myself into regularity. One day, recovering from illness, I let my eyes slide over the print, hardly caring if they found sense or not—what matter the meaning of 'brauchbarred' or the distorted references to Troy or Ballybrack. Then suddenly I heard the Dublin voices, caught the rhythm and general meaning as one does in scrambling over the lines of a newspaper in a partly known language to get something of the news. I began to laugh. . . .

'Well, you know, Joyce wanted people to enjoy *Finnegans Wake*,' Stuart Gilbert said to me. There was also Joyce's reassurance on p. 119: 'cling to it as with drowning hands, hoping against hope all the while that, by the light of philophosy, (and may she never folsage us!) things will begin to clear up a bit one way or another within the next quarrel of an hour. . . .'

There were still great areas of tediousness to be faced, like lumps of clotted paint into which one needed to stir a solvent, but with the main themes now in mind it was possible gradually to break these up. Thousands of references would remain unknown but I was at last reaching the realities from which that extraordinary work had grown.

Joyce himself remarked that what he had to say was always simple but that the technique, dictated by the subject-matter, sometimes created difficulties for the reader. It is hard enough to convey the components of anyone's experience, but often when we come to relate a dream much of it recedes and leaves only a sensation behind, a state of frustration, fear, or happiness. Indeed not enough has been said of those dreams which resolve a problem or the beatific sleep which sends the recipient through the day with confidence.

'If Joyce's sentences do not express a single movement of a mind, it is because there is so often a double movement,' L. A. G. Strong has pointed out in *The Sacred River*, and he illustrated Joyce's method by a reference to the title-page of a certain popular newsreel in which there are a great number of things going on at once in different parts of the screen, which change and overlap each other. Joyce may have come across a description of the principle of colour photography, and he expressed the plurality of consciousness (above or below board) by another photographic image, which his manuscripts show to have been worked over a number of times before it satisfied him. '. . . if a negative of a horse happens to melt enough while drying, well, what you do get is, well, a positively grotesquely distorted macromass or all sorts of horsehappy values and masses of meltwhile horse' (p. 111), which is what happened to the Hen's letter.

Now 'lazy and gentleman', let us suppose that Joyce based *Finnegans Wake* upon a dream of his own. One day he told Nora after the *petit déjeuner* or later talked about it to a friend, for certain dreams bring with them a great need to be communicated.[1]

'Somehow I was back in Ireland again but it wasn't altogether me for I became confused with a number of other people, all our forbears seemed

[1] There is no evidence to show that Joyce did so, but the following summary of the completed book suggests the rough outline for those unfamiliar with '. . . the Strangest Dream that was ever Halfdreamt', p. 307.

to be implicated and although I knew it from the inside I was also changing and yet watching myself.

'At first things were very dark and confused as though I were deeply
asleep and yet there was the noise of a thunderstorm at moments, like God
speaking to the primitive peoples. I could see the central figure landing at
Howth as Sir Tristram, and the hill itself had become the head of a giant
who stretched right across until his toes turned up at Castle Knock beyond
the Phoenix Park—you know how a landscape looks like a sleeping figure
sometimes.

'Now everyone was talking about Humpty Dumpty and his fall, indeed I saw a builder called Finnegan with a load of bricks who lost his
balance on some scaffolding, fell and was killed. In some way this was
connected with Adam and Eve's church on the quays and the garden of
Eden. I knew about his Wake, an enactment of the ballad maybe, perhaps
I was there, and that somehow or other *Here Comes Everybody*, as he was
now called, would be resurrected again.

'Suddenly I found myself over there by the Magazine fort in the
Phoenix Park and I'd a great sense of guilt. We were soon being shown
over the Wellington Museum like the one at Waterloo, by a guide who
jumbled up the facts in an amusing way, and the monument itself had
become a phallic symbol and my feeling of shame (Earwicker's rather)
was somehow connected with two girls going behind a bush in the Furry
Glen; a boy's curiosity and a man's sexual interest were mixed up in it.

'Then Earwicker—that was now another name for H.C.E.—like my
father long ago met a fellow, rather a cad, who asked him the time, perhaps in Irish, and he seemed to know about the peeping Tom episode and
obviously would soon spread it through the town. The voices of the
dream became terribly confused but I could hear a remark or two here
and there, an absolute deluge of gossip about the man. Then we seemed to
be in a court and three Tommies of the Coldstream Guards and the girls
in the park gave evidence!

'Afterwards everything became a sort of film; oh, I'm not clear about
what happened next . . . there was something about a coffin in Lough
Neagh based on that legend of wood being turned into stone when
immersed there. Somehow or other Earwicker managed to get out and
was hunted like a fox across the countryside until they locked him up. All

this was in a primitive period, with wars and thunderstorms, and the most absurd rumours as to what had become of him. I forgot to tell you that as a commentary to all this, I heard the rambling old voices of the Four Masters (and inside them, as it were, the first four evangelists), as the preservers of tradition remembering and remem*boring*. One of the things on their minds was how Tristram made love to Iseult.

'Oh yes, there was also a woman in the story, but she had many shapes and voices, sometimes she was Iseult, another moment just the babbling of the Liffy, her hair was like Nora's, auburn as it used to be when we first knew each other, then at moments she was my daughter. Her voice was always there throughout the dream, sometimes confused with the others or opposed to the romantic silliness of the Gerty McDowell kind of girl. (You know, I can always hear a word or expression in a dream but do not see a person so clearly; not lately anyway; must be something to do with my sight.) I forgot—the principal woman was also rather like Signora Livia Schmitz,[1] so I called her Anna Livia.

'Now there was a great deal about a letter she'd dug up, like a hen scratching at a midden heap! You laugh! Well, in the dream there was nothing incongruous about it. This letter was based on the *Tunc* page of the Book of Kells and I could hear Sir Edward Sullivan's description in a garbled way. He soon turned into a Professor giving a series of riddles to a class of boys, one of them Bruno de Nolan—something about a fable from the Javanese. It had to do with Pope Adrian and the *Laudabiliter* and Lawrence O'Toole being bullied in Ireland. Funnily enough, Wyndham Lewis had become Henry II and I was myself Ireland and the bishop all at the same time. We had it out on the banks of the Liffy until Anna Livia and the washerwomen appeared——'

Here Joyce might stop to ask his listener if he'd had enough of it; aware that nothing can be more irritating than the narration of other people's dreams. Nora may have got up and said, 'Well, Jim, that comes of staying out late with your friends,' and she would add with a laugh, 'Anyway, you shouldn't be dreaming of other people's wives. . . .'

'Then I came into it, quite clearly,' with a little encouragement Joyce might go on, 'as one of the two sons of H.C.E. We had all sorts of different names but Shaun the Post and Shem the Penman summed up

[1] Wife of the novelist whose pen name was Italo Svevo.

the position. He was the active one, running round delivering letters, getting mixed up with the affairs of the world. I was writing it out in terms of objects and traditions, songs and the odd junkshop furniture of life. Then in the dream there was a good bit about my youth in Dublin, *Ulysses* and conflict with Shaun, who was a bit of Stanislaus and other people, yet had something of me in him too. It was as if we were struggling to become one complete personality again—the father. Then our mother came along, more of a universal figure than an individual, and she embraced us but wouldn't take sides; she'd her own song to sing.

'I think it must have been seeing those women washing on the edge of the river in the country the other day [1] put it into my head. I remember thinking how primitive it seemed and yet so inevitable, the talk as they worked, the chatter of the waters. It seemed to me that all rivers, all peoples and periods were the same, flowing into one another. I connected it too with Vico and his idea of cycles of history repeating themselves. Yes, there was some kind of logic to my dream but it was not that of the daytime, and I never had any certainty.

'We came now to a children's hour, the family playing singing games and later the boys doing their prep., during which they ask the riddles of life, death and procreation. It finished up with a great clap of thunder, as a reminder of the powers overhead maybe. When they had gone to bed H.C.E. remembered how the previous night he found himself involved in a dispute in his pub near the Phoenix Park. That Norwegian captain my father used to talk about was there telling stories and became confused with Persse O'Reilly of the ballad. There was also a television show— the Charge of the Light Brigade was part of it—and henceforth the dream seemed to enter the story of Buckley and the Russian General.'

'What was that?' the listener might say.

Joyce would perhaps outline another of his father's tales, apparently based on fact, about the Irishman who could not bring himself to shoot while the man he was told to snipe had his trousers down.

'The tavern keeper having turned out his customers,' Joyce continued,

---

[1] Arthur Power remarked that Joyce said he had seen them on the way to Chartres. A letter to Valery Larbaud, June 1928 (?), mentions a drive there with Sylvia Beach, a point which might be worth investigating. No regular washing is done in the rivers in Ireland nowadays.

'slumps drunkenly on the floor and dreams about young Tristram sailing away with Iseult, watched by the Four Masters with a mixture of disapproval and regret for their own youth. Now he sees his own sons put on trial and reveal their characters through an election campaign. I had running through my mind Aesop's Fable of the Grasshopper and the Ant which seemed to describe their relationship.

'There followed a very curious episode, throwing back to the last supper, the wake and burial themes of the earlier part. Sean was now called Yawn and was alive under the hill of Tara, or Howth or—I wasn't clear for it was all a night landscape. The four old boys and their donkey climbed up to hold another inquisition, and all sorts of voices came out of the earth to answer them as if Finn, H.C.E., Earwicker and myself were still very much alive there. Then a great clap of thunder—the Father voice—woke me up.'

'And I suppose that was the end of it?'

'No; I half came to consciousness but I couldn't remember where I was. For a moment it seemed as if we were back in Trieste and one of the children might cry out so that Nora would get up and go in to them. I felt a mixture of irritation and amorousness . . . and realizing that now there was nothing to trouble us, in a little while, we both went to sleep again.

'This time all seemed to be resolving itself. I now felt part of the consciousness of Alp or Anna Livia. It was her voice which carried my mind along. She moved on through Dublin, away from me too in a sense, towards a solitary completeness, and with a great feeling of peace I thought we had both reached the sea—others would begin the cycle of living again.'

'. . . a commodius vicus of recirculation . . .'

Between the completion of *A Portrait* and the actual writing of *Ulysses* some combination of influences freed Joyce from the restraints of narrative prose. He began to write in terms of thought as it transforms itself into talk. At that time he carefully screened his material, but in *Finnegans Wake*, that 'lingerous longerous book of the dark', all the rubble is deliberately included—stammers, mistakes, repetitions, the distortions of a dozen different accents and as many voices. As James Stephens said in a broadcast of readings from *Finnegans Wake* in January 1947, 'This book is not written in prose, it is written in speech . . . speech moves at the speed of light, prose moves at the speed of the alphabet.' Here and there Joyce defines his methods; the 'meandertale' is full of 'hides and hints and misses in prints' and every word will be 'bound over to carry three score and ten toptypiscal reading throughout the book of Doublends Jined' (p. 20). 'Of the persins sin this Eyrawyggla saga (which, thorough readable to int from and, is from tubb to bottom all falsetissues, antilibellous and nonactionable and this applies to its whole wholume) of poor Osti-Fosti [Joyce himself] described as quite a musical genius in a small way and the owner of an exceedingly niced ear . . .' (p. 48).

There is a story but it is obscure, so that 'if you are looking for the bilder deep your ear on the movietone!' (p. 62). Stuart Gilbert has mentioned taking Joyce to a film studio during the making of *Les Perles de la Couronne*, and perhaps he saw a 'movietone' machine in the cutting-room. This enables the viewer to see the film in miniature and both image and sound can be run backwards if necessary. The effect thus given by the reversed sound-track (I have used one myself) is very odd indeed, most Joycean. Yet throughout 'this scherzarade of one's thousand one nightiness that sword of certainty which would identifide the body never falls' (p. 51).

Those incidents of Joyce's life which come into the reader's view, to his ear rather, as chance associations, can be used as a *recurso* or summary of this exploration of his world which had been undertaken with little knowledge that so many of its fragments could be found scattered throughout *Finnegans Wake*. As the memories of his relatives and schoolfellows (where they arose spontaneously and not from Joyce's books) were often a most valuable comment on his work and personality, so my previous enquiries among people, books, directories or in visiting places described by Joyce, sometimes provided clues which would not have been clear otherwise. For instance, the addresses to which the Hen's letter had been sent (p. 420) could not have been interpreted without a knowledge of the biographical and topographical material to be found in the first part of this study. A number remain obscure and will do so perhaps now that Stanislaus Joyce is dead.

IRELAND. Joyce has many names for his country, and various comparisons to make, not always complimentary; 'The wastobe land, a lottuse land, a luctuous land, Emerald-illuim, the peasant pastured' (p. 62). Various pronunciations are suggested, 'Aaarland', 'Oreland' or 'ourloud's land'. He makes good use of a play on the German *Irre*, confused, indeed mad, in the word 'Errorland'.

CORK. 'Dorhgh' with its 'plovery soft accents' is often named in *Finnegans Wake*. At one moment H.C.E. has 'derry's own drawl and his corksown blather and his doubling stutter and his gullaway swank'. *The Bells of Shandon* by Father Prout provides a form for one of the riddles of Alp's Manifest. The position of the family is perhaps reflected in 'ones propsperups treed now stohong baroque', carrying the suggestion that they were also in Stoney Batter, a Dublin district. That Joyce was aware of Frank O'Connor's reaction to his picture of the city and its frame is perhaps contained in 'The crack (that's Cork!) by a smoker from the gods' (p. 221).

DUBLIN. It is chiefly Dublin that echoes through Joyce's life and background, reproduced in different accents, the Frenchman's 'Dyoulong', for instance, or 'Dear Dirty Dumpling', which becomes 'Dumplan' or 'Dumbil's fair city'; and there are earlier associations: 'Danadune' (fort of the Dane) or distortions of the Gaelic name, *Ford of the Hurdles* becoming 'Caeddurbar-atta-Gliath'.

RATHGAR—BRAY. If he did not forget 'his birdsplace' (p. 231), there seems to be no mention of Brighton Square, Rathgar. The Joyces' house in Castlewood Avenue is named (p. 420), but No. three is given instead of twenty-three as shown by *Thom's Directory* of the period. Nor is there a word about Martello Terrace, Bray. Joyce's schooldays at Clongowes Wood were not forgotten, for 'we were all under that manner barracksers on Kong Gores Wood together' (p. 348), and 'for Seamus, thought little, a crown he feels big; a tibertine's pile with a Congoswood cross on the back for Sunny Twinjim' (p. 211), seems to contain a reference to 'Half-Past-Six' and that tuckshop chocolate which gave Joyce such trouble in the first editions of *A Portrait*.

BLACKROCK—BELVEDERE. The period at Leoville, Carysfort Avenue, so well delineated in *A Portrait*, seems to have been ignored (contributions to this game will be gratefully received), but Blackrock and Seapoint crop up several times in various ways. From Blackrock the Joyces had moved to FitzGibbon Street and in the list of the Hen's addresses there is mention of '13 FitzGibbets. Loco. Dangerous', so that perhaps Joyce was right and *Thom's Directory* for that period contains a mistake as to the number. As to Belvedere College, where Joyce had his day 'at triv and quad and writ our bits as intermidgets', the list of essays (p. 306) certainly owes something to the pages of *The Belvederean*. There is perhaps a link between Joyce's refusal to enter the Church, the remark in *A Portrait* that in Ireland there are nets flung at a soul to hold it back from flight, and the passages in *Finnegans Wake* (p. 447), 'Fine attractable nets, their nansen nets.'

The cul-de-sac off the South Circular Road which is so clearly described in the story 'Araby' in *Dubliners*, becomes '12 Norse Richmound. Nave Unlodgeable. Loved noa's dress' (p. 420). ['Name unreadable. Left no address.'] 'Buck Jones the pride of Clonliffe' gave his name to the road where Joyce and his schoolfellow quarrelled over the merits of Byron and Tennyson.

DRUMCONDRA—FAIRVIEW. 'Drumcondriac' is also 'Draumcondra's dream-country where the betterfies flow' (p. 293) and '2 Milchbroke. Wrongly spilled' might be derived from the two dairies which used to be in Millbourne Avenue. 'Goosna Greene' (p. 533), however, is hardly likely to be connected with the old name of Goosegreen Avenue, near the house with a porch where the children sang in the damp Dublin evenings.

Fairview is given the Dublin pronunciation of 'Fearview' and Joyce was aware that Royal Terrace, where he had written to Ibsen, had later been renamed Inverness Terrace. 'Royal Terrors. None such strait. Shutter up. Dining with the Danes' (p. 420). This probably means that the family had moved. 'Noon sick parson. 92 Windsewer. Ave. No such no.' may mean Windsor Avenue where the family stayed, the landlord being the Rev. Mr Hugh Love.

ST. STEPHEN'S GREEN. '—Steving's grain for's greet collegtium' (p. 550) is a reminder of how Joyce figures in the College magazine as 'the Mad Hatter'. 'Mystic Joacax', or 'The dreaming one of Nola', 'His pseudo-jocax axplanation' (p. 63) and 'Words . . . from the sufferant pen of our jocosus inkerman' (p. 433) would seem to come from the same source, although in *Ulysses* (p. 17) Malachy Mulligan is mentioned as reciting the ballad of 'joking Jesus', and 'inkerman' might here be 'Eckermann'.

Earlier it seemed that Joyce had derived something of the Gerty McDowell tone—the Maggies, Margareena, Marge of *Finnegans Wake*—from the skits of Arthur Clery in *St Stephen's*. Yet on glancing at the women's magazines published during that period, it is clear that Joyce drew directly from their romantic and beauty-hintful pages. At times his mockery is highly localized, talk of clothes which are 'the peak of Pim's and Slynes and Sparrows' (p. 548), all well-known Dublin shops; or there is the amusing passage in which 'Pouts Vanisha Creme' [Ponds Vanishing Cream] is mentioned, and a direct link with the 'Nausicaa' of *Ulysses*, 'And never mind me laughing at what's atever. I was in the nerves but its my last day.' (p. 461).

Although *Emma* Clery of *A Portrait* has merged into *Anna* Livia—the Christian name carried undertones of that attachment—there is a suggestion that marriage would have forced Shem into respectability. Perhaps there remains a memory of their evening walks 'along the quiet darkenings of Grand and Royal', the Dublin canals. At other moments the tone is derisive, 'a lovelooking leapgirl, all all alonely, Gentia Gemma of the Makegiddyculling Reeks, he wan and pale in his unmixed admiration, seemed blindly, mutely, tastelessly, tactlessly, innamorate' (p. 92). As it seems that *Gemma* is the botanical term for leaf bud, there comes to mind Proust's *A l'Ombre des Jeunes Filles en Fleur* and its implications. There is a story still told in Dublin how Joyce, in his 'barmedical' student days, was carrying two Chinese scrolls which he was about to sell. On O'Connell Bridge he met some friends—the narrator inevitably among them—and as they talked a woman with an empty pram pushed into Joyce from behind. He collapsed into it, turned round and said 'Going far?' I mentioned this to Stanislaus Joyce who said there had been some such incident. There it is again in *Finnegans Wake*, p. 490. 'Way way for his wehicul! A parambolator ram into his bagsmall when he was reading alawd, with two ecolites and he's been failing of that kink in his arts over sense.' [1]

KILDARE STREET—SANDYCOVE. When he came to write his life dream Joyce mocked at his youthful seriousness. 'Nero or Nobookisonester himself, ever nurse such a spoiled opinion of his monstrous marvellosity as did this mental and moral defective' (p. 177) who talked of all he could do, in

[1] See *May it Please the Court*, by Eugene Sheehy, for a slight variation of the same story.

fact another 'Shakisbeard', better than all the 'teashop lionses' of London. There is also a deliberately confused account of the Feis Cheoil singing competition at which he 'squealed the topsquall', followed by a long list of the ills which prevented him from sight reading, which suggest Joyce's highly nervous state at the time.

Although the characters of *Ulysses* flit in and out of the dream, there is nothing of the sharp portrayal of the previous books. If Gogarty gets a crack or two, Joyce had worked his resentments out of himself—and became the author-god paring his fingernails, yet fully aware of what was happening to the publican, his sons (or Joyce's younger selves) and the many forms of H.C.E. and surely—Here Comes Everywoman.

CABRA. That fusion of places, names and periods which is characteristic of Joyce's method is illustrated by an oblique reference to 7 St Peter's Terrace, Cabra, where Mrs May Joyce died. As I have pointed out, this became Peter Street [1] later and it appears as '7 Streetpetres' in *Finnegans Wake* (p. 420). When Joyce met Frank Budgen and other friends in Zürich they talked within sound of the great gold-handed clock in Peterstrasse and Joyce, in writing his saga many years afterwards, let one memory overlie the other.

CLARE STREET—HOWTH. Stephen Dedalus' white cap appears again on page 322, worn perhaps by Persse O'Reilly, who was dangling his 'old Conan over his shoulder' rather like Hall the reporter, on the 'hippic runfields of breezy Baldoyle'.

Somewhere, hidden away carefully, is an account of how Nora Barnacle first met Joyce. Finn's Hotel, where according to one account she worked, is mentioned a number of times, but perhaps this is deliberately confused with Wynn's Hotel in Middle Abbey Street, also named, and where talk has it she was the 'most prim and proper girl you ever saw'. The Hen's letter finds its way to 'Finn's Hot.' (p. 420), for Joyce may have stayed in one or other hostelry when expelled from the tower. There are many other echoes, 'onevenersderg in junojuly, oso sweet and so cool and so limber she looked' with her hair 'that was deep-dark and ample like this red bog at sundown' (p. 203).

Several commentators have pointed out that the dream is a confession,

[1] It was also in Peter Street, Dublin, that the Invincibles met after the assassination of Lord Frederick Cavendish. Was this another change of name?

a form of analysis to which Joyce promised he would leave the keys to open all the locked doors. It also contains much of the secret language of lust and love, together with that mixture of guilt and joy from which life is born again, 'O Phoenix culprit!' and 'Finn, again!'

AUSTRIA. There are several allusions to their elopement in the autumn of 1904, confused with the partition of Ireland: 'he even ran way with himself and became a farsoonerite, saying he would far sooner muddle through the hash of lentils in Europe than meddle with Ireland's split little pea.' The period when Joyce was teaching in Pola and later in Trieste is reflected in references to 'the beerlitz' and 'his educandees' (p. 182). Their cries of girl-glee might be compared with a remark by Stanislaus Joyce that his brother frightened off a few lady pupils by making them work and they then transferred their lessons to him. Meanwhile in drafts of A Portrait he 'scrabbled and scratched and scriobbled and skrevened name-less shamelessness about everybody ever he met' (p. 182) and wrote the mystery of himself in furniture (p. 184).

DUBLINERS. The trouble with Maunsel and Roberts, whose office was in Baggot Street—a name distorted in various ways—is suggested in: 'Robber and Mumsell, the pulpic dictators on the nudgment of their legal advisers, Messrs Codex and Podex, and under his own benefiction of their pastor Father Flammeus Falconer,[1] boycotted him of all mutton-suet candles and romeruled stationery for any purpose, he winged away on a wildgoup's chase across the kathartic ocean and made synthetic ink and sensitive paper for his own end out of his wit's waste' (p. 185). Joyce thus likened himself to one of the Irish aristocracy, the wild geese, who left Ireland after the defeat of Kinsale in 1601.

Joyce's memories of Trieste were not pleasant. He plays on the theme of sadness, 'And trieste, ah trieste ate I my liver! . . . All moanday, tearsday, wailsday, thumpsday, frightday, shatterday. . . . How diesmal he was lying low on his rawside laying seige to goblin [Dublin ?] castle' (p. 301).

ZÜRICH. When the Joyces reached Zürich in 1915, they were not well provided against the winter and their shortage of clothes is perhaps con-tained in one of Joyce's parodies of newspaper advertisements, 'Jymes wishes to hear from wearers of abandoned female costume'. A number of

---

[1] The printer who destroyed the first edition of Dubliners.

allusions to 1916 have become overlaid by subsequent developments; for instance Easter Week and what is known as 'Bloody Sunday' appear to have been deliberately confused. Shem, we note, 'in a bad fit of pyjamas fled like a leveret for his bare lives' (p. 176). Joyce had no use for violence, each side of a dispute, as he says, being 'on the purely doffensive since the eternals were owlwise on their side every time' (p. 78). Nor had he a great deal of respect for national assemblies. 'The mad long ramp of manchind's parlements, the learned lacklearning, merciless as wonderful' (p. 252). In 'Anna Livia Plurabelle' we find 'Yssel that the limmat!', a play on river names which pleased Joyce for he often mentioned it to people on walks in Zürich. There are other traces of these years there, such as the 'acoustic and orchidectural management of the tonehall' where The English Players performed. The prompt box and various stage directions are also reminiscent of that period. The remark, 'I can psoakoonaloose myself any time I want' (p. 522) takes us back to Mrs McCormick and her interest in the work of Dr C. G. Jung.

LONDON—'THE EGOIST'. 'as unbluffingly blurtuburskblunt as an Esra' (p. 116) perhaps suggests Ezra Pound. One of the Maggies, or Marge maybe, declares, 'I'm so keen on that New Free Woman with novel inside. I'm always as tickled as can be over Man in a Surplus by the Lady who Pays the Rates' (p. 145). When providing Stuart Gilbert with a note on James Henry Cousins, whom Joyce had known in Dublin, I noticed in the directories of that period that his wife, a suffragette, was also entered as ratepayer for their bungalow at Sandymount, thus the sentence in *Finnegans Wake* combines the name of the magazine which had preceded *The Egoist* with the suggestion that men are surplus and an instance of feminine independence. It may contain the reflection that in winning her freedom woman also takes on her share of responsibility. As part of another advertisement we find a reference to Wyndham Lewis's story which appeared in *The Little Review* and first caused the magazine to be banned. 'You will enjoy cattlemen's spring meat' (p. 172). His criticisms of Joyce's work in 'Spice and Westend Women' are used amusingly throughout the book, and Shaun the Post derives in part from their relationship.

EUSTON—AND W.8. Joyce's visits to England during the twenties provided him with a number of associations. The 'dolightful Sexsex

home, Somhow-at-Sea' on page 291, with the footnote 'Just one bige
booty's pot', might apply to Bognor, Sussex, where drafts for the book
were worked upon in 1923. There does not appear to be very much about
Stonehenge and Joyce's visit there, except for a word 'stonehinged' on
page 69, but in the manifesto of Alp (Anna Livia Plurabelle), pages 113–14,
there is a long paragraph commencing 'I am a worker, a tombstone mason,
anxious to pleace averburies' which seems to have been based on a description of Avebury.

He evidently visited 'Madame Toshowus waxes largely more lifeliked
(entrance one kudos; exits, free)' (p. 57). Districts, streets and shops are
mentioned: 'St Joan's Wood' for instance, 'as british as bondstrict', carrying
the overtone of an Englishman's word being as good as his bond, or 'Sing
Mattins in the Fields'. Shem is an escapemaster from all sorts of hiding-
places; 'if he outharrods against barkers, to the shoolbred he acts whitely'
(p. 127). He dreams of 'the flushpots of Euston and the hanging garments
of Marylebone' (p. 192), evidently a description of railway hotel and
environs!

FRANCE. Joyce promises to tell us the 'story of his entire low cornaille
existence' (p. 173), which is perhaps a combination of his Grand Hôtel
Corneille days as a student and the expression *canaille*, or 'low-down'. His
life in Paris is mentioned here and there—the 'Irish plot in the Champ de
Mors' (p. 119) and 'from Porta Lateen to the lootin quarter' we will find
'his ikom etsched tipside down' (p. 205). There is a certain amount about
the singer 'Jean Souslevin', the French pronunciation of his name, but I
have yet to find Eugene Jolas and his other friends there. Indeed, the book
is rather like one of those puzzle-pictures for children which you turn
about and discover faces hidden in the clouds or among the bushes!
There is a hint of Stanislaus Joyce's criticism of his life on page 464, 'with
his Paris addresse!' Ernest Boyd is thrown in half-contemptuously much
earlier, in relation to the Feis Cheoil or music generally, in taking off the
expression 'just like a bird'—'juice like a boyd!' There are several references to the explanation of his work undertaken by Stuart Gilbert and
others, the most open being, 'His producers are they not his consumers?
Your examination round his factification for incamination of a warping
process', i.e. *Work in Progress*. At moments he had great pleasure with 'his
usylessly unreadable Blue Book of Eccles, *édition de ténèbres* . . . telling

himself delightedly . . . that every splurge on the vellum he blundered over was an aisling vision more gorgeous than the one before . . .' (p. 179). At others we meet the difficulties Joyce encountered, his despair of finishing his experiments, and the cry that 'his pawdry's purgatory [St Patrick's Purgatory] was more than a nigger bloke could bear, hemi-paralysed by the tong warfare. . . .'

Because the book took so long it probably contains shifts of emphasis inherent in Joyce's own life. The Tristram and Iseult theme began with the seagulls mocking King Mark—the adultery of *Ulysses*—but later Earwicker identifies himself with the older man's wish to become the son, to satisfy a spirit loving another without hope of union. This emotion is related to that of Stephen and Emma, Molly Bloom's memory of Mulvey, and again to the story of *The Dead*, based on Nora's similar experience as understood by Joyce. He may also have been aware of W. B. Yeats' feeling for Iseult, Maude Gonne's daughter, who might have been the poet's own child.

I was told of an evening in Paris when an observant friend noticed Lucia's listless stare. 'I would have been disturbed if she had been my daughter' was her comment. For a time Joyce was not aware of what was happening beside him, then he passionately wished that he could make things right for Lucia, suffering as he had once done. 'Oh Joyce was a romantic,' Madame Jolas emphasized, but his period was not in favour of his declaring it. Therefore in *Ulysses* Joyce transferred Nora's acceptance of him to the idea of spiritual fatherhood, and later, by letting certain elements in his work appear incestuous, he was again protecting his deepest nature.[1]

Yet for all its darkness, *Finnegans Wake* is a book of the living, wherein Joyce overcomes the nightmare of the inherited and individual past and delineates but makes no attempt to change the conscience of his race. In achieving through his work 'wholeness, harmony and radiance' Joyce came to an acceptance of the suffering and optimism of Christianity (p. 259), 'Loud, heap miseries upon us yet entwine our arts with laughters low!'

[1] See the 'word of warning' (p. 115).

It is in Ireland that this exploration of Joyce's world should end and his work once again be set aside for the everyday reality from which it grew. I returned there, as it happened, by the train from Belfast through that beautiful Ulster landscape of fields and spruce farms, the ridgy gap in the Mournes above Dundalk and the long, solitary strands of the eastern coast. Nothing breaks the continuity of this run—the mill pool like a hand-mirror, the painted harbour of Balbriggan, the dramatic bridging of Drogheda and the Boyne. There is Malahide like a water-colour by Nathaniel Hone, and soon the fingers of the Pigeon House. Even the gasometers and warehouses of the quays, seen from Clontarf, form a unity with the church spires and the misty background of the Dublin hills.

Seen from the steps of Amiens Street Station, Nelson and all he symbolizes is more removed than ever from life beneath him, with street names written in Irish and over in Kildare Street the parliament of a Republic. Trams no longer run out from the Monument to Dalkey and Donnybrook and Rathmines. Yet the voices are the same, all the accents to be found in *Finnegans Wake* from Trinity to the Coombe, and if we move within another Viconian cycle, the human situations of love and greed, generosity and denigration repeat themselves as they have always done.

The complexities of Joyce's dream-book had become a challenge. In Upper O'Connell Street a man tells me that the Chapelizod distillery where John Stanislaus Joyce was manager used to be called 'the Phoenix', and he outlined how the smaller firms have disappeared. 'In those days a man would know where his whisky came from by the taste of it, each had a recognizable flavour . . . but most of that's gone now.' As there are echoes of Sheridan Le Fanu's *House by the Churchyard* here and there in *Finnegans Wake*, I was interested to find in the National Library in Kildare Street a memoir of the family by T. F. Le Fanu, privately printed, which mentions that as a child the writer lived at Chapelizod, not far from the Phoenix Park where soldiers of the garrison drilled in the uniforms they had worn at Waterloo. There, when Joyce himself was only a year old, the killing of Burke and Lord Cavendish had led to that horrible tangle of information and revenge—that confusion of motive which represents the darkest side of our national character.

Yet the Park, whose name is derived from the Irish for a spring of fresh water, is peaceful enough, for all its memories, with the deep green of old trees about the Island Bridge Gate and boys playing football on the 'fifteen acres'. Below the Magazine Fort there runs a stout wall of that grey, rough-hewn stone used so much in the neighbourhood, screened by old, low-sized thorntrees which hide the lovers lying there. Through the larches the river shows silver as a fish as it passes over the salmon weir. From this high point the Liffey can be seen broadening towards Chapelizod. The mind's eye follows it along by the back road to Lucan, passing the Strawberry Beds, which perhaps reminded Joyce of those donkey-and-cart excursions along the river with his cousins, until at Leixlip the river runs under beech trees near the house where Vanessa lived. On other occasions he had taken the steam train up to Poulaphouca and maybe walked as far as the wild, heather-covered slopes where the Liffey rises, 'On the spur of the hill in old Kippure, in birdsong and shearingtime'. Then 'just a young thin pale soft shy slim slip of a thing', she gradually becomes powerful in passing through Kildare to the lower lands, 'by Tallaght's green hills . . . happy as the day is wet, babbling, bubbling chattering to herself . . . giddygaddy, grannyma, gossipacious Anna Livia'. This was the voice which Joyce heard as the daughter-mother of all the rivers of the world, moving on towards that strange confusion of evil and good which men and women build around them as a city, with its beautiful squares and 'the slime of their slums and artisaned dwellings', past Adam and Eve's, the riverine heads of the Customs House, the confusion of wharves and shipping to reach the Bay, to curve round by the seeping giant of Howth and at last to reach the open sea.

APPENDIX A

Changes in *A Portrait of the Artist as a Young Man*

It is likely that the novel had undergone many changes in evolving from the softer outlines of earlier versions, such as the fragment of *Stephen Hero*, to the clearly lit, almost shadowless prose of the published book. Joyce probably copied it several times and had plenty of opportunities to rub off corners and sandpaper down his style to considerable smoothness. Ironically enough, in writing the last part of *Ulysses* he was to suffer from the other extreme, a printer calling for copy.

A comparison between the serial version in *The Egoist* and the published novel shows that most of the changes made were part of Joyce's war against commas, hyphens and unnecessary capital letters. Several factual alterations illustrate Joyce's search for accuracy. In *The Egoist* when Stephen Dedalus visits Cork with his father he tries to think of Clongowes Wood and how he had eaten chocolate out of his cricket cap, and much later the incident is again mentioned in the interview with the Rector of Belvedere. Either Joyce recollected or asked a school-fellow for the name of a particular tuck-shop delicacy called 'slim jim'. After various attempts by Joyce the word was altered in the third edition of the novel. Stanislaus Joyce tells me that his brother did not eat chocolate and at a cricket match at Clongowes he remembers James bringing over in his cap some of those slim bars with a cross on them, and he demolished them. Slight as this detail may seem, Joyce used the word as part of his method of linking one phase of Stephen's life to another. The word occurs in *Finnegans Wake* (p. 211), 'a tibertine's pile with a Congoswood cross on the back for Sunny Twimjim'.

A further alteration also relates to Clongowes Wood. Chapter I as published on February 2nd, 1914, shows Stephen wondering 'from which window Hamilton Rowan had jumped'. Evidently further information came Joyce's way for the first edition reads: 'He wondered from which window Hamilton Rowan had thrown his hat on the haha.'

This took me eventually to Harold Nicolson's *The Desire to Please* (Constable, 1943), which deals with Hamilton Rowan and his escape from Dublin in 1794 because of his association with the United Irishmen. To my surprise I found on page 136 the following passage:

> One day during the last war I was reading James Joyce's *A Portrait of the Artist.* . . . I was reading the book dreamily, as James Joyce should always be read, allowing my imagination to float at ease among the interior monologues of young Stephen Dedalus. Suddenly my attention was arrested by the following phrase. 'It would be better to be in the study hall than out in the cold. The sky was pale and cold but there were lights in the castle. He wondered from which window Hamilton Rowan had thrown his hat upon the haha, and had there been beds at that time under the windows.'

This episode was not mentioned in Hamilton Rowan's own autobiography, but there appears to have been a tradition that before escaping to France he had visited his family and been pursued into a gentleman's house; opening a window, he threw out his hat and hid while the soldiers thought he had left by jumping out.

Therefore in February 1934, as Harold Nicolson relates, he set out to run both Joyce and the legend to earth in Paris. However, as shown on page 178, he found Joyce preoccupied with the problem of getting *Ulysses* into England and eventually agreed to help, forgetting to ask about Hamilton Rowan. Later a friend in Dublin sent him the correct version of the story, which of course had reached Joyce long ago.

Sean O'Casey and James Joyce

Herbert Gorman records in a footnote on page 344 of his biography that *Finnegans Wake* was listed under 'Books Received' in a Dublin newspaper, as being by Sean O'Casey. 'This mistake, however, brought Joyce two friendly letters, one from Sean O'Casey, who believed it was intentional, the other from the editor who said it was unintentional.'

Sean O'Casey, when I asked him to comment on the incident, in a letter of January 14th, 1955, mentioned that Joyce had written to him twice but unfortunately he was then unable to search for the letters. He had never met Joyce. John Dulanty, then Irish High Commissioner, asked him to join him at dinner with Joyce but he had already arranged to dine with 'the great poet of Scotland, Hugh MacDiarmid, and so, very regretfully had to miss meeting the other great man'. (Such a pity the parties had not amalgamated, with some Boswell of the time listening to their talk!)

Within the Gates had been attributed to James Joyce, in Sean O'Casey's opinion deliberately, 'to hurt Joyce and me. It didn't hurt either of us: instead it linked us happily together'. A letter from Joyce saying that he hoped Sean O'Casey had not been offended prompted the following reply, which is now in the Lockwood Memorial Library, Buffalo University:

> *Tingrith Station Road,*
> *Totnes,*
> *Devon,*
> *England.*
> *May 30th 1939.*

MY DEAR JAMES JOYCE:

I was very glad to get a letter from you, and to find that you weren't annoyed at *Finnegans Wake* being put against my name. My mind is still far away from the power of writing such a book. I wish I could say that such a power is mine. I am reading it now, and though I meet many allusions, the book is very high over my head. A friend here (a painter) and I often read it (or try to) together; and I, it is fair to say, am better than he, and lead him into many a laugh and into the midst of wonder and wonderland. It is an amazing book; and hardly to be understood in a year, much less than a day. I've had constant contact with you in *Dubliners* and *Portrait of the Artist*; and in *Ulysses*—that great and amazing work. As you see, we are now living in Devon,—meself and herself, two kids and another coming, so I don't suppose you'll ever be near here. But God is good, and we may meet some day, I sincerely hope so.

I don't think the reference was a misprint. I know many of Dublin's Literary Clique dislike me, and they hate you (why, God only knows), so that 'misprint' was a bit of a joke. Well, Oxford's (or Cambridge) going to hang the coloured gown of a D.Litt. over the shoulders of Wodehouse, whom, Belloc says, is the greatest living writer of English. So *Finnegans Wake* will, I fear, be a wake in earnest.

Them and their Academy of Letters—all in all, and in spite of all,

A deep bow to James Joyce,

Yours very sincerely,

SEAN O'CASEY

I do hope your wife is all right or much better by now.

APPENDIX C

Press Comments on *Finnegans Wake*

Friends who saw Joyce after the publication of *Finnegans Wake* on May 4th, 1939, found him depressed at the reception of his book. Messrs Faber and Faber have retained a cuttings file which makes interesting reading.

A number of reviewers had recourse to *Our Exagmination . . .* which was re-issued at the time, but several complained that the publishers did not provide a summary of the subject-matter on the dust-jacket. Most of them were defeated by the book, a few were driven to anger. The popular papers either quoted derisively or concentrated on the fact that Jimmy Dorsey, 'King of Swing (U.S.)', used its title for a piece of music.

Oliver St John Gogarty skilfully presented his attack in *The Observer* as *Roots in Resentment*—Joyce's resentment against his family, his country and upbringing, perhaps the doctor himself. He concludes 'This is the most colossal legpull in literature since Macpherson's *Ossian*. Mr Joyce has had his revenge.'

Robert Lynd wrote in *The News Chronicle* '. . . to the ordinary reader it will remain a sealed book, and seem merely symptomatic of the chaos into which the modern world has fallen'.

In *The Spectator*, under the heading 'A private document', Derek Verschoyle pointed out that it was too sombre for a hoax and suggested 'a mind trying to free itself from obsessions by prolonged analysis'. Edwin Muir went into the subject in more detail in *The Listener*. This was 'an attempt never attempted before, which could only have been undertaken by a man of Mr Joyce's genius and perseverance . . . The book has the qualities of a flowing stream, sound and rhythm . . .'

The Irish Times provided a leader and the following day a long review with the heading 'Endlessly exciting in its Impenetrability'. 'The reader was faced by acute bewilderment but "It is the endless folding and unfolding of a dream. It makes its own space in which to have unlimited freedom to complicate itself . . . in this book a new language may have been born. The extent to which *Finnegans Wake* may begin to influence the English language will be the measure of its reality and the only proper test of its importance." ' At the same time, the writer doubted if Joyce had much more to say than was already implied by *Ulysses*.

Bonamy Dobrée wrote in *The New English Weekly*, 'It is a vision extraordinary, rigorously controlled by the intellect as to its just discernible emotional form; with free association severely disciplined and pruned after the event, determining the words'.

It was in the by-ways that the book found friends. Mr Beddow, assistant editor of *The Schoolmaster and Woman Teacher's Chronicle*, wrote: 'I have in my hands the biggest masterpiece of this century.' A long article, evidently the result of careful study, 'Literary conventions challenged in Finnegans Wake', by Norman Hudis, appeared in *The Hampstead and Highgate Express*. *The Morning Herald* of Sydney contained a good analysis in which it was pointed out that 'The weakness of this enterprise lies in the lack of visualization'. *The Library Assistant* strongly recommended the book and an interesting review in *Theology* declared, 'The eye must indeed be blind that does not see in this author's lonely journeying a spiritual pilgrimage.'

Certain critics preferred to be non-committal. B. Ifor Evans wrote in *The Manchester Guardian*: 'The author of *Dubliners*, *A Portrait of the Artist as a Young Man* and *Ulysses* is obviously not a charlatan but an artist of very considerable proportions. I prefer to suspend judgement. If I had had to review Blake's 'Prophetic books' when they first appeared I would have been forced to a similar decision. . . . Mr Joyce in a parody of Jung and Freud ('Tung Toyd') mentions "Schizo-phrenia". One might imagine that Mr Joyce has used his great powers deliberately to show the language of a schizophrenic mind, and then he alone could explain his book, and I suppose, he alone review it.'

Extracts published in *The Egoist* compared with Ulysses in Book Form

Miss Weaver recollects chapters of *Ulysses* arriving at the office of *The Egoist* in typescript, some direct from Mr Joyce by post, others from Ezra Pound, and believes these were destroyed. At this distance she is uncertain if it was decided not to try it on with the printers or if they made certain deletions. A comparison of *The Egoist* extracts with the first and second Paris editions of the book show that a number of sentences were probably added by Joyce, or, as the subject-matter of several of these suggests, they were not included by the printer of *The Egoist*.

Although a detailed study of the development of Joyce's work will not be possible until all the extant manuscripts are available, it has been interesting to read *The Egoist* version with an eye upon its later presentation. In one or two instances this work has led to the discovery of how Joyce corrected errors of fact.

(The second edition of *Ulysses* was printed on plates made from the first Dijon-Paris edition, and Joyce's Errata list of 726 items was not incorporated in the text until the book was reset for the eighth edition. These were chiefly printer's errors, but here and there Joyce added a word or two. I have not consulted this list.)

The first chapter of *Ulysses* did not appear in *The Egoist*. The January-February number of 1919 contained the Nestor episode. The sentence 'His mother's prostrate body the fiery Columbanus in holy zeal bestrode' might well have been a deletion. The description of the French library does not contain the phrase 'under glowlamps, impaled, with faintly beating feelers', and the paragraph 'Glorious, pious and immortal memory. . . . Croppies lie down' is probably an embellishment. It is interesting to find that Joyce added the last part of that now famous remark.

'History, Stephen said, is a nightmare from which I am trying to awake.' In book form this continues. '*What if that nightmare gave you a back kick?*' [1]

There is one change of fact in this section. 'O'Rourke's wife, Prince of Breffni' in *The Egoist* later becomes 'MacMurragh's wife and her leman O'Rourke, prince of Breffni'.

The Proteus episode appeared in *The Egoist* for March-April, 1919, and contains several extensions of interest. The printer of course may have objected to 'Papa's little bed-pal' and 'Unfallen Adam rode and not rutted'. The joke 'Il est Irelandais. . . . She thought you wanted a cheese Hollandais' is surely an addition. On the other hand the description of the dog was either extended by Joyce later or met with disapproval, together with the last group of sentences wherein Stephen finds himself without a handkerchief.

During April Ezra Pound told John Quinn that he had received the fourth chapter of *Ulysses* 'and deleted about twenty lines before sending it off to New York; and also wrote Joyce my reasons for thinking the said lines excessive'. Unfortunately Joyce's reply is not available. This was probably 'Hades', published in *The Egoist* for July 1919, and a comparison with the book form shows considerable extension by Joyce in places. The serialized version was much easier to read because the continuity of narrative was not broken by what might be called pendent associations. Sometimes Joyce's extension of the text serves to tie up certain themes more closely, to relate the parts to the whole, as we have seen in *A Portrait*.

As an instance:

The Egoist	*In book form*
Mr Bloom entered [the carriage] and sat in the vacant place. He pulled the door to after him and slammed it tight till it shut. He passed an arm through the armstrap and looked seriously from the open carriage window at the lowered blinds of the avenue. One	Mr Bloom entered and sat in the vacant place. He pulled the door to after him and slammed it shut. He passed an arm through the armstrap and looked seriously at the lowered blinds of the avenue. One dragged aside: an old woman peeping. *Nose flattened against the pane. Thanking her*

---

[1] My italics.—P. H.

The Egoist (cont.)

dragged aside: an old woman peeping. Job seems to suit them. Huggermugger in corners. Then getting it ready. Laying it out. Wash and shampoo. I believe they clip the nails and the hair. Grow all the same after. Unclean job.

In book form (cont.)

stars she was passed over. Extraordinary interest they take in a corpse. Glad to see us go we give them so much trouble coming. Job seems to suit them. Huggermugger in corners. *Slop about in slipper-slappers for fear he'd wake.* Then getting it ready. Laying it out. *Molly and Mrs Flemming making the bed, Pull it more to your side. Our winding-sheet. Never know who will touch you dead.* Wash and shampoo. I believe they clip the nails and hair. *Keep a bit in an envelope.* Grow all the same after. Unclean job.

There are one or two slight changes in the description of the drive to Glasnevin, with its underlying rhythm of the carriage wheels. Berkeley Road has become Blessington Street at one point, because a whole paragraph relating to The Mater Hospital, Eccles Street and the death of old Mrs Riordan has been inserted in the book.

Another addition later in the episode which might be mentioned is where Bloom daydreams of going to see Milly by canal. The tramp sitting on the curb-stone, part of the Homeric pattern as Stuart Gilbert points out, was also introduced later. The second part of 'Hades' appeared in September, 1919. Here certain themes are slipped into the text to relate the episode to other parts of the book, such as 'Felt heavier myself stepping out of that bath' or 'Did I write Ballsbridge on the envelope I took to cover when she discovered me writing to Martha? Hope its not chucked in the dead letter office.' Bloom's random thoughts at the burial are considerably lengthened—the joke 'Come forth Lazarus! And he came fifth and lost the job!'; speculations as to the caretaker's courtship and marriage, the paragraph on widowhood, most of the long sequence of Bloom's thoughts as he walks past the graves, did not appear in *The Egoist.*

Much more important was the extension of Hynes' remark, '—Parnell will never come again, he said. *He's there, all that was mortal of him. Peace to his ashes.*' One or two phrases may well have been deleted by the printer of *The Egoist*, such as 'Burst sideways like a sheep in clover Dedalus says he will. With a belly on him like a poisoned pup' or 'Catch them once with their pants down'.

The Egoist

Solicitor, I think. I know his face. Menton. Dignam used to be in his office. Mat Dillon's long ago. Got his rag out that evening on the bowling green because I sailed inside him. Pure fluke of mine: the bias. Molly and Floey Dillon linked under the lilac tree, laughing. Fellow always like that, if women are by.

In book form

Solicitor, I think. I know his face. Menton. *John Henry. Solicitor, commissioner for oaths and affidavits.* Dignam used to be in his office. Mat Dillon's long ago. *Jolly Mat convivial evenings. Cold fowl, cigars, the Tantalus glasses. Heart of gold really. Yes, Menton.* Got his rag out that evening on the bowling green because I sailed inside him. Pure fluke of mine: the bias. *Why he took such a rooted dislike to me. Hate at first sight.* Molly and Floey Dillon linked under the lilac tree, laughing. Fellow always like that, *mortified*, if women are by.

The first part of The Wandering Rocks episode appeared in *The Egoist* in December 1919. Again there are several additions worth mentioning. Mr Denis J. Maginni, professor of dancing, and Lord Talbot de Malahide are introduced, the lady in the tram, so well described, comes to smile 'tinily, sweetly'.

Joyce's wish to be accurate is illustrated in the description of the man on the barge under the trees of Charleville Mall, who stares, in *The Egoist* version, at the branch of an *elm*. By the time the book is out Joyce had discovered, or remembered, that this should have been *poplar*. This group of trees (their great soot-dark trunks in the early spring with small, surprising spikes of green) are still there to the left of the bridge over which Stephen Dedalus walked from Fairview towards the city.

Another point which illustrates Joyce's search for accuracy is the correction of the Christian name of the first Countess of Belvedere. The name Ellen appears in *The Egoist* and she is mentioned as walking along the shores of Lough Owel. When I asked Stanislaus Joyce, these were the names which he also gave me, yet evidently Joyce had some doubts for he appears to have written to Dublin to get the matter right. In his papers at the Lockwood Memorial Library, there is a letter on Belvedere College notepaper, dated 3.x.21 and signed Charles Doyle, S.J., in which it is shown that the wife of the first Earl of Belvedere was Mary, the daughter of Earl Molesworth. After the divorce court proceedings she was confined in Gaulstown, Co. Westmeath, the old seat of the family, near Belvedere House by the shore of Lough Emel, a new residence just completed by the Earl. The Countess Mary died about 1780. Belvedere House (now Belvedere College) was not completed and occupied by the second Earl (the builder of it) until 1786. In *Ulysses* (Ed. 1941, p. 211) the names have been corrected to *Mary* and *Lough Emel*.

The Egoist	*In book form*
The gay sweet whistling within went on for a bar or two, ceased. The blind of the window was drawn aside. A plump bare generous arm was seen, held forth from a white petticoatbodice and taut shiftstraps. A woman's hand flung forth a coin over the area railings. It fell on the path.	The gay sweet *chirping* whistling within went on for a bar or two, ceased. The blind of the window was drawn aside. *A card Unfurnished Apartments slipped from the sash and fell.* A plump bare generous arm *shone*, was seen, held forth from a white petticoatbodice, and taut shiftstraps. A woman's hand flung a coin over the area railings. It fell on the path.

Another small but significant point might be mentioned concerning Miss Dunne's telephone conversation with Blazes Boylan. In volume form only it runs, 'Mr Lenehan, yes. He said he'll be in The Ormond *at four*.' Thus Joyce emphasizes the hour of the rendezvous.

APPENDIX E

The Egoist Press

'After the suspension of the journal', Miss Weaver's note continues, '*The Egoist Press* (as it was now called) expanded to some extent its book publication, bringing out some special books, most of them small, the work of young writers who had been connected with *The Egoist* in some way. A book by Ezra Pound, *Quia Pauper Amavi*, was published in an ordinary and a special edition, and Mr James Joyce's other three early books were taken over: *Chamber Music* from Mr Elkin Mathews and *Dubliners* and *Exiles* from Mr Grant Richards, neither of whom was disposed to bring out further editions. And in the autumn of 1922 *The Egoist Press* arranged for a curious London–Paris edition of Mr Joyce's *Ulysses*. This was printed in France from plates bought from Miss Sylvia Beach, owner of Shakespeare and Company, Paris, who had very courageously brought out a first edition on February 2nd of that year which had quickly been subscribed and sold out. The London–Paris edition was handled for *The Egoist Press* by Mr John Rodker who distributed the copies from Paris.

'A good supply was sent in bulk to London and I had the amusement of storing some of these for greater safety at my private address and of delivering others to the back department of a number of bookshops. By these devious means the whole edition of 2,000 was disposed of, though unfortunately some 500 copies were seized by the New York postal authorities and are said to have been burnt. It was to replace these that a third edition of 500 was printed, 499 of which were confiscated by the customs authorities at Folkestone. The surviving copy had been sent by post to me and duly received and apparently two extra unnumbered copies escaped destruction.

'Early in 1924 *The Egoist Press* was wound up, the books on hand being distributed in various ways. Mr Joyce's first four books were taken over by Mr Jonathan Cape, in whose hands they still are.'

FURTHER NOTES

THE CINEMA

(see p. 80)

Details concerning the Italian films shown by Joyce in Ireland are to be found in *Blanco y Negro*, 7–8, Rome, 1952.

Joyce told Miss Weaver that a film on astronomy, in particular some sequences dealing with the moon, gave him an idea for the rhythm of Molly Bloom's monologue in *Ulysses*. Madame Jolas remarked that among other productions seen with Joyce they had discussed *Man of Aran* at length and Joyce appeared to have liked it. Another film was *Wuthering Heights*, Joyce already being disposed in favour of Emily Brontë. Eugene Jolas also recalled seeing the film version of H. G. Wells's book, *The Island of Dr Moreau*, with him. Both emphasized that these recollections were fragmentary and should not be quoted as Joyce's decided preferences.

During the production of *Les Perles de la Couronne* (see p. 222) Joyce met Sacha Guitry and, according to Stuart Gilbert, spoke to an elderly Italian actor whom he knew already. This was probably Ermite Zacconi, associated with films since 1912. Joyce discussed with Stuart Gilbert the possibility of putting *Ulysses* on the screen and they worked out a number of ideas, agreeing that only Eisenstein or Walter Ruttmann could do so effectively. Between 1934 and 1935 they were in touch with a Hungarian director, whose name Stuart Gilbert has forgotten, and planned a film to be based on the Anna Livia episode. A few pages of a draft scenario were reproduced in *The James Joyce Year Book, 1950*, and Stuart Gilbert pointed out that it was undertaken at the request and with the encouragement of Joyce, who made suggestions for improvements.

By the thirties, *Ulysses* had influenced much contemporary writing and it would be interesting to trace the use of the interior monologue in early sound films. Sergei Eisenstein greatly admired the book and stated in *Film Form*, 'It has been left to Joyce to develop in literature the depictive line of the Japanese hieroglyph.' According to Marie Seton, the

Russian director went to see Joyce in the winter of 1932 and found him one of the most remarkable men he had ever met, being much impressed by his reading *Ulysses* aloud to him. 'Joyce was intensely interested in my plans for the interior film-monologue, with a far wider scope than is afforded by literature.' He considered that in *Work in Progress* Joyce had made heroic efforts to overcome the problems of dual-level writing, but that it led to the entire decomposition of the literary method itself. 'Only the film element commands a means for an adequate presentation of the whole course of thought through a disturbed mind.'

H. G. WELLS AND VALERY LARBAUD

(See p. 160)

A reflection of Joyce's attitude is to be found in Thomas McGreevy's contribution to *Our Exagmination . . .* A traditionalist, Joyce was regarded as revolutionary by the academic and also the ultra-scientific 'whose attitude towards the biology of words is not what, if they were consistent, they might wish it to be'. An undated fragment of a letter, now at Buffalo University, written by Valery Larbaud to Joyce, provides an illuminating comment upon Joyce's experiment:

> . . . Dante was certainly haunted by the idea of a common Vulgar; and in fact one Canzone at least is written in 'lingua trina'—Latin, Provençal and Italian. Whitman too seems to have felt the necessity of an international tongue based on English. But what you are doing could only be done in English, I think, because there are as many Latin roots as German roots, so that a Spanish or Italian, a Norwegian, or Dutch word, may be brought into it without seeming utterly out of place. At least one of the two or three meanings or allusions of the word thus coined, will be readily apprehended. While you were reading to me I had an impression of going along a vineyard, where the words were the [bunches of] grapes,—each word the full-grown 'Racème', of which I hastily picked one 'grain', with the intention and the wish to go back to it later on and pick other 'grains' from it. I don't see how the same thing might be done on a large scale in a purely Latin or purely Teutonic language. See how *déplacés* look French words in German! But an inter-Latin language is possible, and, perhaps, an inter-Teutonic one; but they meet only in English.

REBECCA WEST AND JAMES JOYCE

(See p. 182)

Joyce's attitude to criticism of his works requires a more detailed study than has been possible here. Rebecca West, when asked about the controversy which arose from her essay on Joyce in *The Strange Necessity* (1928) and Joyce's references in *Finnegans Wake,* said that it must be taken into account that her essay, though it expressed deep admiration for the genius of Joyce, began with an unfavourable opinion on one of his poems, and that writers are often most sensitive about their lesser works; and that the essay, because of its particular form, perhaps seemed to Joyce too familiar in tone for a writer not of his stature. But Miss West added that there was something mythic about the resentment. Joyce appeared to be under the impression that Miss West and her American publisher, George Doran, had called on him in Paris and had behaved unpleasantly. But Miss West never met Joyce; and he could not have met Miss West and Mr Doran at someone else's home without her being aware of it, for so far as she knows she never was in Paris at the same time as George Doran.

INDEX